# DANIEL GROSE

(c.1766-1838)

# THE ANTIQUITIES OF IRELAND

First Published in 1991 by
The Irish Architectural Archive,
73 Merrion Square, Dublin 2.
Telephone +353-1-763430.

Designed by Ted and Ursula O'Brien, Oben Design.
Phototypeset by Oben in Baskerville II on Compugraphic® MCS8200.
Photography of Original Manuscript by David H. Davison.
Reproduction of Photographs by Master Photo Engraving.

Printed by W. & G. Baird Ltd, Antrim.

ISBN 0 9515536 4 X (Cased Edition)

ISBN 0 9515536 5 8

# DANIEL GROSE

(c.1766-1838)

# THE ANTIQUITIES OF IRELAND

*A Supplement to Francis Grose*

*Edited and Introduced by*

## Roger Stalley

*Published by*

The Irish Architectural Archive

The editor and the publisher would like to thank

**Rohan Holdings Ltd**
**Mark Fitch Fund**
**Office of Public Works**

without whose generous sponsorship
publication of this book would not
have been possible.

# Contents

# Editor's Acknowledgements

The preparation of this edition of Daniel Grose's Supplement would not have been possible without the help of numerous people, many of whom generously spent a great deal of time answering my queries. I must particularly mention Terence Barry, the Reverend Canon Ian Biggs, Cormac Bourke, Tony Cains, the Very Reverend H. Cassidy, Con Costello, Maurice Craig, Anne Crookshank, Brendan Dempsey, Colm Donlon, Cecil English, Hugh Gibbons, Tom and Mary Gibbons (Cornaveigh), the Very Reverend James Grant, David Griffin, Ann Hamlin, Peter Harbison, Richard Haworth, David Newman Johnson, Heather King, Elizabeth Kirwin, Chris Lynn, Mary McAuliffe, Mrs C. McCarthy (Dungarvan), Con Manning, Cathal Moore, Íde Ní Thuama, Cathal Ó Háinle, Siobhán O'Rafferty, Mr and Mrs F. O'Rourke (Manorhamilton), Nigel Ramsay, John Scattergood, Mr Dudley Snelgrove, Rebecca and Clare Stalley, Mrs Jennifer Strevens, David Sweetman and Martin Timoney.

Special thanks must go to Ann Martha Rowan who, as well as editing my typescript, undertook the tedious and exacting job of transcribing Daniel Grose's original text. At a time when it seemed the book would never be finished in time, Rachel McRory came to the rescue with great energy and imagination. She also undertook much of the proof-reading. I must also mention Ann Lynch, who guided me on pre-historic matters (but must take no blame for my errors), and Raghnall Ó Floinn, who furnished me with a comprehensive report on the artefacts included in two of the plates. I could not have visited the islands in Lough Ree without the navigational skills of Harmon and Ann Murtagh. The painstaking task of photographing the watercolours was undertaken by David Davison with great skill. Ted and Ursula O'Brien, together with Paul Bennett, laboured for many a long night on the layout of the book and the outstanding quality of the design is almost entirely due to their committment and expertise. The colour separation was done by Master Photo Engraving who took exceptional care in reproducing the delicate colours of Grose's painting. In printing the book, W. & G. Baird showed their long-established concern for quality. From the start the project has been sustained by the enthusiasm of Edward McParland and Nicholas Robinson and it would never have been completed without the support of my wife, who had to endure Daniel Grose as a companion in the household far longer than any of us expected.

# Preface

Nicholas K. Robinson

As chairman of the Irish Architectural Archive, I am pleased that we celebrate fifteen years of the Archive's existence with the publication of Daniel Grose's *Antiquities of Ireland*.

The sudden appearance of a completely unknown manuscript, which is both beautiful and significant, is the romantic side of archival work. And there is no doubt of the excitement that was felt when Lord Rossmore first brought to us Daniel Grose's hitherto unknown supplement to the magisterial work of his uncle Francis Grose, whose own *Antiquities of Ireland* was published 200 years ago.

After the romance of discovery comes the hard work of editing, commenting on, photographing, designing and publishing the manuscript appropriately. The Irish Architectural Archive sees its publishing programme as an essential part of its work, whereby it reaches out to a larger public than the thousands of visitors who can study its collections in person. *Vanishing Country Houses of Ireland* (published in collaboration with the Irish Georgian Society) celebrated domestic architecture in Ireland of the 18th and 19th centuries, and documented its losses. *The Architecture of Richard Morrison and William Vitruvius Morrison* told the story of Ireland's greatest domestic architects of the early 19th century. *New Lease of Life* is a monographic study of Thomas Ivory's Blue Coat School in Dublin. With Roger Stalley's editing of Daniel Grose's *Antiquities of Ireland*, the Irish Architectural Archive extends its scope from the classical to the medieval and, beyond, to the archaeological.

The *Antiquities of Ireland* is by far the most ambitious of these undertakings, and in its publication we have relied on assistance from many friends. While Professor Stalley lists his own acknowledgements elsewhere, as chairman I would like to thank here Lord Rossmore for bringing his manuscript to us and for allowing us to publish it. And we are grateful to all those who have supported the project financially, especially Ken Rohan of Rohan Holdings Ltd, the Marc Fitch Fund and the Office of Public Works. High standards, such as those maintained by the Irish Architectural Archive in its publications, put a heavy financial burden on the Archive and on its supporters; it is our goal to establish a revolving fund to support future publications.

If Daniel Grose's *Antiquities of Ireland* is part of our celebration of fifteen years' work in the Irish Architectural Archive, there is another. In 1991 we moved to new premises in 73 Merrion Square, Dublin, made available to us by the generosity of government and the Department of the Taoiseach. So in saying good-bye to the Royal Society of Antiquaries of Ireland who were hospitable landlords to the infant Archive, we look forward to a still more exciting future in our new home. With the continuing support of government, the Irish Architectural Archive intends to consolidate its position as the principal source of information on Irish architecture, past and present.

# Foreword

Ken Rohan

The history of construction in Ireland is a long and honourable one. From prehistoric times to the present day Irish architects, builders and artists have designed, erected and decorated buildings of all kinds: their legacy illustrates our history. Some of these buildings have vanished. Many — even of the greatest antiquity — survive both for our use and pleasure. As chairman of Rohan Holdings Ltd and as a director of the Irish Architectural Archive I am delighted to be associated with this important and beautiful book.

In the late 18th century, Francis Grose set out to examine the country and its ancient buildings, and to record their appearance and history. His original volumes, published in the 1790s, are now definitive works of reference. Here for the first time is published a supplement to this work, prepared in the early 19th century by Francis Grose's nephew Daniel, who collaborated with him on his earlier work. Here are nearly 100 watercolour views of the Ireland of nearly 200 years ago, showing her monasteries, her castles, her towns, her sculpture as well as her boats and her fishermen and her frock-coated tourists.

The patient work of recording this great stock of building has been inherited by The Irish Architectural Archive. From cottage to country house, from mill to church to factory to village street, it documents — in pictures and words — the legacy of Irish builders. Rohan Holdings is proud to help it in its work and to wish it well.

'... without a competent fund of Antiquarian learning, no one
will ever make a respectable figure, either as a Divine, a Lawyer,
Statesman, Soldier, or even a private Gentleman .... it is the
*sine qua non* of several of the more liberal professions, as well as
many trades.' (Francis Grose)[1]

# Introduction

In July 1989 the staff of the Irish Architectural Archive received a visit from Lord Rossmore, who
brought with him a rather unusual leather bound book that had long been in the family library. The
staff of the Archive is used to encountering surprising and often beautiful things, normally architectural
drawings or photographs, but this was altogether exceptional. Written in longhand, the volume
contained an account of Irish monuments by Daniel Grose, nephew of the celebrated Francis Grose
(1731-91), best known for his studies of medieval antiquities. Lord Rossmore's book consisted of a
third volume or supplement to Francis Grose's *Antiquities of Ireland* (1791-5), a volume hitherto unknown
to the general public. The chief delight of the new discovery was the presence of eighty-nine watercolours,
all painted by Daniel himself. These were pasted into the book as it was being written, and several
of them depict monuments which have since been drastically altered or destroyed. Although a few
watercolours by Daniel Grose are preserved in Dublin libraries,[2] this is by far the largest collection
of his paintings to survive.

As the first instalment of Francis Grose's *Antiquities of Ireland* appeared in 1791, the Directors of
the Archive felt it would be appropriate to mark the 200th anniversary by publishing Daniel's third
volume in 1991. When approached with the idea, Lord Rossmore very willingly gave his support.
It has not proved possible to publish the supplement in the same format as the earlier volumes, since
none of Daniel's illustrations had been engraved and his text would have required considerable revision.
Instead the text is being published as it was written, complete with spelling mistakes and other errors.
It was also felt that the interest of the watercolours would be enhanced if they were accompanied by
a modern commentary. The book is thus neither a facsimile of the original manuscript, nor does it
repeat the format of the previous volumes. It does, however, follow Daniel's intentions as closely as
possible and we trust he would not be disappointed by this belated publication of his work.

\*      \*      \*      \*      \*

Although information about Daniel Grose is sparse, there is a reliable record of his death, which occurred
at Carrick-on-Shannon in May 1838.[3] He had evidently been living in Ireland for many years. Had
it not been for his uncle's passion for antiquities, however, he might never have set foot in the country.
It was the sequence of events in May 1791 that brought Daniel to prominence and eventually
transformed him into an expert on Irish monuments.

The early weeks of May 1791 had been a frenetic time for Francis Grose, who was busy preparing his great work on Irish antiquities. This had been announced to the public earlier in the year. An advertisement of March 25th explained that the forthcoming publication would contain a 'Collection of Views of the most remarkable Ruins and Ancient Buildings, Accurately drawn on the spot' and that to each view would be appended a historical explanation, 'with every interesting Circumstance relating thereto'.[4] The book was to be published in instalments, at intervals of about a month and the cost would be 3s 6d per number. Early in May 1791 Francis was hard at work, together with his servant Thomas Cocking, collecting material at sites between Dublin and Dundalk. On the 12th of the month he was back in Dublin. That evening he set out to dine with Horace Hone, the son of his old friend, the painter Nathaniel Hone, but on arriving at Hone's house in Dorset street, 'he was seized with an apoplectic fit, which in a few moments ended his life'.[5] Three days later Cocking was still at work in the country, apparently unaware of his master's demise.[6] Francis Grose was buried on May 18th in the churchyard at Drumcondra, in a plot belonging to the architect James Gandon, his grave inscribed 'To the Memory of Captain Grose FAS Who whilst in cheerful Conversation With his Friends Expired in their Arms without a sigh'.[7]

Francis Grose was an astonishing character: writer, artist, antiquarian and *bon vivant*. He was also an astonishing sight. He possessed an immense girth, weighed twenty-two stone, yet stood a mere five feet high. With 'his Falstaffian wit and good humour', he made a marvellous companion and was renowned as 'a great eater and drinker'.[8] He was also fond of sleep. By 1791 he was one of England's most celebrated antiquarians and his four volumes on *The Antiquities of England and Wales* (1773-6) had been so successful that two extra volumes were prepared. Having recently completed further volumes on *The Antiquities of Scotland* (1789-91), it is no surprise that he turned his attention to Ireland. His unexpected death was a calamity for the new project, as only twenty-four views had been engraved and a mere seven pages written. The *St James's Evening Post* recorded the news with the firm pronouncement: 'Death put an end to his Views and Prospects'.[9] Francis Grose was a hard act to follow, but, thanks to the intervention of four people, *The Antiquities of Ireland* survived.

The first was the publisher Samuel Hooper of High Holborn, who had invested substantial sums on engravings and the high-quality paper needed for the work. Publishing in the eighteenth century was a precarious business, as Hooper well knew, having experienced bankruptcy in 1778-9.[10] For good commercial reasons he was anxious to see *The Antiquities of Ireland* finished. The second person was the Reverend Edward Ledwich, vicar of Aghaboe (Laois), a distinguished, if controversial, antiquarian. A year earlier Ledwich had produced his own volume on Irish antiquities, and it was no doubt because of this that the publisher invited him to write the historical entries in place of Francis Grose. The third individual was William Burton Conyngham of Slane Castle, who had a large private collection of antiquarian drawings. 'With unexampled munificence, generosity and patriotism' he allowed these to be used for the work.[11] The final person was Daniel Grose, whose part in seeing the project through to completion has never been adequately recognised.

Daniel, who was twenty-five when his uncle died, was a captain in the Royal Engineers.[12] Perusal of his book leaves no doubt about his passion for guns and battles. When describing a medieval castle, his first instinct was to consider its strategic position, in particular whether it was exposed to artillery from surrounding hills. (The anachronism of this approach, given the age of some of the castles, did

To JAMES GANDON, & SAMUEL WALKER Esq.rs Mr HORACE HONE & RICHd EDWd MERCIER who attended the funeral of the late FRANCIS GROSE Esq.r to the Church of DRUMCONDRA, near DUBLIN where his REMAINS were deposited 18 May 1791.
N.B. the figure of Capt Grose in this Print
is placed on his own Grave.
This View is inscribed by their
Humble Servant
SAMUEL HOOPER

*Drumcondra church, with the portly figure of Francis Grose standing on his own grave.*
*The engraving, published in September 1791, was taken from a drawing by Daniel Grose.*

not apparently occur to him). His *Supplement* includes lengthy accounts of the siege of Kinsale (1601) and the siege of Dunboy Castle (1602). As a military man with an interest in antiquities, Daniel was following a long tradition in Ireland, two obvious precursors being (Colonel) Charles Vallancey (1721-1812) and (Lieutenant-Colonel) William Burton Conyngham (1733-96). Daniel evidently enjoyed fishing and sailing; in 1833 he recounted a visit to a site near Castletownbere (Cork) as a member of a fishing party.[13] Fishermen appear in no less than seven of his pictures, and he rarely lost the chance of drawing a boat. Indeed one has to report that he showed more concern for the rigging of his vessels than for the subtleties of medieval architecture.

By 1791 Daniel had turned himself into a competent topographical artist. There is no record of his receiving any professional training, which perhaps explains his shaky grasp of figure drawing and the finer points of perspective. He may have been taught to paint by his uncle Francis, who is known to have had some skill as a teacher. It was a matter of comment that Francis had managed to make a decent painter out of his servant, Thomas Cocking, whom he otherwise referred to disparagingly as his 'Guinea-Pig'.[14] Alternatively Daniel may have learnt to draw in the Royal Engineers. Some of his training no doubt took place at Woolwich, where the distinguished landscape painter Paul Sandby was chief drawing master from 1768 until 1797.[15]

Daniel's style of painting, which did not change significantly during his career, includes a number of recognisable mannerisms. He tended to exaggerate ashlar masonry, particularly quoinstones, giving a classical edge to his depiction of medieval architecture. Shadows were painted with scrupulous consistency. Sunlit walls were modelled in broad washes of olive, pink and apricot, the distinctiveness of which can be seen when Daniel's pictures are compared with those of other artists. (His near contemporary, Angelo Bigari, the Italian scene painter, who was active as a topographical artist in Ireland, preferred to depict masonry in large blocks of bright colour, as if he was painting Tuscan marble.) Occasionally Daniel gave an autumnal feel to his work, with minute touches of deep tan, a colour used more extensively by his uncle. When depicting rivers he used a series of inked horizantals, sometimes leaving the paper unpainted to suggest reflections. He adopted a number of standard conventions, painting clouds in three distinct gradations (white, light grey and a more opaque grey-blue). Such techniques were welcomed by the engravers, and it is important to remember that Daniel Grose prepared his watercolours with engraving in mind. What is most impressive about his work, however, is the sense of unity he achieved through the use of a restrained and limited palette. Although he struggled with perspective, subtle changes of tone allowed him to achieve a real sense of distance in his landscapes, while at the same time suggesting a hazy warmth.

Many of his pictures include a couple of spectators, usually well-dressed gentlemen in top hats, who are sometimes engaged in lively discussion. On ten occasions the artist himself is shown at work. Although these figures are conventional enough, they are more than just visual props.[16] The presence of the artist helped to underline the 'faithfulness' of the work, the fact that the paintings were actually based on sketches made at the site. The figures also introduce a sense of immediacy, as if the characters were modern witnesses to a long forgotten past. Although these figures include a couple of gravediggers, plus a man with a pick and a labourer carrying hay, the local working population are for the most part excluded.

Daniel's style of painting remained rooted in the techniques of the eighteenth century. He was as talented as most of the other topographical artists of the day and superior to many. His handling of colour, for example, was more sophisticated than that of Gabriel Beranger, his compositions were generally more coherent and he could create a far more convincing impression of distance. It is important, however, to remember the huge gulf separating these amateur watercolour artists from those who painted large landscapes in oils, a medium in which William Ashford (1746-1824) and Thomas Sautell Roberts (1760-1826) reigned supreme.[17]

Strickland states that Daniel attended his uncle's funeral on May 18th 1791.[18] There is no doubt that he prepared the famous illustration of Drumcondra church, with the portly figure of Francis Grose standing on his own grave, published as an engraving in September (Plate 1). It was not until the following year that Daniel turned his full attention to Irish topography. During the summer of 1792 he travelled throughout Ireland, energetically making sketches to illustrate his uncle's book. In May and June he was in Galway and by early August he was concentrating on Carlow and Laois. September took him to Meath and Louth. He worked at a frenetic pace. In the space of 23 days from 28th August

*Drawing of the castle at Ballyloughan (Carlow), one of many ink sketches made by Daniel Grose in 1792.*
(*National Library of Ireland*)

until 19th September he covered at least 200 miles, often visiting several monuments each day.[19] His pen and ink drawings, many of which are in the National Library, have a spontaneity which tends to be lost in the later watercolours (Plate 2). On occasions he made notes on the drawings as reminders to himself — brick, hay, blue slate, grass etc. These drawings were copied at a reduced scale, then painted in watercolour, ready for the engraver. The reductions were not necessarily made by Daniel Grose himself; several of his sketches were in fact reduced and coloured by Thomas Cocking. Attribution of the finished paintings to individual artists can thus be a hazardous operation, but it seems that fourteen of Daniel's drawings formed the basis of engravings in the first volume of the *Antiquities*, along with twenty-five of Thomas Cocking's. In the second volume forty-one of the engravings ultimately came from Daniel's compositions, almost a third of the whole. The latter were all products of his 1792 campaign.

In addition to these newly prepared views, both volumes of *The Antiquities of Ireland* relied heavily on drawings from the collection of William Burton Conyngham. As early as 1778 he had embarked on a plan, together with Charles Vallancey, to collect drawings of Irish antiquities, with a view to

*Monastic ruins on Saints' Island, Lough Ree, from Daniel Grose's Supplement.*

publishing them in a 'handsome book'.[20] The project was taken up by the Hibernian Antiquarian Society, formed in 1779, but it foundered when the Society broke up in 1783 amidst quarrels between Vallancey and Ledwich over the interpretation of Irish history. Drawings had nevertheless been acquired from a wide range of artists, including Gabriel Beranger, John James Barralet and Angelo Bigari. William Burton Conyngham must have welcomed Grose's initiative as an opportunity to publish his collection, and it is no surprise that he gave the project enthusiastic support. One oddity is that no works by Beranger were included in the book, despite the fact that Burton Conyngham had commissioned many drawings from him. The publisher may have felt that Beranger's rather naïve style had become outmoded, though the reasons were probably more personal. It seems that Beranger had plans to publish his own work and he certainly prepared books of watercolours for sale.[21] He may also have taken Vallancey's side in the furious arguments that broke out after 1783; Ledwich's association with the Grose project must have been the end of it as far as Vallancey and his supporters were concerned.

After 1792 it is difficult to follow Daniel Grose's career in any detail. With the outbreak of the French Revolutionary Wars the following year, he may have been involved in military service, but

*Saints' Island today: the west gable of the church has fallen since Grose's visit and the ruins are now encircled by a phalanx of polished gravestones.*

as he makes no mention of foreign places in his antiquarian writing, it is unlikely he spent much time abroad. He continued to travel in Ireland and before long took up permanent residence in the country. He was in Cork around 1800,[22] and a view of Carlow is specifically dated 1804. Late in his life he referred to 'his progress through Ireland, in search of monastic activities', which suggests a degree of financial independence.[23] The editor of the *Irish Penny Magazine* in 1833 described him as 'a learned author' with 'splendid talents'.[24] Daniel's articles for the magazine, together with the text of his supplement to the *Antiquities*, indicate his knowledge of the Irish countryside and the range of his personal experience.

There is strong circumstantial evidence that his later years were spent in the neighbourhood of Carrick-on-Shannon. This is where he died in 1838 and three members of the Grose family are recorded in the registers of the local parish of Kiltoghert (Leitrim).[25] Monuments in the vicinity of Carrick-on-Shannon are heavily represented in the book, and his son, Daniel Grose Junior, made sketches of local monuments at Cambo, Annaduff, Kilbarry and Lough Rynn, giving the impression that the family home was not far away.

Following the publication of the first two volumes of *The Antiquities of Ireland*, twenty-five years elapsed before Daniel began to prepare his supplement. We know he was working on it after 1823, as he refers to Edward Ledwich (who died in that year) as his 'late worthy friend'.[26] Other references in the text confirm the impression that it was written in the 1820s. In his account of Cloondara (Longford), for example, he enthuses about the construction of the Royal Canal, which reached the town in 1817.[27] Although written late in his life, the book was based on the accumulated experience of forty years, and on occasions he goes to some lengths to explain that his paintings illustrate views which have now changed. The actual watercolours in the book were probably made in the period 1823-38, though they were based on drawings and sketches going back as far as 1792. Thus his drawing of Carlow was made before the partial collapse of the castle in 1814, and the view of Kilronan was prepared before the construction of Castle Tenison. Twenty-three of the paintings are derived from the work of other people. Two rather weak compositions (of Elfeet and Clonmacnoise) came from the Reverend Charles Moore, and all four Armagh views were supplied by Benjamin Bradford. One of his relatives, Lieutenant Arthur Grose of the Royal Navy[28] was the author of eleven drawings, and his own son, Daniel Grose Junior, provided a further six. One gets the impression that Daniel organised family outings to visit antiquities.

The way that Daniel prepared his book, complete with an introductory vignette and apposite verses from Byron, suggests that it was designed for immediate publication, but if so, why were the watercolours stuck into the book and not mounted separately for the engraver? Was the volume just a personal scrapbook rather than a serious publishing enterprise? The answer to this question can be found in the dimensions of the watercolours, which, with two exceptions, are painted to a uniform size, approximately 17.0 x 13.5 cm. These are exactly the dimensions of the paintings prepared in the 1790s for the engravings of the first two volumes,[29] leaving no doubt about Daniel's intentions.

Yet his scheme was thirty years too late. Samuel Hooper, publisher of the earlier volumes, had died in 1793 and his business collapsed within a few years.[30] Major changes had taken place in the social fabric of Ireland after the Act of Union, and the supporters of the original publication were either dead or extremely aged. Moreover Daniel's style was old-fashioned compared with the work of the new generation of topographical artists, not least that of George Petrie (1790-1866). In comparison with Petrie's painstaking, observant technique, Daniel Grose's art seems unsophisticated. It was Petrie who was asked to provide the illustrations for Thomas Cromwell's *Excursions Through Ireland* (1819), and six years later it was Petrie who supplied the drawings for Brewer's *Beauties of Ireland*. These books provided a more varied and comprehensive guide to the country than the traditional antiquarian volumes. Furthermore, Daniel Grose's text was a *pot pourri* of old ideas, some of which lacked the credibility they would have had in the 1790s. Daniel was no scholar and what he writes is frequently muddled. If he submitted his book to potential publishers, it would be no surprise to learn that he got a negative response.

In his preface he explains why he decided to prepare a supplement to his uncle's work. He admits that the text is really a 'vehicle' to convey his drawings and that his prime motive is 'to rescue from oblivion so many curious monuments of the pristine grandeur of this Kingdom', the standard cry of antiquarians of the day. Moreover, he was concerned to give 'some idea of the face of the country'.

But there must have been an element of nostalgia in the enterprise, as he looked through his collection of drawings late in life and wondered what use he could make of them.

The *Supplement* has a wider scope than the earlier volumes. More space is devoted to prehistoric monuments, and Daniel was ready to look at the high crosses, one of the first antiquarian artists to do so. He also included a number of seventeenth-century houses. To widen the interest of the book and enhance its antiquarian status, four pages of 'Miscellaneous Antiquities' were introduced, a heterogeneous collection of stone sculpture and archaeological artefacts. In its geographical spread, the volume has a heavy emphasis on monuments in Cork and Waterford and the upper reaches of the Shannon. This may be explained by Daniel's personal familiarity with these areas, not least the fact that he evidently lived in the neighbourhood of Carrick-on-Shannon. But it also makes sense in terms of the gaps in earlier volumes, which included only one monument each from counties Cork and Longford and only two fom Waterford. Although a few sites are repeated (Strancally, Timoleague, Fenagh, Grandison and Carlow), the views are quite different from those published before.

Many of the paintings are of great interest from an architectural and archaeological point of view. They include a number of monuments which have vanished from the scene, including the great castle of the Mac Coghlans at Cloghan (Offaly), the plantation castle at Aughry (Leitrim) and the stone circle on Hungry Hill (Cork). Other buildings have been dramatically altered since his visit. The parish church at Clonmel (Tipperary) was subjected to a brutal restoration in the nineteenth century, and Daniel's painting is a precious record of its ancient appearance (Plates 5 and 6). A substantial section of the main tower at Grandison (Kilkenny) collapsed in 1823, not many years after his visit. Equally valuable are the depictions of seventeenth-century houses, a badly neglected aspect of Irish architecture. Daniel provides an instructive view of Dromana (Waterford) and his painting brings home the scale of the buildings at Rathcline (Longford) and Manorhamilton (Leitrim). Even his paintings of sculpture are of interest, despite their uncouth style. They include pictures of a missing knight effigy from Molana (Waterford) and a lost piece of Romanesque sculpture from Kilbarry (Roscommon). The painting of the chancel arch at Tuam (Galway) is one of the first attempts to record a complex Romanesque arch in its entirety.

When writing the text of his book plagiarism was of little concern to Daniel, substantial sections being lifted word for word from other authors. The range of quotations suggests that he had a decent library of his own, or at least ready access to one. He borrowed heavily from Smith's *History of County Cork* (1750) and from Mervyn Archdall's *Monasticon Hibernicum* (1786). So much did he trust Archdall's lists of religious houses that he failed to realise that they did not include parish churches. In his account of Youghal, Clonmel and Naas, he assumed the medieval parish churches were local abbeys or friaries, with confusing consequences. It is hard to believe he could make such a mistake since he had visited all the places in person, albeit a long time before. For his general ideas about antiquity he was more dependent on Ledwich than Vallancey, subscribing, for example, to the view that there was little improvement in Irish sculpture until the English arrived. There is no sign that his library contained any books on architecture, a subject of which he had no formal knowledge, finding it difficult to distinguish between the styles of different periods. Admittedly this type of expertise was rare at the time, despite the publication in 1817 of Thomas Rickman's lectures on the styles of English

*The parish church at Clonmel as shown in Daniel Grose's Supplement. The watercolour was based on a drawing made before the reconstruction of the church in the nineteenth century.*

architecture.[31] As a consequence, Daniel could not recognise a latrine chute when he saw one and was deceived into thinking that the eighteenth-century tower at Naas was medieval. Yet on occasions he could be quite perceptive, as when he noticed the evidence for wattlework centering at Cornaveigh and Inisbofin.

The chief value of Daniel's writing lies in other areas, in particular his descriptions of folklore and his romantic approach to the past. He gives a fascinating account of the mythology associated with the relics on Saints' Island and the veneration in which they were held: 'Whoever takes an oath falsely, on any of these pieces of wood, the offenders mouth is immediately transfered [sic] to the back of his head' (p. 84). He was equally intrigued by the 'miraculous trout' that lived in the holy well at Kilronan, and there is an account of the disturbing 'Mad House' at Kilbarry, where the insane were brought in search of a cure through the intervention of St Berach (or St Barry, as Grose calls him). Daniel, always partial to a good anecdote, was impressed by the way cattle could climb the spiral staircase in the castle at Kilnatoora. Elsewhere he discusses the techniques of salmon fishing on the Blackwater, where he was also interested in a local manure called 'trusker', 'being a collection of weeds, grass and other matter, that forms itself into a kind of dung' (p. 53). He seems to have had

*The parish church at Clonmel today. Apart from the octagonal tower,*
*the building is almost unrecognisable from that depicted by Grose.*

a particular affection for the town of Youghal, clearly enjoying the facilities of the new Mall House, complete with its ballroom, orchestra and elegant cut-glass chandeliers.

When he was not quoting from other sources, Daniel was capable of florid prose, dwelling on the 'awesome grandeur' of the landscape or the 'melancholy atmosphere' of ancient buildings. His account of Lottery Castle is not untypical of his style: 'a large Elder Tree springs from the midst and seems to flourish as in scorn over this scene of desolation, and appears to glory in the contrast between its fresh and lively verdure, and the gray [sic] and mouldering ruins time has made: the rank nettle and broad leaved Dock lend their aid, and grow with wild luxuriance in and about the masses of masonry, a great portion of which they hide' (p. 179). His romantic spirit is very evident in his attitude to the past. Even the most substantial buildings, he stresses, are destined to decay. He goes on to explain that the reflective mind 'cannot but be struck with the impotence of mans [sic] best efforts to perpetuate his most durable works, which are little less evanescent than himself, and fade away after a few revolving years, and leave no trace that they had ever been' (p. 92). Ruins provided a salutary reminder of the transitory nature of man's activities and served to rouse the emotions, particularly that of melancholy. With many antiquarian artists a sense of decay was thus an important element in their work, and

Daniel Grose was no exception. His description of Molana, which includes an admission that the ruins were probably more impressive than the architecture of the original monastery, demonstrates that he was not preoccupied with the archaeological details of ancient buildings. Although he stresses the 'faithfulness' of his drawings, his work is generalised and unspecific when compared with contemporary English watercolour artists like James Malton (d.1803) or Michael Angelo Rooker (1746-1801).[32] More important was the evocation of the past and the power of the landscape in which the monuments were set.

There are some hints that Daniel was aware of the literary basis of Romanticism.[33] His picture of the stone circle at Hungry Hill, for example, where 'solitude reigned triumphant in all its horrors' (p. 118), includes an apparently ludicrous attempt to depict rocks and mountains. Is this Daniel's amateur version of the 'Sublime', the frightening, overwhelming nature of the terrain? Elsewhere his landscapes follow more traditional formulae, but they remain as deceptive as a modern holiday brochure. The cheerful rhythm of the hills, the fields bathed in perpetual sunshine and the clean, tidy roads portray a happy tranquillity which scarcely accorded with life as it really was. Instead of the well-dressed gentlemen, attired in top hats and brightly coloured clothes — hardly suitable dress for clambering over dirty monuments — Daniel Grose on his travels must in reality have encountered 'a mass of filth, nakedness and squalor'.[34] Nonetheless his paintings and writing provide a reassuring view of the world. While he was ready to castigate absentee landlords and was alarmed by the peasantry's overdependence on the potato, his view of Ireland was essentially comforting and optimistic, a point made abundantly obvious in his account of Strancally:

> 'the rough and barren sides of a mountain of russet hue, the lively prospect of a well cultivated country yellow with grain; the ancient Castle rising in proud preeminence looking defiance th'o in ruins, towards the peac[e]ful, snug and comfortable cottage, wood and water, these are all here to be met with. At present we can look upon these relics of former tyranny with tranquillity, and bless our happy constitution that circumscribes the power of the lord of the soil, within due bounds, and makes the Peer as accountable to the Law as the peasant' (p. 139).

Daniel Grose combined this blissful idealism with a liberal social outlook. He made no secret of his admiration for William Wilberforce and he had a philanthropic, if patronising, concern for the welfare of the Irish peasantry. On reading his book, one gets the impression of an elderly man, kindly and amusing, but rather detached from the realities of the world.

When examining Daniel's watercolours from an archaeological or architectural point of view, it is easy to be irritated by the lack of precision and detail. But Daniel Grose was not painting for the *cognoscenti* of the 1990s and it is important to remember the restraints under which he operated. In an unpretentious way he sought to create images of Ireland's buildings which conveyed both the drama of their history and the grandeur of the landscape. The rediscovery of Daniel's book is a major event in Irish antiquarian history, not least since it was written and illustrated by the same man. Much of its fascination lies in the ideas and preconceptions which link the pictures and the prose.

## Technical details of the manuscript[35]

The manuscript is bound in brown reversed calf, with a blind-tooled panel border. The title is written on a piece of paper, pasted on the cover. It reads: 'Supplement to the Antiquities of Ireland by Daniel Grose, unpublished, Rossmore'. The pages are sewn on thin vegetable cords at random sewing stations. The volume was clearly acquired as a commercial blank book, with the edges trimmed and sprinkled with fine red ochre. There is no head or tail band. There are ten gatherings with fragments of an eleventh, each complete gathering containing eight leaves. In total there are 140 pages, numbered at the top of each page by the author. Several pages have been removed, particularly between 139 and 140. The first and last leaves are pasted on to the front and back boards. The book itself was manufactured with laid paper, creamy in colour, and the watercolours were painted on a separate thick wove paper, very white in appearance.

The paintings are executed in ink, with ink washes and watercolour. All are surrounded by a black border in heavy ink. A few of the pictures are tipped in, but most have tabs cut at the corners. One painting (the chancel of the parish church at Youghal) has been inlaid into the original page (i.e. a hole was cut into the original page to receive it), an experiment that was not repeated. The painted area of the frontispiece measures 21.5 by 15.6 cm, the vignette 11.0 by 13.8 cm, and all the other watercolours are approximately 13.5 by 17.0 cm. The watercolours have been protected by interleaving in a thin hand-made paper of contemporary date, but with some modern additions.

The text was written in ink with red-ruled margins on all four sides, into which it often runs. The titles were written in a blacker ink, with a thicker nib.

The general condition of the manuscript is good, although the leather of the binding spine has decayed. The watercolours, painted on a stable, neutral cartridge paper, are in pristine condition, with no obvious alteration to their colour values.

# Notes to the Editor's Introduction

1. *The Antiquarian Repertory*, vol. I (1775), p.iii. I first encountered this quotation in Conner (1984), 69.

2. National Library of Ireland (1976 TX) and the Royal Irish Academy (3C 29). There are three watercolours attributed to Daniel Grose in the private collection of Mr Dudley Snelgrove of Ewell, Surrey. Illustrations after Daniel's drawings appeared in the *Irish Penny Magazine* for 1833 and 1841.

3. Strickland (1913), 416. Notices of his death appeared in the *Freeman's Journal* (May 23rd) and the *Dublin Evening Post* (May 22nd).

4. The advertisement is bound into the Trinity College, Dublin, copy of the second volume of *The Antiquities of Scotland* (1791), xxiv. Two different formats were envisaged, but the smaller octavo size at 2s. 6d. does not appear to have been published. There is a general misconception that the two volumes of *The Antiquities of Ireland* were not published until 1794 and 1796 respectively. This is when the volumes were completed, but individual numbers were appearing from 1791 onwards.

5. Strickland (1913), 418.

6. A drawing by Cocking of Timon Castle (R.I.A., 3C 29) is dated May 15th 1791.

7. Quoted from McParland (1988), 190.

8. Strickland (1913), 418; M. Craig (1947), 56-8.

9. Strickland (1913), 419.

10. Maxted (1977), 114.

11. Edward Ledwich's Preface to *The Antiquities of Ireland* (1791).

12. See note 3. Strickland (1913), 415, states that Daniel Grose was a lieutenant in a battalion of Invalid Artillery, but this is incorrect. Strickland has confused Daniel the antiquary with another Daniel Grose, who is indeed listed in the Invalid Artillery, being commissioned in 1763 and promoted to Captain in 1772, when Daniel the antiquary was six years old. This Captain Daniel Grose was killed in 1816. Was he the father of Daniel the antiquary?

13. *Irish Penny Magazine*, II, no. 8 (February 19th 1842), 58 (published posthumously).

14. Craig (1947), 58.

15. Herrman (1986), 25-6. Most of the records of the Royal Military Academy at Woolwich were destroyed by a fire in 1873, so it is no longer possible to confirm whether Daniel Grose

was taught by Sandby. I am grateful to Anne Crookshank for pointing out the relevance of the link with Woolwich.

16. There has been much discussion of late about the sociological importance of such figures: Barrell (1980); for an alternative view see Conner (1984), 55-6.

17. Crookshank and Glin (1978), 127-50.

18. Strickland (1913), 418.

19. The comments about Daniel's travels are based on the dates noted on his drawings.

20. Love (1962), 420.

21. Strickland (1913), 57; Wilde (1870), 63; Harbison (1991), 8-9.

22. In 1833 he refers to being in the area of Cork harbour thirty years before, *Irish Penny Magazine*, I, no. 47 (November 23rd., 1833), 369.

23. *Irish Penny Magazine*, II, no. 6 (February 5th 1842), 47.

24. *Irish Penny Magazine* I, no. 36 (September 7th 1833), 285.

25. Susanne Grose of Annaduff died 1817, aged 21. Charles Grosse of Rosebank died 1862, aged 61. Marriage of Frances Margaret Grose to Wilson Bourns 1834. I am grateful to the Reverend Canon Ivan Biggs for checking these references for me.

26. Preface to the *Supplement*.

27. Delany and Delany (1966), 86.

28. The full identity of this gentleman has yet to be established, despite a search of the army and navy lists.

29. R.I.A., 3C 29. This volume contains the watercolours as they were sent to the engraver. It provides a marvellous cross-section of Irish watercolour painting between 1775 and 1795.

30. Maxted (1977), 114.

31. Rickman (1817).

32. Conner (1984).

33. There is an excellent essay on Irish landscape painting and Romanticism by John Hutchinson (1985), 11-26.

34. Comment by George Nicholls, quoted by Cullen (1968), 126.

35. This report could not have been written without the advice of Mr A.G. Cains, Director of the Conservation Laboratory, The Library, Trinity College.

# Editor's Note

Daniel Grose's punctuation was ambiguous and inconsistent so in the interests of clarity the editor has made a number of minor alterations. These include the removal of underlinings, plus a plethora of redundant hyphens, dots and full stops. Adjustments have also been made to Grose's erratic paragraph structure. Spelling mistakes have not been corrected unless the word is almost unrecognisable. In these cases clarification has been given in brackets afterwards. For technical reasons associated with the design of the book it proved necessary to rearrange the order of some of Grose's entries. The original order is given in the appendix. A general view of Kilronan, which serves as a frontispiece in the original, has been placed towards the end of the book alongside the passage describing Kilronan.

# Description
# of the
# Vignette

This plate displays those images alluded to in the lines beneath from Lord Biron; on the distant hill to the left is the desolated Cottage which the figure (the stranger) has left behind him disregarded, and in haste ascends the eminence on the right, to satisfy his curiosity by viewing nearer the ruined Tower, bent by the tempest, or devastating hand of war; the Tower leans considerably from the perpendicular, thus rent and thrown by the force of the gunpowder with which its former haughty strength was demolished; one of its battlements alone is left, but enough remains to show it was once a post of consequence — erected to defend a pass from the sea, an arm of which is seen in the background. In the front is a solitary Pillar against which once hung ample gates, of that description generally found about old Castles in this Island, behind the Tower is an Ivied Arch supposed to be the remains of one of the ports of the Bawne or Court of the Castle, the ruined wall of which is seen beyond it.

Most of the strong Castles in Ireland were blown up, and demolished by Oliver Cromwell and his Army.

Instances of leaning towers of this description occur at Ballynamona a Preceptory of Knights Templars between Cork and Mallow,[1] and at the Abbey of Elgin in Scotland where a tall tower is much more out of the perpendicular than that represented in the Vignette,[2] and has continued so beyond the memory of the oldest man, in those parts.

# SUPPLEMENT

## TO THE

## ANTIQUITIES

### OF

## IRELAND

### BY DANIEL GROSE ESQ.[r]

The roofless cot. decayed and rent,
Will scarse delay the passer by. —
The tower by war or tempest bent,
While yet may frown one battlement,

Demands and daunts the strangers eye
Each ivied arch — and pillar lone,
Pleads haughtily for glories gone!
............................. Byrons Giaur. ...

# Preface

The author of the following Supplement feels a great degree of timidity in appearing before the Public, after the learned labours of his late worthy friend Doctor Ledwich in the two first Volm:[s] of the Antiquities of Ireland;[3] his only motive for hazarding such an attempt is the wish to rescue from oblivion so many curious monuments of the pristine grandeur of this Kingdom, and he considers the few circumstances he has collected of their antient history, as nothing more than as vehicles to convey his drawings, the chief merit of which consists in their faithfulness.

At the same time he has endeavoured to give some idea of the face of the Country, which abounds with many and very striking beauties, and has in consequence not confined his drawing to the ruin alone, but has chosen such views of his subjects as combine in some degree a general prospect of the neighbouring landscape, where it could be procured; he also introduces several Plates of Miscellaneous Antiquities, Druids Altars, Temples &c, in order to acquire a greater degree of variety in the Work.

Such being his motives he submits his labours with less reluctance and forbears to trespass longer on the readers patience.

Dan:[l] Cha:[s] Grose

# An Introduction
## to the
## Monumental Antiquities
### of
## Ireland

In order to illustrate as far as possible every branch of the Antiquities of this kingdom an Introduction to its Monumental remains has been suggested, as an appropriate commencement to the 3:$^{d}$ Vol:$^{m}$ or Supplement to Groses Antiquities of Ireland; th'o this portion is less luminous than those already entered on, in the first parts of the work, it is still a very interesting study, and is only wanting to make the plan compleat, so far and so ably gone into by that master of his art who there so learnedly display'd his knowledge of the subject.(x)

Every nation in the known world, as well Christian as Pagan, has from the remotest ages exhibited a pride in perpetuating the memory of their princes and great men, relatives and friends, by raising Monumental structures over their remains; even the savage Islanders of the Pacific Ocean, participated in this pride, and in the eastern countries the magnificence and magnitude of their sepulchral monuments have been extraordinary indeed.[4]

The Egyptian Pyramids still continue stupendous specimens of this kind, and it would far exceed the limits of an introduction, to notice the instances of this love of posthumous fame, still to be seen in every part of the globe, as well antient as modern.

As the arts spread over the civilized parts of the world, this pride gained strength and th'o at the present day such gigantic monuments as those above alluded to, are not the fashion of the times, the finest labour of the architect and the Sculptor, are lavished profusely on those efforts of human pride, endeavouring to lengthen the evanescent memory of frail man, beyond that narrow space the God of nature and of time has alloted.

Men strain this anxious wish, even to the most absurd lengths, and many instances occur every day, of those whose whole life has been marked by the most miserly meanness, lavishing immence sums on a sumptuous funeral, and superb monument, which at the best can only serve to point out to posterity their former misery and egregious folly.

(x) Doctor Ledwich

The monument adorned by the undeserved eulogy of the venal panegyrist, when seen, brings forth animadversions on the past, and rakes up the memory of those actions best shrouded in oblivion. But when the Mausoleum covers the remains of virtue and honor, when the marble records on its polished surface, the actions of those hero's who bled and fell for their country; or when the patriots fame is recounted, who banished slavery from the traffic of civilized nations, and those efforts enumerated, which gave wholesome laws to a thankful country;[5] then do they answer the best of purposes, and hold forth a powerful stimulous to great and glorious exertions in the Senate and the field, and warm the hearts of those who behold the well earned reward of such generous deeds, and lead them to emulate those noble exploits they see commemorated.

Rude has been the first efforts of art in every country, and particularly in the art of Sculpture, and before it was known the most easily acquired materials were laid hold of, to form Sepulchral Monuments, to perpetuate the memory of the illustrious dead.

Unhewn stones of every description offered themselves without much trouble, and were consequently used for this, and many religious purposes. We still see them composing the temple in which Druidic rights were celebrated, and forming those Cromlechs or Altars on which the Priest crowned with the sacred Missletoe, sacrificed the victim from whose entrails he drew his auguries, and predicted from the figures the blood traced in flowing down the accidental channels in the rough stone, that formed the sloping roof.[6]

The same kind of stones were set up as pillars to perpetuate the enactment of laws, the memory of any great event, or to point out the field of battle; the unhewn pillar stone was chosen to mark to posterity where rested the bones of the general fallen in the fight: nor were greater sepulchral honors paid to the Soverign, or Toparch of a country.

At Broadly in the County of Kildare, is a tall pillar standing on a conical mount, this was Sepulchral; Brugh-lea in Irish is the Stone monument, which was easily changed to Broadley.[7]

A very antient monument appears to be the Carne or Carned, an heap of loose unhewn stones, this was used as a memorial to perpetuate the occurrence of any very extraordinary event, or death, this is a custom of very antient practise, and frequent mention is made of such in the Holy Scriptures,[8] as in use amongst the Patriarchs, as well by the most celebrated heathen authors, and was introduced and established here by the Celtes. It prevails to this day, and on the spot where any accidental death by violence has taken place, a monument of loose stones is immediately raised, to commemorate the circumstance, and every passer by, thinks it incumbent on them to throw another stone to encrease the heap.

The Firbolgs[9] or Belgic Colonies who succeeded the Celtes, formed chambers of dry stones, which they covered with long flags, in them they practised various of their superstitions; at length they became the burial places of warriors and great men. These galleries were sometimes in the shape of a Cross, and contained Urns or earthen vessels, in which were inclosed the ashes of those in honor of whom they were constructed; an instance of this occurs at New Grange near Dublin, a minute description of which with drawings may be found in the Introduction to the 1:[st] Vol:[m] of these Antiquities.[10]

Smith tells us in his 2:[d] Vol:[m] of the History of Cork, that in the year 1737 three large Urns were discovered near Castle Saffron, the estate of John Love Esq:[r] placed in a kind of triangle in the earth, about 100 yards from a Danish intrenchment, made of fine Clay dried by the fire, each Urn 4 feet high, one of these contained the bones of a human skeleton, another a substance like honey supposed to be flesh, and in the 3:[d] a small quantity of Copper pieces as large as halfpence, void of any inscription or stamp. He also mentions the discovery of a number of small urns containing burnt human bones; at Assolas by the Rev:[d] M:[r] Gore in the same County.[11]

Many other instances have occurred of these earthen vessels being found in various parts of Ireland, containing ashes presumed to be those of a human body; and this certainly was one mode of enterment in other Kingdoms, as many of these kind of Urns have been dug up, both in England and Scotland. It is also certain that earthen coffins were made use of at a very early period in Ireland, one of this description was found nearly resembling the usual shape, at Carne the seat of William Bennison Esq:[r] in the County of Cavan;[12] in this Coffin a brazen head of a Javelin and several curious antient Irish ornaments were found.

Sir Ja:[s] Ware in his Antiquities of Ireland gives us the following account of an antient Irish Sepulcher;[13] after endeavouring to prove that the Druids burnt their dead, and no doubt remained, that the same rites were observed by the Irish, he goes on to say ''For in our times, in the year 1646, while they were working the line of fortification in the eastern suberbs of Dublin, an antient Sepulcher was digg'd up; it lay south west, and north east, and was built of eight marble stones, whereof two covered, and the rest supported it. It was in length 6 foot and 2 Inches, and in bredth three foot and one inch, the thickness of the stones was three inches. At each corner was erected a stone 4 foot high, and hard by at the south west end another in form of a Pyramis of 6 foot high, but of rude work, and of that kind of stone we call a Millstone. In the Sepulcher was found a great quantity of coals, ashes and bones of men, some burn'd, some half burnt; a work, as is believed of the Danes, built in memory of some of their nobility, before they were christians. The manner of burning the dead, and collecting their ashes, amongst the Danes, may be seen in Olaus Wormius of antient sepulchers in hills, mountains &c. Of this stone Crypt he gives a drawing illustrative of the description.

Alth'o Ireland abounds in very many beautiful and highly curious specimens of antiquity, both in architecture and sculpture, yet in Monumental Antiquities it is not so abundant, subjects but seldom occur, and those are generally to be met with in Cathedral Churches in cities, where the monastic establishments have been preserved with care, and such relics paid due regard to.

Time the great destroyer must have occasioned this scarsety in religious houses remote from cities, as so many ruins of noble structures to be met with in this Kingdom, must have been adorned with the antient Monuments of those families who were the founders of them, and who it is said, did actually leave their bones beneath their roofs.

This very plainly appears from the many Arches and Niches still to be seen in various religious houses, now empty and entirely divested of the Monumental figures that formerly filled them.

At the suppression of Monasteries in this Kingdom, many of those fine structures were suffered to fall to decay, and no great number of them preserved for the purposes of Protestant worship, except in large towns as before observed, and when parish churches were erected where the Corbieship formerly existed, the old building has totally disappeared, and no vestige of it remains; at least this is in general the case, as they were thrown down for the sake of the cut stone, & materials they afforded for building; and but few instances at present occur where this last sort of devastation has not in some measure taken place. However now and then a tomb appears as will be shown. Many magnificent monuments we may therefore conclude, has been buried beneath the ruins of those buildings they formerly served to adorn, a striking instance of which is exemplified in the Tomb of Saint Kevin at Glandelough County of Wicklow where a small stone roofed Crypt 14 feet in length was entirely buried under the fallen rubbish of one of the neighbouring churches, and every memorial of it lost.

## Tomb of Saint Kevin at Glandelough, Co:<sup>y</sup> of Wicklow.

The discovery of this very curious Monument was made by the late Sam:[l] Hayes Esq:[r] who searching amongst the ruins of the Seven Churches at Glandelough in his neigh-bourhood, found this Tomb in the Crypt above mentioned, where it had been concealed for ages.[14] The face of the Monument is all that at present remains, a stone of a triangular shape, on which is represented the figure of the Saint, sitting in a kind of pulpet, with a book spread open before him, supported by two of his Disciples, habited in long loose robes, the one on the right hand holding a flaggon, and the opposite grasping a pastoral staff.[15]

The Saint is represented in a tight dress fitting his shape, his hair is disposed in rows of curls radiating from the centre, and covering his ears, and his upper lip is adorned with a large pair of Mustachoes. The figures are very rudely cut, and devoid of any proportion, yet are still very prominent; this was the work of the 9:[th] Century, when the art of Sculpture had made but little progress; the tomb as found by M:[r] Hayes has disappeared, and this piece of it, lies amongst a heap of loose stones in the open air.

The Crypt in which this tomb was found,[16] was then entire, and the entrance adorned with sculptures extremely curious, drawings of which are given in the Introduction already alluded to. For a further history of the life of this Saint, and the miracles wrought by him at Glandelough the reader is refered to the plate of historical sculptures found at that place, amongst the ruins of the Seven Churches.

Little improvement in Monumental sculpture seems to have taken place untill the arrival of the English in this Kingdom; before that it is very probable the advancement in this art, kept pace with the progress of Architecture; the first religious houses were constructed of wood, and untill stone buildings took place in lieu of these frail structures, it is probable, that many effigies on monumental works, were of the same materials, as those in stone were but rare. We read in the Preface to the English Antiquities, that figures in wood were frequently found in churches, particularly in the Church of Ayot S:[t] Lawrence in Hertfordshire, and in S:[t] Mary Overy in Southwark. The date of these kind of Monuments is placed in the 10:[th] Century.[17]

When the English settled in Ireland, it is natural to conclude they brought their stile of

## 1. Glendalough: the 'tomb of St Kevin' (Wicklow)

*Two centuries ago this piece of relief carving from Glendalough engendered a huge amount of excitement among Irish antiquaries, many of whom were convinced that it depicted St Kevin himself. At the time it was lying loose among debris and it was not until the 1870s that it was installed over the south door of the 'tomb of St Kevin', a building now generally known as the 'Priests' House'. A large part of the upper left section of the stone is missing and it is not certain whether it was intact in Grose's time. Like other artists, he may have been tempted to restore the missing parts in his drawing. The date of the carving is a matter of controversy, though modern opinion inclines towards the twelfth century. Executed in shallow relief, the sculpture shows an enthroned figure, probably Christ rather than St Kevin, flanked by ecclesiastics, one holding a bell and the other a crosier. It is unlikely that Grose studied the carving for himself, no doubt depending on the drawings of others. As a result he has managed to transform the bell into a flask or 'flaggon', and Christ has been presented with an enormous moustache. The drawing is very inaccurate; even the blue and grey modelling cannot conceal the crudity of the finished work.*

Monumental sculpture along with them, and that it became soon prevalent throughout the Kingdom, the general character, attitude and dress of the figures placed upon Monuments executed after that period, resemble in every respect those found in England and Scotland.

The Knight is represented at full length on his back in Sculpture raised as high as life, over a kind of low Table-tomb, generally higher at the head than the feet. His head rests on a cushion and his feet against a Dog, the emblem of fidelity,[18] his right hand grasps a sword, and the left crosses the breast; he is habited in armour, generally a coat of Mail or Hawberk. Sometimes in this country the Knight is habited in plate armour, but these are not of so old a date. Frequently the hands are raised in prayer, and often crossed over the breast, but this last is not so common.

The specimens generally to be met with in Ireland, consists of the Table on which the figure is carved, removed from the tomb, which has disappeared, and the flag lies on the ground, or is raised against a wall or heap of stones; without any inscription, affording nothing but conjecture to ascertain to whom they belonged. In the Church yard of Old Kilcullen County of Kildare,[19] occurs one of these figures large as life, it represents in high relief a Knight in a compleat suit of Mail armour or Hawberk round his body, his arms and legs, from the elbows and knees downwards are defended by jointed plates, his sword is girded round his body, and grasped in his left hand, the other arm is over his breast; the head rests on a cushion and is covered by an open Helmet flat at top having in the front a figure resembling some animal probably a Lion rampant, possibly the crest of the Knight, and the feet rests against a Dog. It is totally devoid of Inscription, and no clue is left to conjecture who he was.

In the Abbey of Graige-na-managh Co:ʸ of Kilkenny, is a figure greatly resembling the one just described;[20] it is in a much more perfect state, highly raised, and the sculpture fresh and sharp: the country people in this neighbourhood will have it, that this was the effigy of Strong-bow, but the error of this tradition need not be pointed out here — this is also without inscription, but appears with the foregoing to be the work of the 12:ᵗʰ Century.

## Tomb of Reymond Le Gross Abbey of S:ᵗ Molana, Co:ʸ Waterford.

The subject here presented will best give an idea of the kind of Monuments in use in the 12:ᵗʰ Century, th'o differering from those already described; it is supposed to be the figure of Reymond Le Gross, one of the first English adventurers who settled in this Island,[21] we are informed it was placed over the body of the chief in the Abbey of S:[t] Molana, in an Island of the Black-water, about two miles and an half from Youghall; it was removed from amongst the rubbish of this building which is greatly in ruins, and brought to the place where it now stands, reared against the wall of a Romish Chapel, a little way outside the above mentioned town. Reymond was a great benefactor to this Monastery, and History tells us he was actually buried here. The figure is full Six feet high cut on a red grit flag, it is raised and prominent, and the drapery exhibits still a great degree of sharpness, and some skill; the face is almost totally obliterated, and it otherwise shows marks of decay that points out its great antiquity. He is in the act of drawing his sword which is brought before him, the head rests on a cushion ornamented with tassels and is without an helmet or any kind of covering. The body is defended by a Cuirass, and a drapery hangs down from the middle over the thighs; in the armour and drapery it greatly differs from those Tombs already described and certainly these appear to be a pointed distinction.

By the crossed feet of the figure he appears to have been a Crusader, or a Knight of the Crusade (as according to Fran:[s] Grose in His Preface to the English Antiquities) not only those who had actually served in the Holy Land, were intitled to this monumental distinction, but it was assumed by, and permitted to persons who had taken up the Cross, or made the vow to go thither;[22] but died before the accomplishment; and frequently by those who in lieu of personal attendance had contributed a considerable sum of money towards the expences of that service. This might apply to Reymond Le Gros, the great antiquity of the sculpture, its having been brought from the Abbey of which he was the benefactor favors the conjecture; but be this as it may, the figure is evidently the work of those times in which this Chief flourished viz:[t] the 12 Century. I cannot take leave of these times without presenting to the reader a description of one of the rarest specimens of Monumental sculpture perhaps now existing in this Kingdom, and where no doubt can be encouraged in placing its date; this is the Tomb of Felim Mac-Cahall Croudearg, (the red handed) O Conor King of Conaught, in Irish marble, in the Dominican Friary Roscommon.[23] It is a table tomb, and is placed under an arch in the thickness of the wall, on the North near where the Altar stood. The Arch is now plain, but the Tomb was magnificently adorned; the table has been suffered to remain in its proper place, he lies in the usual position clothed in long robes and grasping in his right hand the Royal Scepter.

## 2. Molana: tomb of 'Raymond le Gros' (Waterford)

*This is one of Daniel Grose's most valuable drawings, depicting an impressive effigy from Molana, which vanished in the course of the nineteenth century. Its present whereabouts is unknown. Despite the ungainly character of the drawing, it is obvious that Grose was trying to depict a cross-legged knight in the act of seizing his sword, a type familiar in English and Irish tomb sculpture between 1250 and 1350. The legs and arms were probably defended by mail; a loose surcoat, held by a belt, reached down to the knees. Although Grose has depicted a cuirass over the chest, it is likely that this is a misreading of the upper folds of the surcoat. The extraordinarily agitated drapery, if accurately depicted, recalls that on the famous effigy at Dorchester (Oxfordshire). Raymond le Gros was a member of Strongbow's household and played a prominent part in the invasion of Ireland in 1170. His connection with Molana depends on an uncorroborated statement by the seventeenth-century antiquary, Sir James Ware. As Raymond died before 1200 and the style of the carving suggests a date of about 1300-50, the identification is suspect.*

The head reposes on a cushion and is adorned with what appears a Diadem, under which the hair is nicely disposed; the feet as is common rests against a Dog. Beneath the figure on the face of the tomb, is a row of his body guards, or Gallo-Glasses in shirts of Mail, with open conical helmets, in the act of drawing their swords; each figure is inclosed in a division richly ornamented with tracery work, amongst which are Angels with harps, some praying &c. It is now greatly defaced but the work was finely executed and magnificently ornamented. This Monarch died in the year 1265, and it is natural to suppose the monument was executed shortly after that period.

The armour of these body guards point out the military dress of the times, and being of the same kind as worn by the Knights at Kilcullen, and Graige-na-managh serve to assist us in placing their date with some degree of certainty about the same period.

## Tomb without Inscription in the Franciscan Friary Youghall, Co:ʸ Cork.

It very frequently occurs in works of this description, belonging to the 12:ᵗʰ or 13:ᵗʰ Century, where they are raised over persons of distinction, who were neither of the Clerical or Military professions, that they are represented in long robes, if of the law in furred gowns, if not with a favorite Hawk in their hands, and this was considered as a distincition to point out the nobleman or man of property; of this description is the plate now given. This is also a table-tomb, quite entire and in great preservation, but unusually low, and much more raised at the head, than at the feet.

The figure lies on its back, the head resting on a cushion, and the hair is disposed in rounds radiating from a centre, it is habited in long loose robes flowing to the feet in many folds, the arms are clothed to the wrists, and the doubles of the garment pass round the arm, in the hands is held an Hawk, the feet rests against a Dog.

This tomb is placed on the north side of the Chancel under a window in the Church of Youghall formerly the Franciscan Friary.

There is not the smallest appearance of Inscription on it, even tradition is silent respecting it, and Smith in his History of Cork, mentions this tomb but cannot ascertain to whom it belonged, however from the circumstance of the Hawk, we are led to conlude it to be that of some person of distinction.[24]

We may safely place this as the work of the 13:ᵗʰ Century. About this period monumental brass plates first began to be used, and were common in England the latter

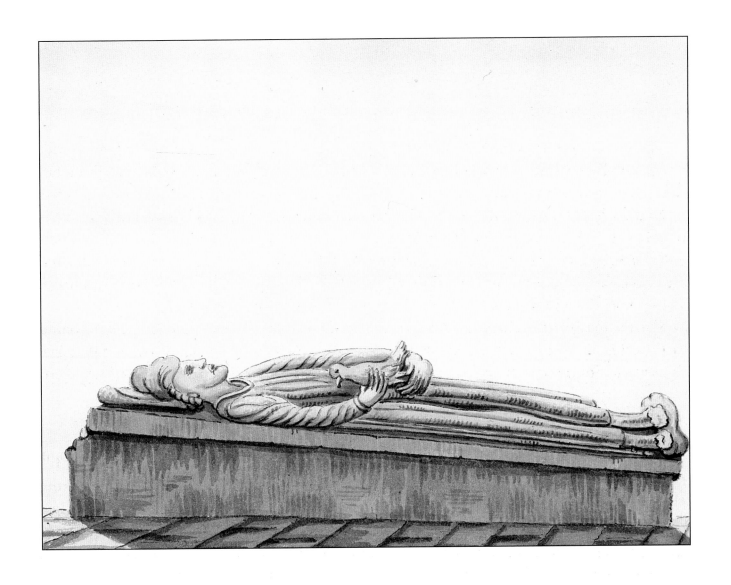

## 3. Youghal: tomb of Thomas Paris (Cork)

*Recumbent effigies are difficult to draw (and photograph) and Daniel Grose has struggled to give a convincing impression of this early fourteenth-century civilian figure. He got badly confused by the churches in Youghal, consistently referring to St Mary's parish church as the Franciscan friary. At the time the effigy was placed in the north transept, but it is now in a recess in the north nave aisle. The sculpture carries no inscription; for a long time it has been identified with Thomas Paris, a member of a prosperous merchant family in the town. The bird, which is not as perky as the drawing suggests, could have been intended as a falcon and, as such, a symbol of lordly status. The curled hair, characteristic of fourteenth-century fashions, has been transformed into a stylish coiffure. When recording sculpture, Grose frequently left the background plain. Here the creamy-yellow highlights add a little sparkle to the otherwise uniform grey-green wash on the carving itself.*

end of the 13:<sup>th</sup> Century,[25] these were generally in laid in flat stones, inserted in the pavement, and were thus placed by the descendants of the deceased who were desirous of prolonging the memory of their ancestors without incurring any great expence. These however are not very common in Ireland, three of them are still preserved in Saint Patricks Cathedral Dublin.[26]

Another very curious kind of Monument which may be esteemed as a work of the 14:<sup>th</sup> or 15:<sup>th</sup> Century, th'o very rare in this Kingdom presents itself in the church yard of Drogheda, formerly S:<sup>t</sup> Laurences Priory.

These are two mural monuments placed in the west wall of the yard, they are said to have been executed to commemorate the dreadful fate of two persons of distinction, man and wife, who were lost at sea, in their passage to Ireland, and whose bodies were sometime after their Shipwreck taken up on these coasts, and exhibited a most shocking spectacle of mortal decay;[27] which the sculptor has but too faithfully endeavoured to represent even to a disgusting degree of accuracy; the crabs and other marine animals are seen feeding on their intestines half rotted away, & creeping out of their flesh, in every part of their bodies, which shows that advanced state of decay, that may be supposed to have taken place after remaining some days, in the dreary caverns of the deep.

If it was the design of those who caused these disgusting sculptures to be executed, and little doubt but it was, to leave them as a lesson against pride to posterity; they certainly well succeeded, and to heighten the effect, tradition goes on to say, these were once of exquisite beauty, in the bloom of life, and the moral must strike home to the thinking observer, for ''to this complexion must we come at last'' and th'o all may not become the prey of, (as in this instance) marine animals, yet the most beautiful and most opulent must inevitably be the food of reptiles equally loathsome and abhorrent.

Table tombs when they are found in Churches, are most commonly placed under arches of various descriptions, hollowed out of the thickness of the wall, sometimes they are fixed under circular arches, these are the most antient; and frequently under the common Gothic arch, and often beneath that kind of the latter, described from four centres richly adorned with ramifications, as may be seen in the Abbey of Clare Galway. The square Festoon occurs in the Abbey of Holy Cross Co:<sup>y</sup> of Tipperary magnificently ornamented with tracery, and projecting beyond the wall;[28] in many religious houses, Gothic Niches are found inclosed half way down with tracery, in these the monumental figures were placed upright, and in these kind of niches were preserved the shrines of

Saints: of this description, where the figure stood upright is that fine Gothic niche to be seen in the Priory of Drumlane Co:ʸ of Cavan and as it is adorned at the top & sides with mitres, it probably contained the effigy of some dignified Ecclesiastic.

It is very probable that in Ireland, those high altar tombs found in the open air, removed some distance from the Church, were sheltered by Festoons, that spred over them in a roof like shape, supported by pillars at the angles, this may account for their being in so good preservation in such exposed situations, th'o the writer has never seen in Ireland one that retains its original covering.[29]

## Tomb of Lord & Lady Roscommon Abbey of Newtown, Co:ʸ Meath.

The high Altar tomb with recumbent figures may be dated about the 16:ᵗʰ Century, of this period is that of the first Lord and Lady Roscommon, in the yard of the Abbey of Newtown near Trim County of Meath.

Here his Lordship is represented as large as life in plate armour bare headed, with his arms over his breast, and hands joined in prayer, the head rests on a kind of bloster, and his sword is suspended from his middle by a belt; the feet has no support, and the figure stretches the whole length of the monument.[30]

At his left side lies his Lady in the same attitude, her head resting on the bolster, which is common to both; she is habited in the costume of the times, stiff ruff, peaked waist, with her sleeves down to her wrists, the plaits going round the arm, her robe opens from the waist downwards, and displays a cord that depends from her middle, and terminates in a tassel near her feet.

Th'o time or accident has greatly defaced these figures, the excellency of the sculpture is very evident, they are raised as high as life, and the plates of the armour, and the folds of the drapery were finely executed, and still appear sharp and distinct.

The sides of the Tomb is adorned with armorial bearings in divisions, separated by fluted pillasters of the Doric order, the foot is occupied by a slab which contained an inscription now too much defaced to be made out.

At the head is represented Lord and Lady Roscommon in relief, kneeling on cushions at a desk, on which is placed before them open books, he on the right hand, and she on the left, behind the father is placed the sons, three in number, and in like manner five daughters with the mother. His Lordship is in plate armour with his sword by his

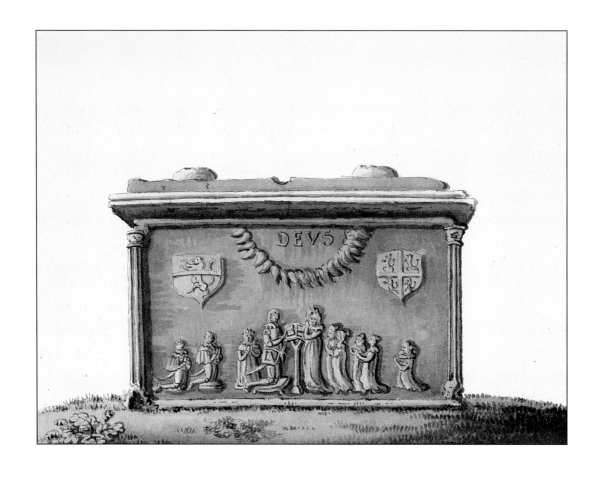

## 4. Newtown Trim: tomb of Sir Lucas Dillon (Meath)

*The tomb of Sir Lucas Dillon and his two wives, Marion Sharl and Jane Bathe, is one of the finest pieces of Renaissance sculpture in Ireland. It is located in the ruins of the parish church at Newtown Trim, just to the east of the cathedral. Making a plea for better conservation (as relevant now as it was then), Daniel Grose in his text complains about the lack of a 'festoon' or canopy, apparently failing to realise that the tomb was once protected by the roof of the church. On the top of the tomb chest are effigies of Sir Lucas together with his first wife Jane, and the whole monument is embellished with crisply cut strapwork, swags and putti. Grose's drawing shows the west end of the chest, with a family group kneeling on both sides of a lectern. By his first marriage Sir Lucas had five daughters, who are shown behind his wife, but only three of their seven sons are lined up on the opposite side behind Sir Lucas himself. One of the sons, James, was destined to become the first Viscount Roscommon, hence the description of the tomb as that of Lord and Lady Roscommon. Sir Lucas died in 1595, over seventeen years after Jane Bathe, and opinion varies as to whether this elaborate memorial was erected in the 1580s or the 1590s. The second wife of Sir Lucas, Marion Sharl, was previously married to Sir Christopher Barnewall, with whom she is also commemorated in an equally splendid tomb not far away at Lusk.*

side, the son nearest him presents a full face, habited in a long Cloak, the two youngest are placed in succession in profile, dressed in short cloaks with swords on, all three in the attitude of prayer, and bare headed. The Lady is dressed in long robes and ruff, and the daughters in long cloaks, and their hair curiously arranged. In the centre over their heads is a glory encircling the word Deus and on each side shields with armoreal bearings. This family piece is much defaced, but is here given as a specimen of what is frequently to be met with on tombs of the same period, in this Kingdom. The Roscommon Monument being without any kind of covering (nor does it appear that it ever had a Festoon over it) & entirely exposed to the weather, together with the rude hands of mischievous curiosity is fast hastning to decay, a circumstance much to be regretted, as such beautiful remains of antient monumental sculpture is very rare, and well deserves to be preserved with care & veneration; it was erected about the latter end of the 15:[th] or beginning of the 16:[th] Century:[31] and is of Irish marble.

The collected figures of a family thus disposed is no uncommon circumstance, they are frequently to be met with sometimes placed as above, and often the daughters under the Mother and the sons beneath the Father; the Aylmer Monument adjoining the Church of Donadea in the County of Kildare is of the same description as our last plate, with this difference that the Father & Mother do not face each other; it bears date 1617, of this a good drawing is given in the Anthologia Hibernica for the month of Aug:[st] 1793.[32]

It now remains for us to describe & produce a few more specimens of Monumental Sculpture incident to the 16:[th] Century.


## Tomb of Richard Bennet & Ellis Barry Church of Youghall, Co:[y] Cork.

The Monument we shall here present was originally of a much older date than the Century in which it is here placed, but the Effigies on it are the work of the year 1619. It is a table Tomb quite plain without any kind of ornament, of unpolished free stone, much higher at the head than at the feet, on it are the figures of a man and woman at full length with their hands joined in prayer, their heads resting on a bolster common to both, ornamented with tassels. The male figure, on the right hand has his head uncovered, his hair flowing over the ears, with a venerable beard; he is habited in a long loose robe that reaches to the feet. The female's head is also uncovered, and her

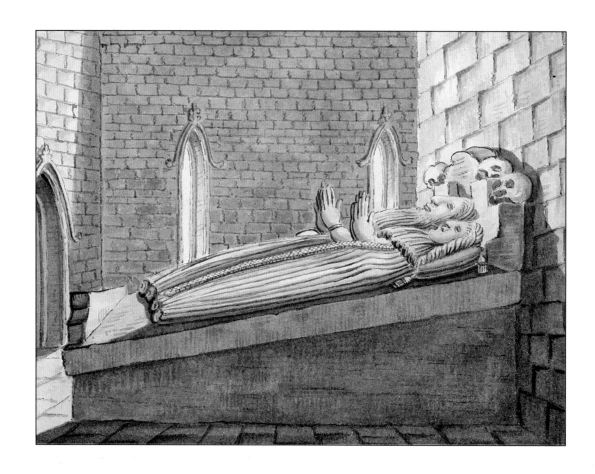

## 5. Youghal: the tomb of Richard Bennett and Ellis Barry (Cork)

*Richard Bennett is said to have been a knight from Glamorgan in Wales, who joined Strongbow on his expedition to Ireland in 1170. He and his wife were early benefactors of the church at Youghal. As an inscription explains, their original tomb was destroyed during the Desmond rebellion of 1579 and the present monument was erected in 1619 on the instructions of Richard Boyle, first Earl of Cork, as part of his restoration of the south transept. It was the work of Alexander Hills, a London sculptor, who also carried out the much larger commission for the Earl of Cork's own tomb nearby. The hands raised in prayer have long since been broken off and the faces are now badly abraded. The macabre stone skulls survive, stored elsewhere in the church, their original purpose apparently forgotten. This is an instance in which one of Grose's drawings provides a valuable record of a monument in its original form. The artist did not bother to record the inscription at the foot of the tomb for himself, merely copying it from Smith's 'History of County Cork' (1750), along with all Smith's mistakes. For once in his paintings of sculpture, Grose has depicted an architectural background, modelling the right wall with strongly marked blocks of yellow and green.*

hair neatly disposed in rolls flowing below her neck, round it is the large ruff and her body is enveloped in a long mantle with a broad edging of raised net work. At their head is a rude kind of pediment, on which is placed several human sculls apparently of great age, probably belonging to those whose figures are there represented, &, to others of their family buried beneath them, & very likely placed there, when Lord Boyle re-edified the monument; at the foot is the following Inscription[33]—

"Here Lyeth the bodies of Richard Bennet & Ellis Barry, his wife, the first foundress of this chapel, which being demolished in the time of Rebellion, and their tomb defaced, was re-edified by Richard Lord Boyle, Baron of Youghall who for the reviving the memory of them, repaired this Tomb, and had their Effigies cut in stone placed thereon. Anno Domini 1619".

It stands in the Chauntry of our Blessed Saviour, Franciscan Friary Youghall. The improvements made in monumental architecture from this period begin to make a very conspicuous figure, and to assume quite a different character, the Greecian orders are introduced, sometimes more than one in the same piece, and more costly materials are made use of, the size of the monuments is inlarged, they are generally reared against the wall & the marble that compose them and the figures, are stained of different colors to represent the life. Where this is not the case, the marble is naturally of various colors brought from foreign parts finely wrought and highly polished.

The attitude of the figures is also altered & a much greater effort to obtain variety of ornaments and design appears throughout.

Whether the profusion of small ornaments, the various colours, the different attitudes of the figures, derogates from that noble simplicity so conspicuous in Monuments of a more antient date, or improves their magnificence, shall be left to the taste of others to determine; but where so many different objects are crowded into a small space, and where so much gilding and glare prevails, the attention is distracted, and the eye wanders without fixing on any object to admire.


## Boyle Monument, in the Chauntry of our Blessed Saviour Youghall Church, Co:[y] of Cork.

This Plate represents the Boyle Monument; it was erected by the first Earl of Cork in his life time,[34] and is composed of colored marbles, and alebaster stained of different colors, the vivid tints of which is now greatly weakened, the whole however (where the hand of mischief has not interfered) is in tollerable good preservation. The principal figure is that of the Earl himself at full length as large as life laying on his left side, his head supported by his left hand, the elbow on a cushion; he is habited in a suit of plate armour, over which he wears a long mantle reaching to his feet; his right hand crosses his body, and his head is adorned with a curious kind of Coronet,[35] his hair long and flowing with a square cut beard and mustachoes, and round his neck he wears the stiff ruff.

This figure occupies the span of a circular niche filled with Inscriptions, Genealogical tables, armorial bearings &c, most of them engraved on plates of Copper,[36] which appear to have been inserted according to the death of that branch of the family they relate to; immediately over the Earl is a black marble Slab with the following Inscription[37]—

Richardus Boyle Miles Dominus Boyle Baro de Youghall, Vicecomes Dungarvan Comes Corcagiensis, Dominus summus hujus Regni Hiberniae Thefaurarius et de privato consilio Domini Regis tam Anglice quam Hiberniae, ex antiquissima Boylorum familia Herefordiensi oruindus, qui patrem habuit Rogerum Boyle Armigerum matrem itidem generosam Joanam Nayleram e solo Cantiano profectam, cum duas sibi invicem junxisset uxores, primam Joanam filiam & coharedem Gulielmi Appesly Armigeri, nulla superstite prole; alteram preclare fecundam Catherinam natum Domini Galfridi Fentoni Equitis Regiae Majestati hoc regno a Secretis postquam varios pro republica cepisset labores, nec immeritos honores, conscendisset, ipse, jam septuaginta septem Annos natus, a mortem indies imminentem expectans sibi & posteris suis, hoc posuit monumentum sacrum memoriae.

Ipse de se
Sic posui tumulum, superest intendere, votis Parce animae, carnem solvito Christe veni.''

At the Earls head and feet are the figures of his two wives, habited in the costume of the times, kneeling on cushions with their hands joined and raised in prayer; the one at his feet has before her a small infant in a cradle, She died bringing this child into the world, and was his first wife Joan one of the Coheirs of William Apsley Esq:[r]. The other at his head is his second Catherine the only daughter of Sir Geoffry Fenton Knight, by whom he had a numerous issue, all of them are here deposited. These figures

## 6. Youghal: the Boyle monument (Cork)

*Richard Boyle, first Earl of Cork (1566-1643) has been described as 'a brilliant, immensely hard working, self-made millionaire' (A. Crookshank) and he used his riches to create a magnificent range of houses and memorials for himself. As baron of Youghal, he purchased and restored the south transept of the parish church. His own tomb there is one of the great sculptural monuments of Ireland. It was made by Alexander Hills, being completed by April 29th 1620 when the Earl recorded 'that the chardges of bwylding the chapples, the Tombe, vault, grate....did coste me (besides dyett for Mr Hill) 507 li. 12 s. ster.' Daniel Grose was obviously impressed by what he saw, though the squashed proportions of his drawing do not do justice to the design. Below the reclining figure of the Earl are ten miniature carvings of those of his children alive in 1619, flanked by his two wives Alice Apsley and Katherine Fenton. The recumbent female near the top of the tomb is Lady Fenton, his second wife's mother. As usual, the details have been drawn very freely, but Grose has given some impression of the sculptural richness of the tomb, with its obelisks, multi-coloured stones, ornate costumes and coats of arms. The drawing is also interesting as it shows the monument before its restoration by the Duke of Devonshire in 1848.*

are in open niches, supported by pillars of red marble, with rich capitals and are formed of Alabaster painted, or stained over. Beneath the Earl are placed a row of small figures cut in Alibaster and stained, in different dresses and attitudes, thus his son Galfridus Boyle who was drowned in the College well of Youghall is represented laying at full length on his side on a long cushion, his hand supporting his head & a human scull beneath him; this is the second figure from his feet; several of these figures have lost their heads and bodies, and are otherwise greatly defaced, this is imputed to the wanton folly (not to call it by a harsher name) of some strangers, who came to view this monument.

Over the circular Niche on a broad Cornice reclines the figure of Joan Nayler mother to the Earl, habited in the dress worn by females in the reign of Queen Elizabeth, the large straw hat, ruff and Fardingale, she lays on her left side her head supported by her left hand and her arm resting on a Bible clasped; the other arm is extended along her side, and her hand grasps a skull; at her head and feet, are [s]mall standing female figures habited in the fashion of the times.

The two at Her head remain (all but the arms of one) entire, seperated by a pyramidical column, but one stands at her feet, the other and the column has fallen down, this from her dress was a nun.

Behind Joan Nayler rises the family coat of Arms, enclosed and supported by pillars and under on the Tablet is the following Inscription —

"Precatio Viventis
Quam Pater, quam prole & gemino quam conguge faustam.
Fecisti, o faustam fac faciendo tuam.

The whole is surmounted by a Pyramidical Column. Besides those ornaments already recounted, are introduced several coats of arms, cherubims, heads, rosets, pyramids &c.

This Monument hands down to us with great accuracy the dress of the times, in which it was erected, and produces some variety, the habit of Joan Nayler is much more simple than those of the Earls two wives, & was probably that worn by old women at the time of her death, but the straw hat, ruff and Fardingale was the general dress in the time of Queen Elizabeth, when the Earl, then M:<sup>r</sup> Boyle, first came into notice; it is likely the younger ladies are represented in more courtly dresses. This highly ornamented piece of work occupies a large space in the west wall of the south wing of the Franciscan

Friary Youghall,[38] formerly call'd the Chauntry of our Blessed Saviour. It was purchased from the Corporation of Youghall 29:[th] of March 1606 by the Earl of Cork and is in the same state of preservation as the Church, in which divine Service is now performed, communicates with it by a door, and is used as a vestry room. The next we shall describe is a mural monument, the Tomb of O'Connor Lord of Sligo in the Dominican Monastery of that town;[39] it is against the wall of the principal Chapel on the North side of the Altar.

## Tomb of O'Connor Sligo & the Countess of Desmond, Abbey of Sligo.

It represents O'Connor and his Lady kneeling on each side of a portable Altar, placed in a centre pillaster, with their hands joined in the act of prayer, he is habited in a suit of plate armour his head uncovered, and his helmet at his feet; she is dressed in the costume of the times, with a large ruff and mantle, and a coronet on her head, they kneel within circular niches, that form the centre of the monument. Above and beneath these niches are long tablets formerly containing inscriptions now obliterated; between the Archivolt of the niches is a shield with an armorial bearing, a coronet for a crest; over this in the front of the pediment, is the Sligo arms & crest, and the whole is surmounted by a vertex on which is delineated the Crucifixion.

Under the tablet beneath the figures is a winged hour glass, the emblem of the swift flight of time, supported by ropes tassels, foliage, a spade and trowel &c terminating in a bunch of grapes. Two pillasters support the Monument ornamented with various devices, on the Ladys side emblems of religious worship, a chalice, open book with beads, cherubims, deaths head and armorial bearings, surmounted by a pinacle on which is sculptured a female figure, probably the holy virgin.[40] On the mans side, military trophies, arms, cherubims, deaths head &c and on the pinacle the figure of S:[t] Peter, bearing the key and the sword.

The Lady whose effigy is here represented is said to be the famous Countess of Desmond who was married to O Connor Sligo, and who lived to the astonishing age of 144, and whose eventful history is too well known to need any rehearsal here, she died A:D: 1656.

The different ornaments thus judiciously assembled together, with the elegance of the design, and the excellence of the workmanship altogether constitute this, a very interesting piece of antient sculpture, and it is greatly to be lamented that it has been, so badly taken care of, and that a few years will probably consign it to oblivion.

## 7. Sligo 'Abbey': the tomb of Sir Donough O'Connor and the Countess of Desmond

*The O'Connor tomb is one of the outstanding pieces of seventeenth-century sculpture in Ireland, a sophisticated and fashionable work which it is remarkable to find so far west. Sir Donough and his wife, Lady Elinor Butler, former Countess of Desmond, are depicted kneeling and facing each other. He is clad in plate armour, meticulously rendered by the sculptor, but crudely abbreviated in Grose's painting. To judge from the accompanying text, the artist studied the monument quite closely without, however, managing to understand all the details. Below the crucifixion are the arms of O'Connor Sligo: a shield bearing a tree erased, surmounted by a knight's helmet with a crowned lion passant guardant as a crest. All this has become meaningless in the drawing, with the lion reduced to the status of a poodle. The monument, which is taller in proportion than the watercolour suggests, was erected by Lady Elinor in 1624, fifteen years after the death of her husband. The presence of the tomb in the Dominican friary reflects the O'Connors' support for the friars in Sligo after the Reformation.*

a grave 7 feet deep at the bottom of

## 8. Armagh Cathedral: base of a medieval font.

This appears to be a unique record of a stone found in the cathedral of Armagh in 1805. Edward Rogers, the nineteenth-century historian, recounts that it was sent to London by Lewis Nockalls Cottingham, the architect in charge of the restoration of the cathedral (1834-40), so that it could serve as a model for the base of a new font. Rogers goes on to explain that the original work 'was retained to enhance the stock in Mr Cottingham's museum, and at his death was sold at a high figure'. Its present whereabouts is unknown. Grose's painting, based on a drawing by Benjamin Bradford, is sufficiently detailed to suggest that the font was carved about 1500. The octagonal stone was divided into bays by Gothic pinnacles, each bay being filled by a winged angel, a popular motif in the later middle ages. The pedestal of Cottingham's new font (1840), which appears to be a close copy of the original, suggests that the angels were placed under flattened ogee arches, with late Gothic foliage filling the space above, details which were misunderstood by the artists.

**Stone found in a Grave in the Cathedral C[h]urch Armagh.**

The last plate we shall present in this Introduction, is a stone found at the bottom of a Grave in the Cathedral Church of Armagh, seven feet deep at the S:W: corner of the West Aisle on the 13:[th] of June 1805;[41] being considered as a great curiosity it was placed on a pillar, which stands opposite the North entrance as described in the view of the Cathedral given in the annexed collection. Round the pillar beneath the Stone is an Inscription setting forth how and when it was found, as above.

This antient Stone is circular and divided into copartments in each of which is portrayed an Angel, with wings display'd, the hands joined in prayer, and over the head a winged dart, surrounded with flames and clouds.

The whole is in great preservation and well executed.

It is hard to determine what this was, if monumental or otherwise, but from its being found in the situation above described it is included amongst the first; it is equally impossible to affix any date with certainty, however from the good proportion of the figures, and the elegance of the Sculpture, we are led to conjecture that it was the work of the 15:[th] Century.

This view was taken by Benj:[mn] Bradford Esq:[r].

# Monumental Antiquities
## of
## Ireland

## 9. Timoleague Castle (Cork).

*The castle at Timoleague was a five-storey tower house which survived relatively intact until 1938, when the upper parts were demolished by Cork County Council, on the pretext that the vibration of the trains on the adjacent railway track (the former Timoleague and Courtmacsherry Light Railway) was dislodging stones and causing them to fall. A certain amount of repointing and consolidation might have been a less drastic solution. The tower is now an ivy-clad stump in the grounds of Timoleague House. In 1907 it was said to be in 'a good state of preservation', but in 1920 it received some damage when a mine exploded beside it. Its subsequent emasculation is particularly unfortunate since it is a dated building. An inscription on a loose stone from the base of a window records the intials DB and ER (David Barryroe and Ellen Roche), with the date 1586. David Barryroe was responsible for burning an earlier castle at Timoleague during the Desmond rebellion, in the belief that it was about to be seized from him. Grose's painting shows the gables and the main chimney intact, with access to the wall-walks provided by a stair-turret at one angle. From a topographical point of view, the landscape is freely drawn, but the picture remains one of Grose's more impressive compositions. The excessively 'gnarled' tree imparts a degree of vigour and coherence to the scene and the tan-coloured leaves add an attractive autumnal touch.*

# Castle of Timolegue, Co:ʸ Cork.

This Castle stands on a rugged rock, near the village of Timolegue (that is Tee molaga, the residence of S:ᵗ Molaga) on the banks of a beautiful little stream call'd the Arigideen or (the little silver stream) which winds romantically between hills prettily improved for better than a mile before it reaches this castle. A large square tower is all that remains of this building, without a roof, every part is much dilapidated, the walls are however of considerable thickness, and the erection appears to have been originally of great strength; it is however but little calculated as a post of defence to resist the modern mode of attack with cannon being commanded by surrounding hills. It was built by the family of O'Shagnassy a powerful Irish Sept in this part of the country.[42] We find that this castle then belonging to Sir Roger Shagnassy was beseiged by the Lord Forbes in 1642 who after burning the town of Timolegue, reimbarked and set sail for the Shannon. It was also taken the next year 1643 on the 1:ˢᵗ of July By Col:ˡ Myn, who beat the Irish on the north side of the river. In the same year this Castle was nominated in the 8:ᵗʰ Article of treaty for a Cessation of Arms, between the Marquis of Ormond and the Irish, to be one of the Garrisons in which the Kings Protestant subjects were to quarter, for the term of one year.

The village of Timolegue is on the sea shore, but the harbour is now only navagable for small craft, the Arigideen here joins the sea, after flowing past the Church, and the venerable Franciscan friary founded here by the Mac Cartys.[43] This village was formerly of some note, being much resorted to by the Spaniards, who came to it to vend their wines. The greatest part of this Barony belongs to the Barrymore family.

The Arigideen abounds in various kinds of fish, particularly Pearl fish call'd by the Irish Closheens.[44]

From the high ground above the Castle you command an extensive prospect of the harbour and the Old Head of Kinsale beyond it, and when the tide is in, and the day clear, the scene is delightful.

D:Grose Fecit

## 10. Kilnatoora or Two Mile Bridge Castle (Cork)

*The castle at Kilnatoora is a magnificent late-medieval tower house, located on a hillside above the river Tourig, three miles north-west of Youghal. The south wall (not visible in Grose's painting) has fallen away, perhaps as the result of the siege in 1645, when it was held for the Confederates against the Earl of Castlehaven. The overgrown ruins are now covered in ivy. Extensive quarrying has taken place around the castle, which accounts for the rocks in the foreground of the picture. Parts of the bawn wall, reinforced by a circular turret, survived in Grose's time, but these have now disappeared. The tower was designed on a grand scale, with major and minor chambers on each storey and barrel vaults at two levels. Grose has exaggerated the batter of the walls and simplified the details, but nonetheless the painting conveys the strength of this impressive fortified house.*

# Castle at Two Mile Bridge near Youghall, Co:ʸ Cork.

Two miles from Youghall is two mile bridge, which crosses a small stream that winds though a glin for some extent until it empties itself into the Black Water near its mouth. Near this bridge stands two Castle's or rather Towers on oppoisite sides of the stream, about half a mile distant from each other. This stream divides the Counties of Cork, and Waterford, and they were erected to defend the entrance of a very strong pass, which commences here, and extends some distance. The one nearest the bridge, and on the North bank of the stream (a view of which is here given) is in a very perfect state,[45] and has only one considerable breach in the north face, which was battered down by Cannon during the time of Oliver Cromwell, and owes its safety to its surrendering after receiving a few rounds.

The different divisions or stories of the Castle is built upon arches, which still remain entire, to which you ascend by a very perfect flight of broad stone steps running from the bottom to the top; in one of the upper apartments you are shown a large square hole, which runs in an oblique direction from it to the lower part of the Tower, and opens on the outside about six or eight feet from the foundation, on the west face, immediately over a deep quarry. Tradition gives the following account of this Hole. The lord of this Castle, having a dislike to a neighbour, or any of his vassals, invited him to feast at his table, and on some pretence or other, decoy'd him into this apartment, and causing his miserable victim to cross the stage that covered the treacherous aperture, he fell head long, and was ejected from this horrid cavity bruised to death, on the outside of the Castle walls.

The lower parts are at present used as a barn, and what is rather extraordinary the owner (a farmer) stables his cattle, in the upper stories of the Tower, and they pass up and down the spiral stairs, with the greatest facility. It stands in a very insulated situation, on the point of a rock, or quarry, out of which in all probability the stones were taken to erecte the building, the hollow forming a deep ditch nearly round the Castle.

The building of this Castle is ascribed to the O'Shealds a powerful Sept in these parts, the Irish call it Kill-na-tworagh.

We read of Fardoroagh mac William mac Brien of Kill-na-toragh being found guilty as concerned in the Earl of Desmonds rebellion as one of his followers.

D:Grose Fec:ᵗ

## 11. Youghal: Dominican Friary (Cork)

*The Dominicans possessed a substantial church at Youghal, but all that is left are the west gable and a fragment of masonry where the chancel joined the south transept. The ruins survive today much as when Daniel Grose painted them two hundred years ago, though the trees have gone, along with 'the air of solemn gloom'. The ancient remains now stand isolated in a bleak modern graveyard. The style of the friary at Youghal, which was founded in 1268 or 1271 by Thomas FitzMaurice, is consistent with a building erected around 1300. Grose has gone to some lengths to depict the architectural details: angle shafts, capitals, shaft rings and mouldings are all carefully delineated. Given that the two surviving parts of the friary are some distance from each other, the artist has pulled the composition together quite effectively. A late Gothic ivory carving of the Virgin Mary, which once belonged to the friary, is now kept in the Dominican house at Cork.*

# Dominican Friary Youghall, Co:<sup>y</sup> Cork.

This ruin is situated at the north end of the town of Youghall, very little of which is now left to ascertain its former magnificence, the only remains still standing is the west end or gable of the nave, with a capacious window, but totally divested of ornamental work; together with a small portion of the east window quite detached, and from the distance these are asunder, we may form some judgement of its original extent which appears to have been considerable.

The capitals of three slender pillars that adorned the east window, are in good preservation, curiously and sharply cut in beautiful foliage, and constitute the only ornamental work to be seen about this ruin.

It stands in a large yard, partly surrounded with walls, and is shaded by some lofty trees that give an air of solemn gloom, to the small portion of the building that remains. Adjoining this inclosure, stands a Romish Chapel, in the yard of which, is a most curious effigy of a Knight grasping his sword, cut out of a solid block of brown grit, near seven feet long; tradition names this to be the figure that covered the tomb of Raymond Le Gross, who was a great benefactor to the monastery of S:<sup>t</sup> Molana on the Blackwater, two miles and an half from this place; and in which he is said to have been buried.

This Abbey was founded in the year 1268 or 1271 by Thomas, the son of Maurice son of John of Callen, son of Thomas, the second son of Maurice Lord Offaly, who was buried here in 1296 or 1298:[46] it was calld the Friary of S:<sup>t</sup> Mary of Thanks.

A:D: 1303, Robert de Percival, an eminent benefactor to this house, was enterred here on 22:<sup>d</sup> of October.

1493. This house was reformed by Bartholomew de Comatio, general of the order.

This house upon the dissolution was granted first to Will:<sup>m</sup> Walsh, and afterwards to John Thickpenny for a term of years, then to Sir Walter Raliegh in fee farm, who sold it to the Earl of Cork.

An image of the Virgin Mary, held in the utmost veneration, was preserved in this monastery; and the general chapter held at Rome in 1644 mentions it in their acts.

## 12. Youghal: the parish church (Cork)

*The parish church at Youghal, which Daniel Grose consistently confused with the Franciscan friary, was devastated during the Desmond rebellion of 1579. The chancel, depicted in Grose's painting, is said to have remained without a roof for the next 270 years. It was erected shortly after 1464, when a college, consisting of a warden, eight fellows and eight singing men, was established to take over the running of the church. The design is dominated by a flamboyant window, with a six-lobed oculus at the apex. The lack of cusps or points within the tracery suggest that the window was an addition to the fabric, inserted sometime after 1550, when such forms became fashionable. Tracery is never easy to draw, and Grose has made things difficult for himself by illustrating the building from an angle, with embarrassing results for the perspective of the window. These weaknesses are compensated by the artist's attention to the fall of light, with the sunshine catching the inside of the tracery bars. The modelling of the south wall in washes of yellow, grey and olive green is particularly effective.*

# Franciscan Friary Youghall, Co:ʸ Cork.[47]

This beautiful specimen of gothic tracery exhibited in the ruin, of which a view is here given, belongs to the chancel of this antient abbey, being the east window, adorned with the greatest taste, and magnificence, and is perhaps one of the finest of its kind in this kingdom. It is adjoining the church in which divine service is at present performed, that is surrounded by several ruined chapels, and a square tower, about Fifty feet high. The south wing of the old building is at present converted into a vestry room, which opens into the church, this was formerly call'd the Chauntry of our Blessed Saviour, and in it are several very fine antient monuments, in high preservation, particularly the Boyle Monument erected by the first Earl of Cork in his life time, and adorned with figures as large as nature, of the Earl, his mother, two wives, and his progeny; but these last are very small, and have been greatly defaced, and mutilated, they are all dressed in the costume of the times (the reign of Queen Elizabeth)[48] in which it was erected, of marble and alabaster, stained to represent life, with inscriptions &c.(x) Here is also an antient tomb of Richard Bennet and his wife Ellis Barry the founders of this chapel, with their effigies cut in stone, as large as life, and placed there, by Richard Lord Boyle A:D: 1619; together with several stones against the walls with inscriptions &c. The north wing is open to the church, and in this also are several antient monuments, especially one, which represents a figure in long robes as large as life, lying on its back, and grasping an Hawk in both hands, which meets across the body; there is no inscription on this tomb, and it appears to be the most antient in the Abbey. Many parts of the antient building are ornamented with grotesque human heads,[49] and also some heads and shoulders, that are represented as bearing up the weight of the roof. The nave of the church is beautified with 6 fine pointed arches on each side, under which are the Pews, Galleries &c.[50] This church and ruins is situated on the south side of the town of Youghall, inclosed in an handsome, and capacious yard, neatly ornamented with trees and shrubs, and surrounded with a broad well kept gravel walk; part of the inclosure is formed by the remains of the antient fortified wall, which formerly entirely surrounded the town, considerable portions of it is still standing and several towers. This yard nearly

(x) This chauntry was purchased by the Earl of Cork from the Mayor & Corporation of Youghall March 29:ᵗʰ 1606.

joins the domains of the College which was erected by the family of Thomas the great Earl of Desmond in the reign of Edward the 4:[th] a short time before the church was rebuilt and beautified; and the Provosts house still stands near the north side of the churchyard surrounded with beautiful gardens.

This monastery was founded for Franciscans in the year 1224 by Maurice Fitzgerald who was induced to perform this pious act by the misconduct of his eldest son, the occurrence is thus related.[51] This Maurice Fitzgerald intending to build a Castle in the town of Youghall, had workmen employ'd digging the foundation, these men on the eve of some holiday, requested from him some money to drink his health; in complyance with which he directed his eldest son to give them what they required, — who instead of obeying his fathers order, violently abused the workmen: this so disgusted & grieved Maurice, that he gave up his design, and converted the intended Castle into an Abbey. This Nobleman after filling the situation of Lord Justice of Ireland in the years 1229 & 1232 renounced the world & sequestered himself in this monastery, taking on himself the habit of S:[t] Francis, he died & was interred here 8:[th] of May 1257. In 1460 this Friary was reformed by the Observantines of the strict Obediance. There is to be seen in the archieves of Christ Church Dublin, a letter dated 1482 containing an indulgence & plenary pardon of all sins, however numerous, from Donald O'Fallon to Richard Skyrret Canon & after prior of this religious house for contributing to the Crusade. Youghall is a sea port town of some extent and was formerly strongly fortified. It is famous for the first Potatoes planted in Ireland, imported by Sir Walter Raliegh.[52]

### 13. Youghal: view of the town (Cork)

*Daniel Grose must have spent a considerable time in Youghal, and eleven of his pictures relate to monuments in the town or its vicinity. As the buildings spread for almost a mile in a narrow band along the west side of the Blackwater estuary, it was not easy to bring coherence to such a diffuse townscape. Grose has overcome the problem, partly by exaggerating the hill to the left and partly by incorporating the foreshore and the boats. Indeed, the sailing boat, with its mauve coloured hull, has been particularly well drawn. Thanks to the artist's interest in shadow, the buildings of the town have taken on a sharp, prismatic feel. The clock tower, 'not badly designed' in Grose's opinion, was built in 1771 and forms the most prominent building on the skyline. Just to the right is the Mall House (now the local council offices), which so impressed Grose with its handsome ballroom, orchestra and 'well regulated coffea room'. Youghal was an Anglo-Norman town, which developed in the thirteenth century with two long parallel main streets. Substantial sections of its defensive walls remain, though these are not quite as dramatic as suggested by Grose.*

# East View of the Town of Youghall, Co:ʸ Cork.

Youghall is a flourishing sea port town, situated on the bay of the same name, formed by the influx of the River Black Water, which flows past the town for its whole length. It extends north and south along the shore, under a steep hill, for more than an english mile, and principally consists of one street, composed of good slated houses, the greatest part of them large and commodious, with handsome gardens extending up the side of the hill, which from the opposite side of the water, makes a very pretty appearance, and highly adorns the town. The principal public erections of this town is first the Clock-gate which is a lofty square building, not badly designed, crowned with a cupola in which is the town clock, the bottom is perforated by an arch under which is the highway and the apartments above are used to confine criminals & debtors:[53] it stands nearly in the centre of the town. The next building of note is the Mall house, erected at the expence of the corporation, and contains an handsome ball, card & tea room, with an orchestra, elegant cut glass chandelier's, and every thing appropriate; under the same roof is two Billiard rooms and a very well regulated coffea room, extensively furnished with newspapers & periodical publications, this is kept up by the voluntary subscriptions of the inhabitants and gentlemen of the neighbourbood, & to which are admitted military strangers gratis. The mall in the centre of which this house is built, is an handsome inclosed walk, shaded by trees, and open to the river, and the refreshing coolness of the sea breaze. Here is several rows of modern built houses, a Presbyterian and a Quaker meeting house. Youghall affords an excellent market for flesh and fish, particularly the latter, which are of the best kinds & in great abundance. This town is much frequented by sea bathers, who find good accommodations, and a Regim:ᵗ of foot is always stationed here. The trade of this town is not at present in a flourishing state, it however formerly rivalled Cork in that particular, this decline is the more to be wondered at, when we consider its advantageous situation on a fine navagable river with a good harbour; the entrance into the bay is however dangerous, there being a bar across it, which cannot be passed till half flood. The town was formerly defended by a small fort or block-house, now totally dismantled, & used as a fish market, this was placed near the Quay, Custom house &c. Youghall was incorporated by King Edward 4:ᵗʰ in the 2:ᵈ year of His reign, through the interest of Thomas, the great Earl of Desmond, it was governed by a Provost & Burgesses.

Ochill Jokile & Youkelain in Latin Ochella, now Youghall, was once strongly fortified, a considerable part of the walls still remaining defended by strong & high towers, & perforated with cross loop holes, under which is a parapet, the whole of great strength & thickness.[54] This line of defence runs along the ridge of the hill already mentioned, & extends for a considerable distance; there is also the remains of a strong castle, near the centre of the main street, seemingly of the same date as the walls.[55] This place suffered much in the wars of the E:[l] of Desmond, it was taken & sack'd by him A:D:1579 & being regained by Cap:[n] White, it was the same year retaken by the Sene[s]chal of Imokilly. An:1582 the Seneschal of Imokilly assaulted Youghall but was repulsed with the loss of 50 men. The Earl of Cork shut himself up in this town in the rebellion of 1641 in which he suffered great hardships, and died in it, during those troubles. The Earl of Castlehaven besieged it about ten weeks, and th'o the town was far from being strong, & the garrison very weak & ill supplied, yet they had the courage to defend it bravely with considerable loss to the Irish army, who were at last forced to raise the siege An 1645. An:1649 Youghall was in the power of Oliver Cromwell & made the place of his residence. Two religious Houses were founded in this town of which an account has already been given.[56] The Colledge of Youghall was founded on the 27:[th] of Dec:[br] 1464 by Thomas Earl of Desmond; the community at first consisted of a Warden, 8 fellows & 8 singing men, who lived in a collegiate manner having a common table, and all other necessaries allowed them, with yearly stipends, the whole donation at the time of foundation being worth 600£ per year. This was afterwards repaired and beautified for a dwelling house by the first Earl of Cork, but it was again suffered to run into decay; it is now however in good repair, and used as a dwelling House, the gardens around it are delightful and well kept. Near this stands an almshouse & free-school also founded by the above nobleman. Not far off is another charity of the same kind built by M:[r] Maurice Ronayne of Dlaughtane in the Co:[y] of Waterford.[57]

## 14. Cornaveigh Castle (Cork)

*The castle at Two Mile Water, better known as Cornaveigh, was a large tower house, just south of the river Tourig, three and a half miles north-west of Youghal. It belonged to a branch of the FitzGeralds; in 1442 a certain Edmund FitzGerald, second son of Richard the first seneschal of Imokilly, was described as 'of Curneveigh'. The tower is likely to be somewhat later, being built probably in the sixteenth century, but its dilapidated condition makes precise dating difficult. A huge barrel vault covers the two lower floors, and there was a straight staircase in the western wall, both features noted by Grose in his text. The old road from Youghal to Tallow, which passed beside the castle, is now only a rough track; as a consequence, Corneveigh is a difficult castle to find. The painting shows two large breaches in the tower, only one of which in fact exists. While the valley of the Tourig is picturesque and secluded, Grose could not resist enhancing the drama of the scene.*

# Castle on Two Mile Water near Youghall, Co:ʸ Cork.

This small remain stands on an eminence at the extremity of a range of hills forming a strong pass, to defend the interior of which, this Castle was erected;[58] the hill on which it is placed is of a very irregular figure, th'o evidently in several places shaped by the hand of art, in order thereby to render the situation of the Castle the more inaccessable; the two mile water winding along the different indentions. The foundations of old walls which can still be easily traced, plainly indicate this building to have been once of much greater extent, th'o nothing at present exists above ground, but the stump of a square tower, in a very ruinous state.

As usual in all erections of this kind the different divisions were built on arches, that covering the lower apartment alone remains, in which may still plainly be discerned in the cement, the marks of the hurdles on which the arch was turned.[59] Out of this room, which extends the full dimensions of the tower, runs off the stairs of ascent that led to the upper stories of the building; from the top of this arch a full view of the pass may be had, which was certainly of considerable consequence as it communicated between the Counties of Cork and Waterford.

It evidently appears that this fortress was demolished by cannon, which battered it on the north and east sides; against this or indeed any other kind of attack this Castle had but little defence, for tho' built on an eminence and once of considerable height, it is placed in the centre of a deep glen winding round it, the sides of which are so high, that of consequence they must have compleatly commanded it on every side; none of its garrison during an assault could venture to show themselves on the battlements, without exposing themselves to certain distruction by Arrows, or even stones so entirely does the surrounding hill overlook it.

Tradition gives this Castle as the seat of a branch of the Fitzgeralds in whose time it was demolished by Oliver Cromwell, and shared the same fate, at the same time, the Castle at two mile bridge was reduced by him.

The Tallow road runs past the north side between which and the Castle flows the river, that divides at this spot by a few yards only, three different parishes. In Irish this Castle is denominatated Cornavagh, and likewise Cul na feeagh, literally translated, the corner of the Deerpark.[60]

## 15. Mount Long (Cork)

*Mount Long is a fine seventeenth-century house, five miles east of Kinsale on the shore of Oysterhaven. It was designed around a square core, with projecting corner towers, an arrangement similar to that found nearby at Monkstown Castle (1636). Although Mount Long was conceived as a fashionable residence, it made some concessions to defence through the installation of musket loops around the door and the retention of narrow windows on the ground floor. The north-west tower has long since fallen and the remaining walls are in urgent need of conservation and repair. The house was built in 1631 by John Long, who ten years later was one of the organisers of the rebel camp at Belgooly at the start of the Confederate Wars. As a consequence, the house was attacked in 1642 by royal forces; one of the besiegers explained how, on arriving at Mount Long, 'we found nothing to do; the people were all run away the best of their provisions with them, only a few empty Chests, Stools, Bed-steads, Hutches and the like were left'. John Long was condemned to death and eventually hanged in Cork in January 1653. It seems that the house was abandoned at an early date and, by the time Grose visited it, the owners lived in the 'neat dwelling house' (now also derelict), visible in the painting behind the main building. With its mullioned windows, emphatic string courses, tall chimney stacks and insistent gables (originally twenty in all), Mount Long is a spectacular building, which understandably caught the imagination of Daniel Grose.*

# Mount Long Castle, Co:y Cork.

About half way up the Eastern shore of Oyster Haven, on the side of a gentle green slope, well sheltered by a lofty wood, stands this fine old Castle, the walls of which is still in a very entire state.[61] It is a strong square erection with square towers at the angles, these as well as the body of the building are entirely without roof; the chimneys are still entire, as well as the stone cases of the windows.

Th'o this building exhibits great strength — in its walls, towers &c — yet is it in the same predicament with almost all other antient erections of the kind, in this County, being commanded by neighbouring hills in several directions.

Adjoining is a neat dwelling house inhabited when this drawing was taken by a M:r Long, who has taken care to improve his surrounding property. Oyster haven is an extensive & well sheltered arm of the sea, about three miles east of the harbour of Kinsale, it is so denominated from its abounding in that shellfish. The shores of this Haven, are highly cultivated and adorned by several pretty villas, and the lands lying high shelter it on all sides from the wind.

The Haven narrows considerably as it approaches the Castle, and after passing it, terminates at the small village of Brownes Mills, having a sweep inland of five miles.

This Castle was built by the Longs; not far from it is Belgooly, where the Irish had their Camp, for the first years of the wars of 1641.[62]

Oyster Haven is in the Barony of Kinalea and Kerrycurihy, now one Barony, the latter formerly calld Maskry Millane, was possessed by Richard Cogan, and came from him to the Earls of Desmond, it was given by James the 15:th Earl to his brother Maurice.

Kerrycurrihy became forfeited to the Crown by act of Parliament 28:th Elizabeth.

On the 19:th of May 1642, Colonel Brocket landed at Kinsale, upon which the Castle of Mount Long was deserted by the Irish.

## 16. *Kilgobban Castle (Cork)*

*Kilgobban Castle is a well-preserved tower house on the west bank of the river Bandon, a few miles from Kinsale. The air of gentility and the well-tended landscape suggested by the painting (perhaps misleadingly) have now given way to scrub and dereliction. The 'spacious modern dwelling house' beside the castle was abandoned in the 1960s. The tower is said to have been built by the MacCarthy Reaghs; in 1576 a Daniel MacCarthy of Kilgobban, along with his brother and son, was accused of oppressing the local people and extracting 'coine'. The tower contains two levels of barrel vaulting, as at Kilnatoora. The painting exaggerates the batter of the outer walls and there appears to be no justification for the offset depicted below the roof line. The tranquil waters of the river are indicated in Daniel Grose's typical manner, with inked horizontals and with the paper left unpainted to represent reflected light.*

# Kilgobban Castle, Co:y Cork.

This Castle is situated on the left bank of the Bandon River, going up, about five miles from the town of Kinsale, it stands on a green sloping bank, formed into a point by the influx of a small stream, that winds down the adjacent country.[63] The view it affords is romantic and pretty, and the few tall trees that are scattered about it add greatly to the prospect; it is a tall square tower of large dimentions, in good preservation, with a slated roof, and a spacious modern dwelling house adjoining: it exactly resembles in construction several other Castles, situated on this river.

The banks of the Bandon abounds with beautiful prospects at every wind of the river, all the way from Kinsale, to the town of Innis-shannon, diversified by antient Castles, modern seats, woods and improvements; immediately in the neighbourhood of Kilgobban above it, are several fine slate quarries, much used affording slate of an excellent quality: this river was antiently named Glasheen. This Castle was built by the Roches and in 1641, we find that it was taken by surprise by Dermot ni Giack, from Littergorman.

On the 4:th of May 1642 the garrison of Bandon, repaired to this castle, and found it deserted by the wardens.

We read of a Saint Gobban a disciple of Saint Ailbe, who was Abbot of an Abbey of Carmelites in the town of Kinsale in the 7:th Century;[64] it is probable this castle derives its name from this saint: these lands are in the Barony of Courcys.

## 17. Ringroane Castle (Cork)

*Ringroane Castle was a four- or five-storey tower house, located on the south bank of the Bandon river, opposite Kinsale. Only one wall remains and even the church behind the castle has fallen into ruin. For centuries this was the site of a ferry, but a modern road bridge now brings traffic sweeping across the hill in front of the castle. The house and cottage to the right have been replaced by a modern dwelling. Grose's viewpoint is in the centre of the river, one of several cases where he seems to have made his sketches from a boat. He was looking south, towards the sun, and his attention to light is particularly evident in the sunlit trees and the modelling of the tower with ochre and turquoise washes.*

# Ringroane Castle near Kingsale, Co:ʸ Cork.

This Castle stands on elevated ground on the left bank of the Bandon River, nearly facing that part of the town of Kingsale, call'd the worldsend.[65] It consists of a large square tower, at present of no great height and much in ruins, and apparently resembled in every particular, the other Castles on this river. Here is a small village, and the parish Church stands near the Castle. A ferry is also established here, which keeps up the communication between the village and Kingsale.

Ringroane was built by and gives the title of Baron to the noble family of De Courcy;[66] this manor had antiently 30 Knights fees, and was of a much greater extent than at present.

By an inquisition taken at Kingsale on the Tuseday next after the feast of S:ᵗ John Baptist A:D: 1372 and 46 Edw:ᵈ 3:ᵈ before Roger Hawkensew the Kings Escheator, Milo de Courcey died seized of the manor of Ringroane, who held the same of the King in chief as of his fee, being one entire Barony.

Miles de Courcey Baron of Kingsale, overthrew Florence Mac-Carty-More with a great army of his followers, at a battle near Ringroane, and drove them into the Bandon River, where many of them were drowned A:D: 1390.

18:ᵗʰ of James 1:ˢᵗ John Lord Courcey and his son Gerald, passed Pal:ⁿᵗ for the Castle and Manor of Ringroane.

## 18. Charles Fort (Cork)

*With his military interests, it was inevitable that Daniel Grose would take a keen interest in the design of Charles Fort, though it was scarcely a building of great antiquity. Built on the site of Ringcurran castle, it was designed to guard the entrance to Kinsale harbour. Permanent stone fortifications were begun in 1678 under the direction of Sir William Robinson, architect of Kilmainham Hospital. The layout follows an irregular star shape, with five great bastions, three facing inland and two guarding each end of the sea defences. Grose's painting shows the fort from the shoreline, with the so-called Charles Bastion in the centre of the composition. The gables behind, one flying the Union Jack, belong to the soldiers' quarters; to the left the roof and upper storeys of the Barrack Stores are visible. The latter is the finest building on the site, though it cannot in fact be seen from this position. Grose's fascination with the architectural details of the fort extends to the projecting sentry posts and the three relieving arches on the Charles Bastion. In 1690 the fort was held for James II, but it was forced to surrender after a two week blockade. Following significant improvements made during the Napoleonic Wars, the fort remained in use as a military base until 1921.*

# Charles Fort near Kingsale, Co:$^y$ Cork.

This Royal fortification is situated about a mile east of the town of Kingsale, and was built for the defence of the harbour on the ruins of an antient Castle call'd Rincurran.[67] It is a regular fortification with a strong Citadel on the land side, commanding the whole work; in it are barracks capable of containing a Regiment of Infantry, exclusive of Artillery and Invalids, store houses, magazine ordnance store, canteen, and in the center a lighthouse, constantly kept well lighted, which communicates with that on the Old Head of Kinsale.

When this view was taken its Batteries were mounted with only 32 pieces of Cannon of different sizes, th'o it was originally furnished with 100 pieces of brass cannon from 24 to 42 pounders; most of the embrasures on the lower works facing the harbours mouth are now stopped up, as is also those of the Bomb-proofs which are under the batteries flanking the work towards the sea, these are calculated to hold the garrison in case of a seige: it has a Governor, and Lieu:$^t$ Governor the latter of whom constantly resides in the fort, and has a commodious house and garden in it: it has also other proper officers.

This fort is so placed that all ships coming into the harbour, must pass within pistol shot of its batteries; the sea washing the foundations on two sides. We find that the Castle of Rincurran on whose scite this fort was built, bore a conspicuous part in the transactions during the seige of Kinsale, by the English, whilst it was in the hands of the Spaniards A:D: 1601. On the 22:$^d$ of Oct:$^{br}$ same year Captain Button commanding the Queens pinnace call'd the Moon, and Cap:$^n$ Wards ships were ordered to batter Rincurran Castle; but their ordnance being too small, they lay by to guard the harbour, & prevent relief from coming by sea to the enemy. On the 27:$^{th}$ & 28 a battery was raised against the castle; the enemy attempted to relieve it but they were prevented by Cap:$^n$ Piercy, that night upon guard, & by a constant firing from Cap:$^n$ Buttons ship of war.

The Castle of Rincurran continued to be battered to the 31:$^{st}$ the Lord President Mountjoy, being well skilled in the art of besieging, directed the gunners; the Spaniards again attempted to relieve this castle, but were driven back, their leader Don Juan de Contreras taken, and on the English side the Lord Audley, Sir Oliver S:$^t$ John, and Sir Garret Harvey were wounded. The ordnance still continuing to play, the besieged towards night beat a parley, and asked permission to march to the town with their arms;

which being refused, the battery kept a constant fire, as did the besieged. About two o'clock, finding the Castle not tenable, they beat another parley, which not being regarded, several of them attempted to escape by the rocks close to the water side; but being observed by the English they were taken prisoners, with several Irish who shut themselves up in the castle. An hour before day, the commander offered to surrender, and quit all their arms, provided they might be sent into the town, which being refused, he intreated that he might carry his Arms into Kingsale; which also being deny'd, he bravely determined to bury himself in the ruins of the Castle: but his garrison mutinying, and threatning to throw him out of the breach, he consented that his men should be disarmed in the castle, and that he himself should wear his sword, until he delivered it upon his knees to the President; which he performed, and he and his men were sent prisoners to Cork.

The new fort was began in the year 1670 the first stone being laid by the Earl of Orrery and was finished at the expence of 73,000£.

On the 25:th of August 1681 the Duke of Ormond who came to review it, changed its name from Rincurran to Charles Fort in honor of King Charles the 2:d.

D Grose

## 19.  Temple Michael  (Waterford)

*Daniel Grose gives an enthusiastic and eloquent description of Temple Michael in his text, but he would be disheartened if he could see the site today. Mr Freeman's 'modern country seat' of about 1800 is now a total ruin, closed off by barbed wire. The masonry quays are gradually disintegrating and the curving avenue leading down to the house has almost vanished from view. Paradoxically the oldest building at Temple Michael, the late-medieval tower house, has suffered least. This was a five-storey tower, barrel-vaulted at the second and fourth levels, with the upper storeys reached by a spiral staircase. It was a Geraldine stronghold, probably of early sixteenth-century date, and two lords of Decies are known to have died here, one in 1553, the other in 1598/1600. During the Confederate Wars the royalist army, led by the Earl of Castlehaven, arrived before Temple Michael in June 1645, forcing the castle into submission. Much of the northern section of the main tower has fallen, apparently as a result of subsequent Cromwellian bombardment. A short distance from the castle is a ruined Protestant church, adding to the all-pervading sense of dereliction at this otherwise idyllic spot on the banks of the Blackwater.*

# Castle & House of Temple Michael, Co:<sup>y</sup> Waterf:<sup>d</sup>.

This ruin stands on the southern bank of the river Blackwater, a few miles from Youghall, it is beautifully situated, imbowered amidst trees, and sloping hills waving with corn, and rich in pasturage; forming altogether a striking and picturesque landscape.

The effect of contrast is here very conspicuous, a modern country seat the property of a M:<sup>r</sup> Freeman, being built at the foot of the ruin, salutes the eye with a pleasing and uncommon variety, between the old and new erection; and both being near the water, the enlivening addition of a noble river flowing past affords a constant moving feature, to the other beauties of this romanitic picture. The banks of the river is handsomely quay'd with masonry and the lands crowned with wood, rise to some height behind the house, intersected by a winding road, leading to the building.

The ruin consists of only one tall Tower of three stories high, one half of which is intirely down, from the materials it afforded, the dwelling house was most probably built, the rest is cleared away, and nothing more appears but the stump of a small round turret, standing at the foot of the large one, partly covered with ivy, consequently nothing now remains to ascertain its original extent and strength.[68]

This was most probably one of Desmonds Castles, as he had several on the Blackwater, and was demolished at the same time with those of Strankally and Drumana. Upon the whole, it does not appear to have been of much consequence either as a place of strength or size, it has the same defect with most other Fortresses of similar erection, that of being commanded by rising grounds in its vicinity; this is overlooked by hills so near, as to be within reach of a Bolt from a Cross-bow. It was evidently built to overlook a pass of the river of consequence to the neighbouring country. The Black Water is here broad and rapid, and navagable for boats; the banks of this beautiful river throughout its whole course, is romantically ornamented with hanging woods, sloping lawns, and broken rocky cliffs, wild and majestic, often enriched with the elegant embellishments of art, handsome seats, picturesque ruins, flourishing towns, pleasant Villages, and crossed by many well built Bridges. It takes its rise in a swampy bog, near the Island of Kerry, and thence pours along to Black-water bridge and so runs, in an easterly direction through Mallow, Fermoy, Lismore, Cappoquin and empties itself into the Sea at Youghall. It abounds with Salmon & Trout, both of which, are caught in great quantities, especially at Lismore, and Cappoquin, and all the way down to the Sea. The Fishermen use a small boat, call'd a Cott, much resembling, and nearly as dangerous as an Indian Canoe; its name is probably derived from Corragh(x) the name of the old Irish boat made of hides of leather, so frequently spoken of by antient Irish Antiquaries.[69] Two of these boats, with one man in each are moored across the stream, some distance apart, and a net is let down between them and suspended, each man holding the rope on which it is hung, who immediately feel when a Salmon strikes, which they are ever sure of taking, and great quantities are procured in this manner. The more than common fertility to be observed on the banks of this River, is owing to a kind of manure taken out of it, call'd Trusker, being a collection of weeds, grass and other matter, that forms itself into a kind of dung.

(x) Corrach or Corragh, The antient Irish had boats and Canoe's, small wicker boats (Fir Fuarch) signifies a boat not well joined. S:ᵗ Isodore calls them Carabs & says they were made of twigs & covered with raw hides which are made use of yet, in coasting along the shores & Islands, they are call'd in Irish Corach or Noemhog. The Irish word Corach seems to be derived from the Latin word Corriune a hide — O Flahertys Ogygia — Cox calls a boat or Cot covered with hides Nevoge.

## 20. Rincrew (Waterford)

*The medieval ruins at Rincrew are magnificently sited on a hill above the confluence of the Blackwater and the Tourig. As Grose explains in his text, the buildings were part of a preceptory of the Knights Templars, the military order founded to defend pilgrims en route to the Holy Land. In one of the more disreputable episodes of the middle ages, the Templars were suppressed in 1312 by Pope Clement V, on the advice of Philip the Fair of France, who accused them of all manner of immoral and heretical behaviour. It is difficult to form much impression of Templar architecture in Ireland. At Rincrew Grose shows two buildings placed at right angles to each other: the structure on the right had a barrel-vaulted basement with a chamber above. The gabled building to the left was apparently single-storeyed and could have served as a church. Since the drawings were made, both gables have collapsed and the site is so covered in impenetrable brambles, ivy and nettles that it is hard to make much sense of the architectural layout.*

# Rincrew Castle, Co:^y Cork.

This very antient remain stands on a promontory which shoots itself into the Blackwater, as it emptys itself into the Bay of Youghall; and th'o the situation is well calculated for defence, being very difficult of access on three sides, yet the ruin displays little of that military character, to be expected in a building denominated a castle.[70] It would be difficult to judge of its former strength, from the ruins that now remain, as they are much confused, and fast hastening to decay.

 The prospect from this height is really beautiful, commanding the bay and town of Youghall, with an extended stretch of ocean beyond, and on the left, a diversified landscape of wood, hill and mountain, in the Co:^y of Waterford.

 We are told Rincrew was a Preceptory of Knights Templars, and consequently partook of the nature of a Monastic, as well as a military erection; this house as well as all others in the County of Cork, belonging to that body, was suppressed by an order of King Edward 1:^st directed to Sir John Wogan then Lord Deputy A:D: 1314, and their lands were given ten years after to the Knights Hospitallars another military order.

## 21. Dungarvan: Augustinian Friary (Waterford)

*The Austin friars, officially known as the Order of Hermits of St Augustine, arrived in Ireland in the second half of the thirteenth century, eventually founding over twenty houses in the country. As Grose explains, the friary at Dungarvan was established by Thomas, Lord of Offaly, in 1295 (or possibly a few years before). In most Irish friaries a substantial tower divided the choir from the nave, and that at Dungarvan is exceptionally well-preserved. Grose has simplified the upper windows (which in reality have twin ogee-headed lancets) and he has exaggerated the quoinstones, a mannerism that occurs throughout his work. In 1750 the decorated rib vault under the tower still contained 'the boards, on which the vault was turned', an interesting structural element which sadly no longer remains. The post-Reformation church behind the medieval building has been reconstructed in modern times and the ground floor of the tower now serves as a porch. The last remnants of the tower house to the left were demolished by a local farmer in the 1950s. Lewis (1837) records that 'in the Abbeyside division (of Dungarvan) are the ruins of a lofty square castle, of which nothing more is known than that it was anciently the property of the McGraths'.*

# Augustinian Friary Dungarvan, Co:ʸ Waterford.

Is situated a small distance from the town of Dungarvan, opposite to it, on the other side of the water and close to the shore; from what remains we may judge that it was once a light and elegant building, together with the cells occupying a considerable space of ground. The steeple appears to have been about 60 feet high supported by handsome arches, battlemented at top & divided into stories, to which the light is admitted, through small pointed gothic windows. When this drawing was made part of the ruin was fitted up, as a place of divine worship.

This Friary for Eremites following the rule of S:ᵗ Augustin, was erected by Thomas Lord Offaley, who was Justiciary of Ireland in 1295; the family of Magrath endowed this house with a Castle (probably the one represented in the drawing) and some contiguous lands, & the O'Briens of Cummeragh, who held the rectorial tithes of the parish, were great benefactors to it.

10:ᵗʰ March 37:ᵗʰ of Queen Elizabeth, a lease of this Friary, with sundry other lands, was granted, for the term of twenty one years, to Roger Dalton at the annual rent of 40£..10s Irish money.[71]

## 22. Dromana House 1 (Waterford)

*Three miles south of Cappoquin, the river Blackwater cuts through a wooded valley, set above which is Dromana, one of the most spectacularly located houses in Ireland. Commanding views both up and down the river, this natural place of defence was once the site of a medieval castle. In the 1780s a large rectangular block was added to an earlier house by George Mason-Villiers, second Earl of Grandison, and this is what is depicted in Grose's view. The nine-bay facade was embellished sixty years later, when pediments were added to the windows and the roof was recessed behind a parapet. The painting is thus an interesting record of Dromana in an intermediate state. The whole block was demolished in 1957. Grose's painting is also valuable as a record of the two riverside buildings, the boathouse and the 'banqueting house'. In reality the latter was situated some distance to the right and this, together with the discordant perspective, reveals the way Grose combined separate sketches into a single composition.*

# Drumanna or Dromanagh Castle, Co:ᵞ Waterford.

This romantically situated pile of building, stands on a steep eminence over the Blackwater, towering over the woods that surround it on every side; it retains nothing of its antient military character, except its commanding site, but must have been when laid out as fortification, a very strong hold. Here the river is broad and deep, sweeping round the wooded point on which the house is erected, on the S:E: side it is very difficult of access, not only from the steepness of the acclivity, but from the thick growth of trees, and underwood, that spring from the foot of the walls, and descend down to nearly the waters edge. (Plate 1:ˢᵗ) represents the N:W: aspect, as you go up the river,[72] and the eminence th'o not so steep on this side, is still very abrupt; here is some appearance of an approach to the Castle, by a water gate, and a strong wall, but even this does not indicate a very antient date. Outside this gate stands a square building called the banqueting house, on a terrace close to the waterside, defended from the stream by a strong wall.

There is some good apartments in the house to which you ascend by an ample flight of stairs, over these, are shown two pair of enormous Moose Deer horns, attached to the skuls, and extending from tip to tip an extraordinary length.

When this view was taken, the house was kept in tollerable good repair, th'o seldom visted by the Earl of Grandisons family, whose property it is.[73]

This Castle was often the scene of action in the different rebellions of Ireland, and frequently changed its masters, we find Drummanna Castle taken by the the Lord Castlehaven on the 5:ᵗʰ of Apr:ˡ 1646 — and also reduced in 1647, the 3 of May, and Capoquin (from which it is about four miles distant) by Murrough O'Brien first Earl of Inchiquin, who commanded an army of 5000 foot and 1500 horse; it was also seized by Col:ⁿ Hastings from Cork AD 1691.

(Plate 2:ᵈ) represents the South East aspect.

Drumana came into the Grandison family by marriage in the right of Catherine, daughter and heir of John Fitz-Gerald of Drumana AD 1676-7. The famous Countess of Desmond who is said to have lived to such an advanced age (some years above 140) was daughter to the Fitz-Geralds of Drumanna, and of whom so much has been said by Sir William Temple, M:ʳ Pennant, and others.

D Grose

## 23. Dromana House 2 (Waterford)

*The medieval castle at Dromana, battered during the Confederate Wars, was replaced by a more comfortable house in the later years of the seventeenth century. With its steep roofs, tall chimneys and dormer windows, Grose gives a good impression of this building, parts of which survive. By the time of his visit, the house had been extended around a courtyard; the gables of the two flanking wings are just visible in the painting. This is one of Grose's most successful compositions, though he has dramatised the scene by narrowing the river and steepening the sides of the valley. The trees silhouetted on the skyline are very effective, and, by using lighter washes for the far bank, the artist has suggested a warm hazy atmosphere. The purple and tan jackets of the boatmen provide a delicate foil, a technique that Grose used regularly in his work.*

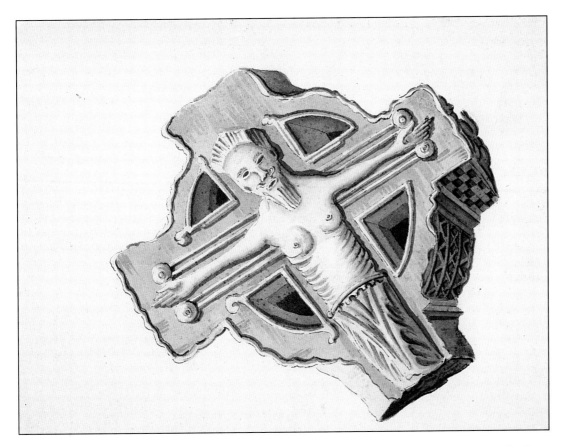

## 24. Tuam: market cross 1 (Galway)

*The twelfth-century cross head, which Daniel Grose saw lying in the undergrowth beside the cathedral at Tuam, was used in the reconstruction of the market cross in the 1870s. As its dimensions do not coincide with the other fragments, it must have belonged to a separate monument. Grose's admiration for the carving is fully justified, for this is an outstanding piece of Romanesque sculpture, with the crucified Christ modelled in high relief. Although the general design is adequately portrayed, Grose's difficulty with figure sculpture is once again apparent. The facial characteristics bear little relationship to the original, and the careful linear geometry of the chest has been misunderstood in an unfortunate way. The 'V' folds of the loin cloth, which are more rigid and angular than the watercolour suggests, provide some evidence that the Irish sculptor based his work on an imported metal crucifix, possibly from the south of England.*

# S:ᵗ Jarlaths Cross at Tuam, Co:ʸ Galway.

The remains of this beautiful relic of antient sculpture, formerly stood in the market place of Tuam, and it cannot but strike the observer with astonishment, that such a rare specimen of the skill of our forefathers in this art, should be suffered to fall asunder, & be totally neglected, when the preservation of it, must have been so easy, and have proved so highly ornamental to the town. It now lies unnoted, the head reared against the east end of the Cathedral Church, nearly obscured with weeds; the shaft has been used as a grave stone in another part of the yard, and the pedestal has totally disappeared. This head is of one solid stone, perforated by four triangular holes, the outside line, forming the arc of a circle, beyond which the arms of the Cross extend.

On this side is represented in strong relief the Crucifixion, boldly th'o rudely executed. On the ends of the arms, is sculptured a figure in a monastic habit, with uplifted hands, the upper and under sides ornamented with chequer work, and the outside of the circle that unites the arms, is also beautifully adorned, regularly wrought, and all in high relief. The shaft is also entire of one stone, th'o much defaced exhibiting equally engenious workmanship, it is divided into square copartments of alternate Lozenge and chequer work, interspersed with runic knots, every square representing a different design.[74] This above described was apparently the front side; the reverse (Plate 2:ᵈ) is occupied by the figure of the Saint himself, in his Pontifical robes, holding in his left hand, the pastoral staff, and the right arm raised, as in the act of bestowing the benediction. On each side of him, are two smaller figures still within the circle, those on the left hand in the same dress and attitude as the one already described, the two on the right, are in a different position, one of them holds in his right hand a Jug, or Chalice, and the other figure has in his left, what appears to be a Loaf of Bread. We may naturally conclude these emblems relate to the Holy Sacrament, and corroborates what Archbishop Usher, and many later antiquaries has proved, that the religion introduced by S:ᵗ Patrick into this kingdom, and set forth by the antient Bishops and Clergy was, as to the main points of doctrine, the very same in substance with that by law now established.[75] But to return to the Cross, over this head rose a smaller one, which was fastened into gro[o]ves deeply cut in the arms, & when both were reared on the shaft, and placed on the pedestal, rose to the height of 20 feet. In this state it is remembered, and was seen standing in the market place of Tuam, by several of the present inhabitants.

S:<sup>t</sup> Jarlath was one of the Comorbans of S:<sup>t</sup> Patrick, Albeus, Columba, Fechin and others, he was the first bishop that fixed his Cathedral see at Tuam; antiently called Tuam-da-gualand. He was a Conaughtman by birth, of the stock of Conmach, and son of Logha, educated under S:<sup>t</sup> Benin or Benignus, second Bishop of Ardmagh, immediate successor of S:<sup>t</sup> Patrick; A:D: 455 — as soon as he had left his master Benignus, he retired to Cluanfois in the territory of Conmaine not far from Tuam, where he founded a Monastery, and opened a school, to which numbers flocked for education and learning, and amongst others the famous S:<sup>t</sup> Brendan and S:<sup>t</sup> Colman, who was afterwards founder and 1:<sup>st</sup> Bishop of Cloyne. He was a learned man, in whom piety and purity of manners vied with his learning. Certain prophecies writ in Irish are extent in his name, relating to his successors in the See of Tuam, but what credit they deserve let others judge.[76] The writer of the life of S:<sup>t</sup> Brendan makes mention of S:<sup>t</sup> Jarlath as follows. "Afterwards S:<sup>t</sup> Brendan came to Bishop Jarlath, then dwelling in Conaught, with whom he abode at that time, satisfying his thristy soul, in that living fountain of saving doctrine," and a few lines after "The holy priest Jarlath, taking a journey in his Chariot, the wheels broke not far from his own cell, and there a Monastery was built call'd Tuam da Gauland.

Ware mentions him to have flourished about the beginning of the 6:<sup>th</sup> Cent:<sup>y</sup> and places his death, the 26:<sup>th</sup> of December, or 11:<sup>th</sup> of February, but in what year he cannot determine (he says). Colgan thinks he died before, or about the year 540. His bones long after his death was sought for, and found, and inclosed in a silver shrine, or Chapel, from thence commonly call'd Temple ne Scrin, or the church of the Shrine. We may I think with every probability place the first erection of this Cross at Tuam, about the same period.[77]

D Grose

## 25. Tuam: market cross 2 (Galway)

*This side of the Tuam cross head faces north in the re-assembled monument. Although Grose has misunderstood some of the details, he clearly studied it quite hard, noticing the slots in the arms and the two projecting tenons near the bottom. The identity of the ecclesiastical figures continues to puzzle scholars. Some people interpret them as bishops, whereas others would agree with Grose in seeing the larger figure as an image of St Jarlath, the founder of the monastery at Tuam. The smaller figures hold books, bells and crosiers, rather than the jug, chalice and loaf of bread identified by Grose, whose speculations in the text about their eucharistic role are thus ill-founded. Nor is there any evidence to support his view that the slots were designed to hold a second, upper cross, which would have transformed the monument into a bizarre and unstable structure. To model the sculpture, Grose has made effective use of a light green wash, but his lack of technical training as an artist was badly exposed when he drew the left end of the cross.*

D. Grose

## 26. Clonmacnoise (Offaly)

*The celebrated monastery at Clonmacnoise was founded in 545 by St Ciaran and, with its ruined churches, round towers and sculptured crosses, it represents one of the most rewarding medieval sites in Ireland. Since it became a popular spot for antiquarians and artists in the nineteenth century, it is strange that Grose chose to rely on a drawing borrowed from the Reverend John Moore. This is a loose composition, unreliable in detail. The doors and windows of the cathedral, for example, bear little relationship to their actual position. Nor does the stone cross correspond in place or design to any of the surviving crosses at Clonmacnoise. Grose has given the painting his own stamp through his treatment of the water, the trees and the fall of the sunlight on the grass. As so often, it is the boat that has been drawn with the most care.*

# Ruins of Clonmacnoise, King's County.

It was said of this monastic establishment that almost half of Ireland was within the bounds of Clonmacnoise; so celebrated was it for sanctity, & so rich in the endowments and gifts bestowed upon it by various Kings and Princes; so holy was it considered, that a belief prevailed throughout the Island, that whoever was so fortunate as to Obtain sepulture within its precincts, ensured to himself the certain enjoyment of everlasting life and happiness in Heaven.

It is not to be doubted that such a belief was encouraged by and produced great benefits to the soc[i]ety, who were regular Canons of S:ᵗ Augustin; & in consequence many solicited so enviable a distinction, and chose this as their place of interment, and Ten Churches exclusive of the principal Monastery were erected here by the Kings and petty Princes of the neighbouring country. The several founders named these Churches as follows. Temple Righ, or Melaghlins Church, built by O'Melaghlin King of Meath; Temple O'Connor, built by O'Connor Dun; Temple Kelly; Temple Finian, or MᶜCarthy, built by MᶜCarthy More of Munster; Temple Harpan, or MᶜLaffys Church; Temple Kieran; these Churches abounded in magnificent ornaments, and many rare works, and was as much celebrated for their rich adornments as for the great holiness of the ground on which they were erected.

Dermid the son of Cervail Monarch of Ireland, having granted to S:ᵗ Kieran, Clonmacnoise, and Inis-Aingin, or the Island of All Saints on the Shannon, together with 100 Churches in Meath; he bestowed the Church of Clonard upon his master S:ᵗ Finian, and the Island upon S:ᵗ Domnan. In the the year 548 he founded an Abbey for himself at Clonmacnoise which afterwards became a celebrated Monastery; but the founder died in 549; his feast is commemorated here on the 9:ᵗʰ of September.[78]

Greatly as this spot was honored for its holiness, and th'o the chosen Sepulcher of so many Kings and Princes, we find it frequently visited by the Danes, Irish, and English for the purposes of plunder, and the Monasticon gives us no fewer than 35 instances of its being pillaged and despoiled; it was also consumed by fire 19:ⁿ times.[79]

These numerous instances of misfortune seems to belie the great care the founder Saint took of this his favorite establishment, as we are told even after death,[80] for in 1130 says the same Work, the jewels stolen from this Monastery in the year 1108, were found in the custody of Gille Comhbhan, a Dane of Limerick, who was taken by Connor O Brien, King of Munster and delivered to the community of Clonmacnoise; at the time of his execution, he openly confessed to the said fraternity, that he was at the several ports of Cork, Lismore, and Waterford, and continued sometime at each in expectation of a passage from thence to another kingdom; that all the other ships left their harbours with a fair wind; but as soon as any vessel he entered into had set sail, he saw S:^t Kieran with his staff return it back again, and that the Saint continued so to do, till he was taken. It is further said that the Clergy of the Abbey made incessant prayers to God and S:^t Kieran (the year the robbery happened) to enable them to discover the guilty person, and their prayers were answered as related. Many other miracles is related of this Saint performed by him to punish the despoilers of this Monastery, such as inflicting unknown diseases and the like, but alas his pious cares were in vain, for whilst the Monastery continued to possess such great riches, the predatory visits continued; nor was his cares confined, to revenge the loss of Gold and jewels, for we are also informed by the annals of Clonmacnoise, that Connor O'Maolseachlain King of Meath, was slain by the son of his brother, & his head was forcibly taken away from this Abbey on Good Friday, by Toirdealbhach O'Bryan, who buried it at Kenncovia, on the banks of the Shannon in the County of Clare; but it is said the same was on the following Sunday, brought back, with two collars of Gold round the neck, which miracle it was supposed was effected by the immediate interposition of God and S:^t Kieran.[81]

These remains are situated on the river Shannon, about ten miles from Athlone, on a gentle undulating eminence; in the view here given is shown two round towers and seven of the Churches which remain; one of the towers still retains its conical roof and is in a very perfect state, this is call'd M^cCarthy's, and is seven feet in diameter within, the wall three in thickness, and is 56 feet high;[82] the roofless tower is every way the largest and measures 62 feet in height, this is partly covered with Ivy and stands on the most elevated ground, they are both built of fine cut stone.

There still exists several old Crosses standing amongst these ruins, which altogether possess an air of venerable antiquity, that cannot fail forcibly to strike the observer, and he treads over the ground, where mouldered the mortal remains of so many Irish Kings and petty Princes, with sensations of respect and deep interest.

We are also told that there existed here a Bishops Palace which was built towards the west;[83] Clonmacnoise was formerly call'd Tipraie, Clone or Cluain, signifies a lurking place, a Cave or Den; Ware tells us the Annals of Inisfale say that it was partly named from Nois Muccaid King of Connaught, and when put together formed Clone or Cluain Nois, or Clonmacnoise.[84] This view was taken by the Rev:^d John Moore.

D:Grose

## 27. Clonbrock House (Galway)

*For the architectural historian, Clonbrock is a depressing place. The seventeenth-century house, depicted by Grose, has vanished completely, and the handsome neo-classical building (1780-8) which replaced it was burnt in 1984. Amidst the dereliction is a vast array of stable yards, walled enclosures and ancillary buildings. The seventeenth-century house was evidently destroyed by a fire in 1807, during over-exuberant bonfire celebrations to mark the birth of the second Lord Clonbrock's son and heir. It is not clear whether this happened after Grose's visit or whether the partially destroyed wing to the right represents the fire-damaged building. In contrast to the more modern structures, the massive late-medieval tower house has survived, and a new roof and new floor joists testify to a recent, abortive attempt at restoration. Grose's painting is not to be trusted for details, and it is difficult to establish the artist's viewpoint, as the geography of the estate was reorganised during the nineteenth century. The sequence of buildings at Clonbrock — medieval castle, seventeenth-century house and neo-classical mansion — illustrates the changing patterns of Irish architectural patronage in a striking, if rather disheartening manner.*

## Clonbrock Castle, Co:ʸ Galway.

The remains of this Castle stands in the fine domain, belonging to the noble Lord whose family once inhabited it, and from whom it derives its origin; here the more modern building is seen to combine with the antient, but both have been in their turn deserted, and exhibit marks of decay, and the family now resides in an handsome structure of the present day, at some distance.[85]

The Castle seems to have been a place of some strength, and covered a considerable space of ground, the keep or dongeon was square, defended by round towers, which were probably at the angles of the bawn, and are still roofed; but the keep is in a state of great delapidation, and partly shrouded in Ivy.

The Domain is well laid out, displaying the agreeable varieties of wood and water. The family of Dillon first settled at Clonbrock about 1577.

## 28. Tuam Cathedral 1 (Galway)

*The cathedral church at Tuam has a complicated architectural history, and Daniel Grose's drawing is valuable as it shows the building before it was transformed by the addition of the Gothic Revival church in 1861-3. Grose realised that the porch-like structure to the left was all that survived of the twelfth-century Romanesque church, to which a large Gothic choir (now known as the Synod Hall) was added in the early fourteenth century. The latter was part of a grandiose scheme to rebuild the whole cathedral and the abbreviated buttresses in the centre of the painting mark the start of work on the transepts. This ambitious project was abandoned after 1312, leaving a peculiarly hybrid building. The oblong-planned tower, added in the fifteenth century, was dismantled by Sir Thomas Newenham Deane when he began the neo-Gothic cathedral. Presumably he felt that the medieval tower would detract from the spire he was building further west. In his composition Grose has conveyed the general form of the cathedral in a bold and effective way, making full use of the space available. As always, however, his depiction of window tracery and other details should not be treated as an accurate record of what was there around 1800-20.*

# Cathedral Church Tuam, Co:ʸ Galway.

Reduced as this Cathedral now appears, and nearly divested of all its antient ornamental architecture, yet once was it famous for its grandeur and size, and was a building such as might be expected to flourish in a city as it is said Tuam once was, the seat of learning and several extensive religious institutions, of which it was the chief. A truly beautiful specimen of its excellence in sculptural magnificence still remains in tollerable good preservation, an accurate representation of which is given in the next plate.

This truly beautiful arch appears to have seperated the body of the antient Church into two parts, the remaining half now forming the present Cathedral.[86]

The old foundations[87] may still easily be traced, and the ground plan appears to exhibit the form of a cross. Immediately under the Belfry is the stone work of several large arches, probably the passages of communication to the cross Chapels, these are ornamented with sculpture, resembling that on the grand arch, but now nearly obscured, by the the repeated coats of whitewash laid over them in repairing the Church, to form the side walls of which these were stopped up.[88] The steeple is lofty but of a singular construction being a narrow oblong stretching from side to side of the building; it is supported on the outside by high and strong buttresses: it was several times destroyed by fire, caused by lightning, the last time it so suffered, it was repaired by Bishop Vasey in 1688, this we are told by an inscription on a large stone placed in the east side of the Belfry, on the outside, near the top.[89]

The Cathedral is well fitted up, with an handsome Organ; against the North wall is a neat monument erected to the memory of Dean Echlin, with a well written Epitaph.[90]

The Church yard in [is] inclosed by a high wall covered with ivy, and in this wall is to be seen the remains of the West gable of the orignal building, which can be easily distinguished by the extraordinary thickness of the masonry in that particular part;[91] this serves to point out its former extent. The corners of the yard are planted with clumps of trees, which together with the ivy mantled wall, gives it a beautiful appearance.

It is unnecessary to repeat more here of the antient history of this Cathedral as much has been said already of it, in the description of S:ᵗ Jarlaths Cross.

D Grose

## 29. Tuam Cathedral 2 (Galway)

*Under the year 1184, the annals have a terse entry recording the collapse of the church at Tuam 'roof and stone'. This may be a melodramatic way of describing a deliberate piece of demolition, but it does provide a clear date for the start of work on the new Romanesque building. This had an exceptionally wide and ornate chancel arch, 'a truly beautiful specimen of our antient architecture', as Grose reported. The style of the carving would now be described as Hiberno-Romanesque, rather than Saxon, and the reference to 'twelve sweeps' is a curiously ambiguous way of describing the six decorative orders. Nevertheless Grose has made a valiant attempt to indicate the different types of chevron and he has also included the human faces carved on the inner capitals. The other capitals were decorated with patterns of interlace, too complex to be attempted in a small drawing. The old cathedral was damaged by fire in 1787, which explains the reddening of the sandstone that Grose noted in his text. The drawing is an unusually early attempt to record a Romanesque arch, complete with all its sculptural detail.*

# Saxon Arch and Ornaments Tuam, Co:ᵞ Galway.

This truly beautiful specimen of our antient architecture, is one of the finest of its kind in this Kingdom, or perhaps in any other. It has been already said in the foregoing description of the Cathedral, that this Arch apparently seperated the grand Choir of the antient building; it is now stopped up,[92] and is on the outside, exposed to all the injuries of the weather, and it cannot but excite our surprise that the ornaments have so long preserved that prominence and sharpness, they still exhibit.

It is composed of twelve sweeps each presenting a different species of ornament in something dissimilar from the others, these are supported by round pillars,[93] with Capitals representing ferocious human countenances, the whole deeply cut, and finely executed. Time however has obliterated the Capitals of most of the outside Pillars, those less exposed and sheltered by the Arch, retain their character.

The ornaments are cut out of a kind of red free stone, which adds greatly to their beauty and the Pillars are composed of the same materials.

The Introduction to Antient Irish Architecture, at the head of the 2:ᵈ Vol:ᵐ of this Work,[94] will amply satisfy the readers curiosity in respect to these truly rare and beautiful specimens of our forefathers skill in the art of sculpture; and it would be presumption in us, to attempt to handle the subject, after so learned an author.

D Grose

## 30. Manorhamilton (Leitrim)

*Manorhamilton was one of the most imposing seventeenth-century houses in Ireland, though in its present neglected, ivy-clad state it is difficult to appreciate this. Daniel Grose's painting gives a reasonably clear idea of the building, which has a rectangular nucleus with four corner towers. The latter have a slightly pointed or spear-shaped form, a layout which links the design with Rathfarnham Castle (1590s) and the Bishop's Palace at Raphoe (1636). This arrangement had its origin in military design and permitted flanking fire along each face of the towers. The main defences at Manorhamilton, however, depended on an outer wall, reinforced by corner turrets, none of which are visible in the painting. The semi-fortified mansion was built about 1634 by Sir Frederick Hamilton, a Scotsman, who had taken over confiscated land. Following the rebellion of 1641, he took vigorous action to defend his interests and he is notorious for a devastating attack made on Irish rebels in Sligo in 1642. According to the Ordnance Survey letters, his house was burnt not long after 'by a family of the name of MagLoughlin, who detested his name and his power'. With its projecting towers, regular string courses and well-dressed quoinstones, Manorhamilton had a geometrical clarity which Daniel Grose obviously sensed. In his view the house is seen from the east, with the steep slopes of Benbo, filling the skyline to the right.*

# Manorhamilton Castle, Co:ʸ of Leitrim.

The ruin here given is the most respectable of its kind in this county, and affords a very beautiful and romantic view; it stands on a small eminence close to the town of Manorhamilton, which takes its name from the Castle, and this fortification must have been in its day, a place of considerable size and strength. It was an oblong square erection, defended at each angle by a square tower, that overlooked the bawn, and th'o now much in ruins, exhibits evident proofs of its excellent workmanship, and the pains taken in the building; the cordon's of every story are of cut stone, and are still in high preservation, and the stone frames are still whole in some of the windows: the quoins are fresh & good and of a stone, that appears to have well withstood the effects of time & weather, they are of a red shining grit, full of mica, and this warm colour gives the building a peculiar appearance, which forms a beautiful contrast with the luxuriant foliage by which it is surrounded.

The lofty mountains that rise beyond it, gives an air of wild grandeur to the scene & it derives no small additional beauty, from its immediate vicinity to the handsome and well wooded domain of Screeney, the seat of the Cullen family, the gate of which is close under the ruins. This fine Castle was built in the reign of Queen Elizabeth by Sir Frederick Hamilton, who bravely defended it, and was the scene of much commotion during the rebellion. Prodigious execution was done here upon the rebels by Sir Frederick Hamiltons reciment AD 1641 and we also find it next year beseiged by the rebel Owen ORourk with 1000 men; in the absence of Sir Frederick Hamilton.[95]

## 31. Rathcline Castle (Longford)

*The ruins at Rathcline, which belonged to an impressive seventeenth-century house, are little known and much neglected. The core of the building was a medieval tower house, which was enlarged in the years around 1600. This new wing, which was furnished with transomed windows and regular string courses, was given a projecting square tower, visible at the left of Daniel Grose's painting. This forms one corner of a vast bawn, square in plan, which was defended by turrets at the other three angles. The entrances into the bawn were embellished with finely moulded arches, one of which has a superb classical console, now buried in ivy. Although Grose claims that the house was 'dismantled' by Cromwell, it was undergoing restoration in 1666-7, when it belonged to Sir George Lane, secretary to the Earl of Ormond. The painting gives a good impression of the size of the place, although the background hills are not as steep as the artist suggests. The shore of Lough Ree is some distance from the castle, and the meadow in the foreground now seems too marshy to produce a good crop of hay.*

# Rathcline Castle, Co:ʸ Longford.

The eye of the draftsman is here amply gratified by a view of one of the finest subjects for his pencil, this county affords. This very extensive ruin is beautifully situated on the banks of Lough-ree, which here forms a small bay or inlet, over which it stands; it covers a considerable space of ground, and consists of several large masses of building, towers and detached pieces of masonry, inclosed by a battlemented wall, which shows a long face towards the lake. Amongst the antient, are scattered the remains of more modern buildings, interspersed with fine trees, whose ample foliage overshadow the ruins, which adds greatly to the romantic grandeur of the scene. Th'o picturesquely situated, it was by no means properly placed as a stronghold, being surrounded on the land side by lofty grounds, that entirely command it, the hill of Rathcline rising boldly over it, within half Musquet shot. This we are told was once covered by a magnificent wood, which has totally disappeared, and a low brake of bushes now spreads over the face of the hill. The building of this Fortress is ascribed by tradition to the family of O'Quin; & is said to be one of the oldest Castles in Ireland, to have stood many seiges, & to have been the scene of much turbulent commotion and bloodshed, during the wars, that so frequently agitated this Kingdom. At length it suffered the same fate as most other Castles, that withstood the Parliament, being dismantled by Cromwell, & afterwards was totally distroyed by fire, during the final overthrow of James by King Williams forces. It was for some time inhabited by the Lanesborough family & in later times, since its final destruction, a modern dwelling house was built from the ruins close to the walls.[96] It is distant from the small town of Lanesborough about two miles, and from thence forms a beautiful object in the view the bridge affords. The prospect from the hill of Rathcline is truly magnificent, the noble river Shannon here spreads intself into an inland sea, broken with beautiful Islands, and bounded by undulating shores; to the right Slieuve Bawn stretches its cultivated sides, and the hill of Kilmane, in the fine domain of that county of Roscommon, immediately opposite the Castle, displays a striking feature in the landscape: nor does the Abbey steeple, bridge and town of Lanesborough, contribute less to inrich the view.

## 32. Inchcleraun 1 (Longford)

*Inchcleraun, a low-lying island in Lough Ree, was the site of an early Christian monastery founded by St Diarmaid in the sixth century. It contains six churches, not seven as Grose believed, and four of these are situated close together inside an enclosing cashel. The largest church is Templemor, a thirteenth-century building, to which a cloister was added in the later middle ages. The gables of this church can be seen at the centre right; the two arches at the left lead into the cloister walks. The tree in the centre of the ruined cloister has disappeared, so too the western gable of the church. At the left of the picture is the so-called Chancel church, a well-preserved Romanesque building and at the extreme right are the remnants of the tiny oratory of St Diarmaid. Beyond are glimpses of the lake. The ancient walls are painted with considerable vigour, using strong shadows and pink and ochre highlights.*

# Abbey of Inis Clothran, or the Island of the Seven Churches. Loughree, Co:ʸ Longford.

The number Seven was considered by the antients as holy and mystical, and was in great repute amongst the Irish in their monastic erections, and this Island is an instance amongst many others of the same description. Here we find the remains of seven churches the whole of them in a very advanced s[t]ate of ruin;[97] these were an establishment of the Culdees, who always prefered insular situations for their religious residences. About the year 540 we find S:ᵗ Dhiarmuit Naoimh or the just, and brother to Fiedlemid bishop of Kilmore, founded an Abbey here, in which he died on the 10:ᵗʰ of January. He wrote a learned and pious work in elegant rhime, in the nature of a Psalter, which as Colgan informs us, was in his possession. A:D: 1010 and 1016. The inhabitants of Munster pillaged, and sacked this Abbey in each of these years, and again in the years 1050 and 1087. 1089 In this year it is said the abbey was wasted by Muircheartach O Bryen and a great fleet of Ostmen. 1155 The Abbey was burnt on the feast of S:ᵗ Peter & S:ᵗ Paul.

1170 Rughry O'Carrol King of Ely was slain by his own brother in the midst of this Island, and in 1103 Gilbert de Nangle plundered and spoiled it.[98]

The ruins of the abbey is about 20 paces in length, and consists of three large gables, some broken arches, and one stone roofed cell still entire, the principal chapel is seventeen paces in length, with a lofty window consisting of two high and narrow pointed arches beneath which some stones of the Altar yet remain together. Here are grouped together several Chapels surrounded and overshadowed by venerable trees, particularly a noble Yew, perhaps coeval with the building it shelters. The Island was surrounded by a wall, and two of the churches are considerably detached from the Abbey, which lies low, and near the water.

(Plate 2:ᵈ) This View represents the N:W: Aspect of the Abbey, and displays a fine ramified window, and the venerable Yew already mentioned, and was taken by Lieu:ᵗ Grose of the Royal Navy.

### 33. Inchcleraun 2 (Longford)

Daniel Grose's second painting of Inchcleraun, based on a drawing by Lieutenant Arthur Grose, illustrates Templemor from the north. Apart from the loss of the 'venerable yew' (still there in 1900), the ruins are depicted much as they are today. The fifteenth-century traceried or 'ramified' window formed part of the reconstruction of the monastery in the later middle ages. Templemor belonged to a priory of Augustinian canons, which survived until 1541, and further buildings must once have surrounded the diminutive cloister garth. The scene, drawn from a consistent viewpoint, is one of the more accurate compositions in the book. In comparison with his first painting of Inchcleraun, the weather appears to have deteriorated, with a watery-yellow sky and ominous clouds to the left. As in modern picture postcards, the sun usually shines in Grose's paintings, but here for once there is the threat of rain.

D Grose

## 34. Inchcleraun 3 (Longford)

*Some distance from the other churches, on the highest point of Inchcleraun, are the ruins of 'Clogás an Oileáin',*
*or 'the bell tower of the island', a simple rectangular church with a western tower. Although vegetation has*
*increased, the scene has changed little over the course of two hundred years. The narrow round-headed window*
*in the east gable is cut from well-dressed ashlar and appears to date from around 1200. The tower is an*
*addition; even in Grose's painting it is possible to see how the later masonry was built on top of the original*
*gable. Not visible in the picture is an ingenious double opening in the thickness of the north wall, which*
*provided access to a mural stair. This is one of Grose's finest paintings. The composition is boldly arranged,*
*there is a convincing sense of recession across the lake and even a hint of heather on the distant mountain.*

# Detached Church Inis Clothran Loughree, Co:ʸ Longford.

This is one of the Seven churches already mentioned, but considerably removed from the Abbey, it stands on very elevated ground, the highest in the Island, and can be seen from a considerable distance;[99] it is in an equal state of ruin with the rest, the belfry was much higher, and from the fragments of foundation walls easily to be traced, must have been a respectable erection: th'o nothing near so large as the Abbey.

   The view this hill commands is truly beautiful, of the lake, and surrounding country, the mountain of Slieugh Bawn rising in the distance.

   This Island, at present commonly called Quakers Island, from it being the property of one of that profession,[100] is good ground, rather more than three quarter's of a mile in length, and something more than half a Mile in breadth, and is inhabited by several families whose cabins are built of the ruined fragments of the Churches.

D Grose

## 35. Saints' Island 1 (Longford)

Saints' Island, which can now be reached by a causeway from the Longford shore, is still a remote and peaceful place. There is no evidence that an early Christian monastery was located here, as Grose and others believed. The existing ruins belong to an Augustinian house, founded sometime before 1244 by a member of the Dillon family, who settled in Ireland after the Anglo-Norman conquest. Most of the architecture dates from the fifteenth century, when the community clearly enjoyed a degree of prosperity. Grose's first painting shows the ruins from the north-east, looking across to the church and the west range. Much of the north wall of the church, where the roof line of the cloister is marked, has fallen since Grose's day, but the fine window, with its switchline tracery is still intact. Scattered in the foreground of the painting are fragments of an exquisite fifteenth-century cloister arcade, almost identical to that reconstructed in the nearby monastery at Fore (Westmeath).

# Priory of All Saints in Saints Island, Loughree, Co:ʸ Longford.

A noble Monastery was founded in this Island by Saint Kieran, so early as the year 544, and in 4 years after he obtained a very considerable endowment for the support of its poor, and having pitched upon S:ᵗ Domnan or Donnan for his successor .He left the Island, for the purpose of erecting the magnificent Abbey of Clonmacnoise.

In 1087 this Abbey was plundered by the Munstermen, and again ravaged by Muir-heartach at the head of a great fleet of foreigners AD 1089: but from this transaction following the former so closely, there is every reason to believe they are one and the same affair.

This first Abbey falling to ruin, we are told that one of the descendants of Sir Henry Dillon of Drumraney, who came with John Earl of Moreton into Ireland, built an Abbey on this Island, most probably on the site of the former; at the suppression of Monasteries this was granted to Sir Patrick Barnwell.[101]

At present this once magnificent pile of building lies a mass of confused ruins,[102] precluding any very accurate conjecture of its original plan, the most entire part is a large Chapel about 30 paces long, and 10 broad, the east window of which was lofty and much ramified, beneath are some remains of the Altar, and in the walls of the building, on each side, are several nitches for holding relics, and holy water, now filled with human sculls, exhibiting great marks of age.

In one of these is carefully kept three pieces of rotten wood, called the Blessed Tree preserved here as tradition says, since the first foundation of the Priory. Many miraculous qualities are ascribed to this blessed Tree which are implicitly believed in, not only by the inhabitants of the island but by those on the mainland, for a great distance. Whoever takes an oath falsely, on any of these pieces of wood, the offenders mouth is immediately transfered to the back of his head, and he remains a conspicuous monument of the wonder-working powers of this miraculous tree. A few days before this drawing was taken, it made a considerable tour, and was soon again to go a round, through three town-lands, in search of stolen timber. It was once taken, we are told, for a similar purpose by a man, who having made successful use of it, carelessly threw it aside, and it was mislaid amongst some nettles at his door, but woeful consequences soon followed this culpable neglect, for in less than a month, the man and his whole family died. So firm a faith is placed in the powers of this tree, that many have been known to fly the country, rather than swear by it; if superstition of any kind can admit of an excuse, surely this may pass without severe sensure, when so good a point is gained, as the suppression of perjury amongst the lower ranks of people. You enter this large Chapel by a lofty arch in the west end, and another door in the north side, near the Altar communicated with the Cloisters or Cells, which together with the other habitable part of the building, appears to have formed a square, with an open space in the centre; several of these cells remain, but fast hastning to total ruin.[103] Beneath the building we are told, extend subterraneans to some distance, but of this there is no outward indication.

On the South side, is another adjoining smaller Chapel, with a tracery window pretty entire, near this and probably communicating with it, stood a lofty Belfry, which fell about 13 years ago, and greatly disfigured the surrounding remains, its fall was occasioned by a quantity of stones being taken out of its foundation to build a Masshouse. The Priory of all Saints when entire must have covered a great space of ground, and was surrounded by a lofty wall with a square and ample gate, near which, part of the porters lodge still remains, and facing stood a stone cross, the stump yet standing in the pedestal.[104]

Throughout these ruins, and about them, lie scattered fragments of beautiful fluted columns, capitals of clustering pillars, and pieces of arches finely moulded, all which plainly indicate the former magnificence of this religious house. It stands on a gentle aclivity sloping towards and very near the lake, which affords a beautiful prospect on every side; and close to it, is a comfortable village, the only one on the Island, built with the cut stone, and quoins taken from the Priory, which in all probability hastened its decay.

From this circumstance which very frequently occurs, we are led to wonder that people (the lower Irish) who have so great a reverance for such buildings, and who attach so many superstitious notions, to places of antient worship, supposing them to be the nightly rendezvous of the departed dead, whose remains they moulder over, and the haunt of Fairy goblins, under whose immediate protection the[y] conceive them to be; should build their houses of the materials taken from those ruins, and thus violate their favorite scenes of nocturnal revelry. This Island is somewhat better than half a mile in length, and about a quarter and an half broad.

Plate 2:[d]. This view which represents the South West Aspect was drawn by Lieu:[t] Grose Royal Navy.

## 36. Saints' Island 2 (Longford)

*The second painting of Saints' Island shows the monastic church from the west. The gable in the foreground has since collapsed, taking with it the Gothic west window. The small traceried window at the extreme right opens into the transept; somewhere in this vicinity stood the 'lofty belfry' that fell thirteen years before Grose wrote his book. Needless to say, the 'three pieces of rotten wood called the Blessed Tree' are no longer to be found in the aumbries or niches. In this case Grose was unusually sympathetic to local belief in the miraculous powers of relics (one trusts their loss was not attended by the sort of ill-fortune he describes in his text). The painting, which was adapted from a view by Lieutenant Arthur Grose, shows the ruins during the morning light; the walls are more shaded than is normally the case, but as always the handling of light is consistent, with the sun catching the edge of the door and casting a pool of light in front of the church.*

## 37. *Inisbofin 1 (Longford)*

*There are two islands named Inisbofin off the Atlantic coast of Ireland, but the Inisbofin that Daniel Grose visited lies in the heart of the country, in the eastern arm of Lough Ree. Despite 'its exposed and bleak situation', it is the only island in the lake which is still inhabited. Although the ruins of two churches survive, Grose was pre-occupied with the larger, northern building, which some authorities believe was the home of a small community of Augustinian canons. In the painting the church is seen from the south, extending from left to right across the picture. The traceried window belongs to a transept that was added in the fifteenth century; the keystone on the exterior of this carries the well-carved bishop's head mentioned in the text. To the left of the transept is a vaulted sacristy, which Grose illustrates in the form of a blocked arch. Many details are loosely depicted, including the delicately carved Romanesque window near the east end of the choir which has been transformed into a late Gothic design. It seems that Grose was more impressed by the 'lofty Ash', but this 'protecting guardian' has long since vanished from the scene.*

# Abbey of Inis Bofin in Loughree, Co:ʸ Longford.

This very antient remain admits of but very little description, and a short time must give it to total oblivion, its exposed and bleak situation lays it open to the powerful effects of every storm that blows. The ruin is small at present, the walls of one chapel, and part of another, all much broken and shattered, together with one stone roofed cell, is all that remains,[105] yet has time spared the stone work of two ramified windows, which were richly ornamented with carved work round the edges, th'o now very faint, from the effects of the weather.[106] The largest of these exhibits on the outside at the point of the arch a mitered head uncommonly well cut, and in high preservation; and the marks of the hurdles on which the arch was turned, in the sement, may still be seen in the roof of the Cell. From the foundation walls which can easily be traced, may be formed a conjecture, that this building once represented the form of a cross, and from their extent, that it was large and respectable.[107]

A lofty Ash grows amidst the ruins, and spreads its ample branches over them as the protecting guardian of the scene, and has most probably from the shelter it affords preserved them many years from total decay, being at least 80 years old and was planted by an inhabitant whose remains it canopies, and whose family has resided in the Island these 300 years.

To the south about 100 yards distant is another small chapel, very much in ruins lying quite exposed and bare.

We find S:ᵗ Rioch, son of S:ᵗ Darerca, the sister of S:ᵗ Patrick, founded an Abbey here, and was himself the first abbot; this Saint was living after the year 530 but the time of his death is unrecorded. In 770 the Abbey was destroyed by fire and in 1010 it was plundered by the Munstermen, again by the same in 1016 and their devastations were renewed in 1087. In 1089 the Danes plundered and destroy'd this Abbey.[108] (Plate 2:ᵈ). This plate represents the N:W: aspect and is taken from the lake giving a general view of the Island, which is of no great extent, and is inhabited by two or three families only. Here the Ash tree already mentioned makes a most conspicuous figure, and from its lofty appearance, and the lowness of the Island, is seen at a great distance, and serves as a leading mark to navigate this part of the lake, which in general is rendered intricate by the many sunken rocks, and stoney points that run out without showing themselves, from every shore. The Islands in Loughree, appear to have been favorite spots for religious erections, and were well calculated for privacy and security, objects eagerly sought after by the Culdees, who fled to insular situations, to protect themselves from the persecutions of the Papal Clergy: who notwithstanding but too soon found means to eject them, not only from their supposed secure lodgements, but altogether from every part of the Kingdom.

D Grose

## 38. Inisbofin 2 (Longford)

*Most of the islands in Lough Ree are encircled with trees, and the churches on Inisbofin are now barely visible from the lake. This view brings into prominence the north transept of the main church, with the traceried window that caught Grose's eye. To the left he has, inexplicably, added an extra gable, a misunderstanding perhaps of rough sketches made on the lake. This is one of the weakest compositions in the book; the two main elements in the picture, the church and the boat, are set a long way apart. Only the ash tree, dominating the ruins, provides much focus to the scene. The boat, however, is a study in itself, with its three sails billowing below the flag of St George and a sleek yellow strip along the hull.*

## 39. Rindown 1 (Roscommon)

*Half way up Lough Ree a promontory stretches into the lake from the Connacht shore. In 1227 this strategic site was chosen by the king's justiciar in Ireland as the seat of a major royal castle. Under the protection of the castle an Anglo-Norman town developed, defended on the landward side by a substantial stone wall, reinforced by flanking towers. Almost all trace of the town itself has gone, but in the southern corner of the vast enclosure lie the overgrown ruins of the parish church, mistakenly identified by Grose as the church of the Holy Trinity. The painting makes it seem extensive, though it was a relatively simple Gothic building. The great mass of ivy shown above the chancel arch in the centre of the picture is still there and, despite Grose's gloomy predictions, the walls have not yet crumbled into dust, though all the dressed stonework has disappeared. The large boulders are still to be seen on the foreshore nearby. The bright green sailing boat is drawn with an affection for detail far greater than Grose permitted himself when painting medieval monuments.*

# Church of the Holy Trinity S:ᵗ Johns Randown Loughree. Co:ʸ Roscommon.

The bay of S:ᵗ Johns in Loughree is a fine deep and broad inlet on the Roscommon or western shores of the lake, formed by the main and a long neck of land that extends itself into the water for a considerable distance narrowing to a point called warrens point.

This neck of land th'o somewhat elevated is low ground in comparison with the other sides of the bay, which form a kind of amphitheatre of hills sloping towards the water, beautifully diversified with wood and inclosures together with a gentlemans house (in the cottage stile) and improvements, which furnishes the landscape, and gives a finish to the whole.

This small portion of ground is rich in antiquarian treasure, and is well worthy the inspection of the curious observer; the first ruin that presents itself nearest the main, is the subject here given, which in its dilapidated and mouldering walls, nearly fallen to total decay, exhibits the all subduing attacks of time, that visits alike with its irresistible powers, the spired Abbey, the turreted Castle, and the humble cottage. A very short space must consign this ruin to oblivion, as no part of it remains, but the shattered outward walls of the Church, the greatest part of which lies leveled with the ground.[109] The antiquary feels a lively interest, in snatching from the destroyer for a short space longer, these venerable relics of antient days, particularly those that are so frequently presented to his view on this extensive lake, as a few years must inevitably from their present general state of decay, and exposed situation, soon mingle them with the dust, when no memorial will be left of them, but this work, and heeps of stones, overgrown with nettles and rank weeds. The reflective mind from such objects cannot but be struck with the impotence of mans best efforts to perpetuate his most durable works, which are little less evanescent than himself, and fade away after a few revolving years, and leave no trace that they had ever been.

The church was placed not more than an hundred yards from the waters edge, and probably was a dependance on the neighbouring Castle of S:ᵗ Johns or Randown, as this with it (in the Monasticon Hibernicum) bears in common both those names, from which we learn that "It appears that Clarus archdeacon of Elphin, who founded the Priory of Loughree, founded also the Church of the Holy Trinity Rinduin".[110]

D Grose

## 40. *Rindown 2 (Roscommon)*

*Daniel Grose gives a good description of the royal castle at Rindown in his text, but it is not easy to grasp the form of the building from his painting. He shows the castle from the north-west; the tallest features are the ruins of the hall or keep. The main gate is visible to the right, and immediately in front is the 'deep and broad ditch', which could be filled with water from the lake. The arches to the left, located on the far side of the inner bailey, served as a support for a defensive wall-walk. During the thirteenth century Rindown occupied a crucial position in the military strategy of the royal government. It guarded the shipping routes along the Shannon and, combined with the fortifications of Roscommon and Athlone, helped to keep the O Conor kings of Connacht in check. It was the scene of much building activity between 1275 and 1302, but until the ruins are cleared of ivy and properly surveyed, it will remain a frustrating monument to study. Remote from the public road, with its walls half concealed by vegetation, Rindown is indeed a place of solemn 'grandeur', uniting as Grose observed 'all the charms of wood, water and romantic ruins'.*

# Castle of Randown or S:^t Johns Loughree.
# Co:^y Roscommon.

Previous to the use of Great Guns, this fortification must have been considered of very great strength and importance; it is situated on a long wooded neck of land nearly surrounded by water, and upon occasion of necessity, could be entirely cut off from the main, it being encompassed by a deep and broad ditch, by means of which the isthmus could be inundated quite across. Over this ditch in the deepest and broadest part on the N:W: side of the Castle which here presents a long extent of front, was thrown a Draw Bridge, the butts of the masses of masonry, from whence this bridge sprung, are still to be seen, and by this, was entered the Fortress, through a circular arch. On the oposite side of the building, a causeway also crosses the ditch, which could easily be removed at pleasure, this was defended by towers; great masses of the masonry belonging to them, are seen scattered around; and by this an entrance was gained into the bawn, or court of the Castle.

The bawn was protected by a strong and lofty wall perforated with loopholes, and parapeted at top, with here and there a tower.

The keep and habitable parts of the Castle, as already noticed, stretch to the N:W: and occupies the whole length of the building, communicating at one end, by a large tower to the angle of the bawn, which inclines in figure to an half circle, the diameter being formed by the keep, that extends a small distance beyond the arc.

The walls of this Castle are still of great height, and speak its once vast strength, part of the lower apartments are still left entire, and sustain by three massy arches the greatest portion of the building, which was sufficiently strong to resist in some measure the powerful effects of Gunpowder, used to distroy it.

Enormous fragments of masonry, some of them containing entire passages, with flights of stone steps within them, lie scattered in the bawn, and bear ample evidence to the goodness of the work, and the solidity of the walls.[111]

A beautiful mantle of ivy covers the greatest part of the building, and communicates an air of grandeur to these truly venerable and picturesque towers.

To add to the strength of the fortress a line of defence was drawn round beyond the ist[h]mus, taking within its sweep, a considerable space of ground, this was defended by square towers at regular distances, and effectually cut off all communication on the land side, and this obstacle must be surmounted, before the Castle could be closely invested: some of these towers remain entire whilst others are quite distroy'd.[112]

At the extreme point of the peninsula to the S:E: of the Castle, about 150 paces distant from it, stands on elevated ground, a detached round tower, with three tiers of loop holes. The appearance of this tower stamps it with a more modern date than the Castle, but from its situation and construction, appears to have been a watch tower, or look out, commanding an extensive view of the lake in every direction, and precluding all approach to the Castle from that side, without alarm being given.[113]

Tradition has not been idle respecting the romantic history of this Castle, it informs us, that a certain King of the Country once took refuge here, and stood a siege, which he sustained for some time with great bravery, but at length, being too closely pressed, and the Castle taken by storm, he was obliged to seek safety in flight, followed by one attendant only; but one way was left for them to deside on and no other alternative but death or Captivity, they were obliged to take to the lake, and actually swam their horses to a small island, East of the Castle, nearly two miles distant, which they reached in safety, and from this circumstance it has borne the name of the Kings Island, which it retains to this day. We are told that a Castle was built here in the reign of King John,[114] for Knights Hospitallars, or for Crossbearers, at his express command, that after many vicissitudes, the English strongly fortified it in 1226, and in 1237 Phelim O'Conor plundered and pillaged the same; AD 1334 the Constable of this Castle John de Funtayn's was retained at the annual stipend of 40£ Sterling.

The many beautiful varieties the situation of the Castle presents to the eye of the artist, is well worthy his labour, and when combined furnishes him with a subject wherein is united all the charms of wood, water, and romantic ruins.

## 41. Clonmel: St Mary's parish church (Tipperary)

*Daniel Grose had difficulty writing about towns with more than one medieval church. At Youghal he confused the parish church with the Franciscan friary and he did the same thing at Clonmel. Nevertheless his picture is of enormous historical interest. It shows the parish church before a series of drastic restorations in the nineteenth century, which deprived the building of most of its medieval character. The church is now almost unrecognisable from that depicted by Grose. The roofless chapel in the foreground, the White Mortuary Chapel (1622-3), was demolished in 1805, and in the same year the octagonal tower was substantially rebuilt without the wooden flèche and belfry. The picturesque dormer windows in the aisles have gone, so too the nearby porch and crenellated battlements. Most of these alterations took place in 1857, when the church was remodelled according to the designs of Joseph Welland. The arches of the town wall can be seen at the extreme left of the picture and in the foreground the energetic gravedigger, smartly dressed in a green jacket and blue breeches, makes a lively contribution to the composition. Daniel Grose's skill as a colourist is particularly evident in the painting of the tower, with its delicate touches of green, yellow and pink.*

# Franciscan Friary Clonmell, Co:ʸ Tipperary.

Clonmell is an handsome town, the Capital of the County, and is a bustling thriving place, being on the high road from Dublin to Cork and consequently a considerable thorough-fare. It lies on the right bank of the river Suir which adds greatly to its appearance, and the salubrity of the air. It has an excellent market for every kind of provision, and the neighbouring river supplies it plentifully with fine Salmon and Trout, nor is it too far from the Coast, to want a good share of sea fish.

Clonmell was once fortified and underwent many of the chances of war; it was taken by the Lord Deputy, Earl of Kildare A:D: 1516, and again besieged and surrendered after a vigorous defence, which cost Cromwell Two Thousand men A:D: 1650.[115] In it was two religious houses a Dominican and a Franciscan Friary,[116] the last of these, is the subject now before us we are told was a truly magnificent structure, and esteemed one of the finest in Ireland; but its celebrity consisted most in a miraculous Image of Saint Frances, that worked many wonders, and was resorted to from far and neer. The building extended a considerable space, containing a Church and Steeple, dormitory, hall, Chambers, Kitchen, Stable &. It is aledged to owe its foundation to several different people, but its true benefactor was Otho de Grandison, in 1269; in 1536 this friary was reformed by Friars of the strict observance.

The 8 of March 31:ˢᵗ of King Henry VIII, Robert Travers then guardian, surrendered this house containing as above recited, the whole in a ruinous state, and of little value. Afterwards in the same reign a moiety of it, and all its distant possessions, was granted to the Sovereign, and commonalty of Clonmell, and again the other moiety to Ja:ˢ Earl of Ormond, each at the yearly rent of 12 Pence Irish. Th'o still venerable, the Church of Clonmell has lost much of its former magnificence the Dormitory, Chambers, Kitchen and Stables have disappeared,[117] and the body of the Church, with part of the Steeple, and one small Chapel alone remain, these (except the chapel) have undergone various modern repairs and additions, it is now fitted up for a numerous congregation and Divine Service is performed in it.

The Church still retains its curious battlemented walls, and with the ramified windows, and octagon Steeple, leaves room to form a fair estimate of what the general building must have been in its flourishing state. It is surrounded by a large yard planted with trees, and inclosed by an high wall, in part of which may still be seen, arches that formerly composed part of the Cloisters, and points out the extent of the old building.

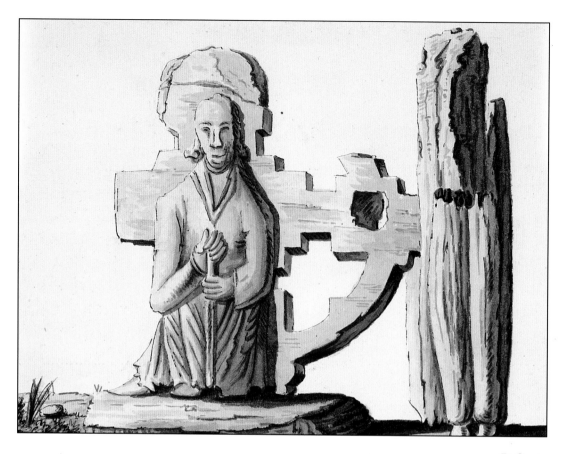

## 42. Roscrea: stone cross (Tipperary)

*The site of the monastery at Roscrea, founded by St Cronan in the seventh century, is marked by a round tower and the facade of a Romanesque church. It is not the most tranquil of early Christian sites, for the main road from Dublin to Limerick slices between the two buildings. The stone carvings drawn by Grose belonged to a twelfth-century high cross, now re-assembled (incorrectly) to the south of the church. The design of the cross was typical of the twelfth century, with a large figure of an ecclesiastic on one face and the crucified Christ on the other. Local tradition holds that the ecclesiastic represents St Cronan, but, as Roscrea was advancing its claims to a bishopric in the twelfth century, the sculpture may have been intended as a more general image of episcopal authority. The cross head is badly damaged and the whole of the left arm is missing (it has been restored by a new piece in the reconstituted monument). The inside of the ring was cut in a stepped pattern, an unusual feature, but one that is repeated on the contemporary cross at the neighbouring monastery of Mona Incha. The fragment to the right formed part of the shaft. On each side was a tall figure, cut in heavy relief, of which Grose gives some indication. The best preserved sculpture on the cross is the abstract ornament on the underside of the ring, which seems to have escaped the attention of the artist.*

# Saint Cronans Cross at Roscrea, Co:^y Tipperary.

This mutilated cross at present exhibits but little of its former magnificence, but enough still remains to convince us, that it was once a very curious and elaborate piece of workmanship.[118] The half of the Saints figure remains, a fragment of the head and one limb of the cross, with an indented perforation, the outside of which forms a segment of the arc of a circle, and when compleat, must have been of considerable size.

The saint is represented in his pontifical robes, leaning on a staff, in very high relief, and th'o greatly defaced, was very boldly executed, as the folds of the drapery are still very plain and deep, and the hands and arms greatly raised. The face is considerably injured, and the features nearly obliterated, but the remains of the hair is discernable, which flows in curls below the ears.

This fragment is placed upon a flat flag, perhaps part of the pedestal, and is supported against a piece of the shaft, which has been fixed upright close to it, on this is to be seen the lower extremities of the figure, the feet resting on the ground.

It is impossible to ascertain its original altitude, as this appears to be only a part of the shaft, but there is every reason to conjecture that when the whole was put together and erected, it must have been of considerable height.

These fragments stand near the Church door of Roscrea on the high road, and from its exposed situation, and already decayed state will soon be totally demolished.

We find but little mentioned of this Saint. Sir Ja:^s Ware, in his Antiquities says that Saint Cronan was a Bishop, otherwise called Abbot of Rosscrea, the writer of his life, stiles him the Glorious Abbot Cronan born in Munster, whose father name was Odran. Cronan died the 28:^th of April, he flourished in 580. And again in his lives of the Bishops. It is most certain that S:^t Cronan, who was a Bishop, or as some say — Abbot was the founder of the Church of Roscrea, and flourished about the year 620. This Saint had the honor [of] baptizing S:^t Kevin who was of a family of high rank.

D Grose.

## 43. Castletownbere: Castle Dermott (Cork)

*With his military experience, Daniel Grose was fascinated by stories of ancient battles and he showed a particular interest in the gruesome siege of Dunboy Castle in 1602 at the end of the Nine Years War. Plagiarism was of no concern and he copied his account word for word from Smith's History of County Cork (1750). To illustrate his text he chose not Dunboy itself, but the neighbouring castle of Castle Dermott at Castletownbere. This appears to have been a standard late-medieval tower house, perched on a cliff above the harbour. It had already disappeared by 1837, and so Grose's activities as a painter once again provide valuable information about a lost monument. The various 'good and neat houses' stacked above the shoreline make an attractive composition, and the artist appears to have enjoyed painting the undulating hillsides with their hazy tones. This is one of the rare occasions on which Grose omitted his favourite white-edged clouds.*

# Castle-town Castle, Co:ʸ Cork.

Th'o retired and difficult of access, this neighbourhood was the scene of many military operations, and the Castle of Dunboy not above a mile from the subject now before us, affords the Antiquary some interesting events, not unworthy the page of history. The two places here mentioned, are so near each other, and their fate were so linked together, it would be unpardonable to pass over such circumstances in silence, when the account of one of the Castles is attempted: the more especially, as the total ruin of Dunboy (scarce a vestige of it remaining) precluded its being taken as a distinct subject.

Castle-town or as it was antiently call'd Castle Dermott, is a small scattered village amongst which at present are some good and neat houses, that from their being white-washed, make a showey and clean appearance, inspiring comfortable ideas, when put in comparison with the dreary aspect of the bogs and mountains that spread around it.

It is situated partly along the side of a small sheltered bay, formed by the Island of Dinish containing some acres which shuts it from Berehaven Bantry bay. Nearly opposite the Centre of this inlet, stands the remains of the Castle, whose walls are immediately upon the bank over the sea, but little of it is at present to be seen, except part of the walls of a square tower greatly in ruins, and the butts of two small flankers; a much more considerable part of it was standing, within these few years past, but as we are told, the walls having a great inclination from the perpendicular, the neighbouring inhabitants, dreading its sudden fall, there being a much frequented landing place just under it, pulled it down by force with ropes &c; but the true state of the case appears to be, that this Castle was reduced to its present ruinous state, more from the depredations committed on it, for the sake of the cut stone in which it abounded, than from the effects of time.[119]

This was once a fortress of note and strength, it probably originally belonged to the O Sullivans, commonly call'd O Sullivan Bear a powerfull family in these parts, and was of such consequence together with the Castle of Dunboy, as to call for the presence of the Lord President himself with a strong army to reduce them. M:ʳ Richard Boyle, afterwards the 1:ˢᵗ Earl of Cork and Orrery, says in his life written by himself as follows

"At my return into Ireland AD: 1602 I found my Lord President (Sir George Carew) ready to march to the Siege of Beerhaven Castle then fortified and possessed by the Spaniards, and some Irish rebels, which after battering, we had made assaultable, entered and put all to the sword''.

At the same time Sir George Carew invested Dunboy Castle. of this siege Smith gives us the following account.[120] O Sullivan having taken possession of the Castle of Dunboy, and surprised what arms, and ammunition the Spaniards had in it, fortified himself in it, and wrote an account of his success to the King of Spain.

The army under the Lord President, scarce exceeded 1500, being much diminished by the winter seige of Kinsale, marched along the sea coast towards O Sullivan and arrived at Bantry, where they waited for the Shipping with the stores; and were there joined by Sir Charles Wilmot, who made a most dangerous march over Mangerton mountains, notwithstanding Tyrrells having boasted to intercept him, now offered to parley with the president, but was refused. The forces did not embark till June for Bearhaven, the weather proving wet, but on the 6:th they landed near Castle Dermot, notwithstanding an attempt made by the enemy to hinder them. Dunboy was defended by one Richard MacGeoghegan for O'Sullivan, who proved a brave commander. On the 13:th Tyrrell alarmed the Camp about midnight, having poured in some shot, which did little hurt; but next day the principal officers had a very narrow escape, for the President, the Earl of Thomond, and Sir Cha:s Wilmot, as they were riding in a rank along the shore, for their recreation, observed a gunner traversing a piece of ordnance, in the Castle; that fellow, said the President, will make a shot at us, and he had scarsely spoke the word, when the piece was discharged. Sir George Carew reigned his horse and stood firm, but the Earl and Sir Charles started forward, so that the ball grazed at their horses heels and beat the earth about them. The President seeing them past danger, laughing said, that if they had been as good mechanical Cannoneers as commanders, they would have stood firm as he did, for a good gunner always takes aim before a moving mark.

The battery which consisted of 4 pieces of Cannon, having beat down a tower of the Castle, on which the enemy had an iron Falcon planted that much annoyed the besiegers, the Irish offered to surrender upon quarter but their messenger was hanged, and the breach ordered to be entered. It was mounted by Lieu:t Frances Kirton of the Presidents Regiment, who received three Shot, and a wound in his right arm; but he valiantly maintained his post, till he was supported by Lieu:t Meutas. The Presidents colours were soon after planted upon a turret of the Barbican, from whence they drove the enemy, into another turret on the South side, which with the former was rampered with earth, well manned, and defended by a demy-culverin, and saker of brass, both which the enemy charged with hail-shot, and kept continually firing upon the English, who were masters of the other turret; but their gunner being shot, obliged them at length to retreat, under the east part of the Castle. The passage to which being narrow, was maintained with great obstinacy for an hour and a half on both sides: the Irish defended themselves both with Shot and stones, kill'd numbers of the assailants. During this dispute, Captain Slingsby's Sergeant, who had gotten to the top of the vault of the South West tower, by clearing the rubbish, found that the ruins thereof, had made a passage which commanded that part of the Barbican of the Castle. By this passage the English made a fresh descent upon the besieged; and gained ground, they being then in a desperate situation, about 40 of them salley'd out of the Castle towards the sea, but being intercepted, they were all put to the sword, except 8 who swam for their lives, and these were most of them killd, by some forces placed in boats for the purpose. After some hours of defence and assault on both sides the top of the Castle was gained, on which the English planted their Colours. The remaining part of the ward being 77 retired into the Cellars, into which, there being no descent but a narrow pair of winding stone stairs, they defended the same, but offered to surrender if they might have their lives. Soon after one Dominick Collins a friar born in Youghall, who was brought up in the wars of France, served there under the League, and had the command of some horse in Britany, surrendered himself upon mercy.

The sun being set, and strong guards left upon the enemy, the Regiments withdrew to the Camp. Next morning 23 more surrendered to the guard, with the two Spanish Gunners; the remainder of them made choice of one Taylor to be their Captain, who drawing nine barrels of powder, into the vault, sat down upon them, with a lighted match in his hand, vowing to blow up the Castle and all in it, if he and the rest had not quarter given them, and promise of their lives; which being refused by the President, he ordered a new battery to be erected against the vault, with an intention to bury them in the ruins. The bullets entering amongst them they compelled Taylor, by force to deliver himself up, who with 48 more being ready to come out, Sir George Thornton and others entering the vault to receive them, found Richard Mac-Geoghegan lyeing there mortally wounded, who at the instant of their coming in raised himself up, and snatching a lighted Candle, staggered with it to a barrel of powder which stood open. Captain Power perceiving his intent, held him in his arms till he was killed; whereupon Taylor and the rest were brought prisoners to the Camp. The same day 56 were executed, but the Friar, Taylor, Turlogh-Roe Mac Swiney and others were yet spared; in hopes of their performing some future service. This Garrison consisted of 148 select fighting men, the best of all their forces, of which none escaped; but were either slain, buried in the ruins, or executed, and so obstinate and resolute a defence was never made before in this Kingdom. Tyrrell hearing that some of the rebels lives were spared sent to the President to ransom them: but the President finding that they did not intend to do any further service, caused them to be hanged, being 12 in number. Taylor was soon after executed in Cork, as was Collins the Friar, at Youghall the place of his birth. Dunboy being thus reduced, the President caused it to be demolished. It was however thought a post of so much consequence, that Lord Orrery in 1665 wrote to the Duke of Ormond proposing to have Dunboy Castle rebuilt.

D Grose—

## 44. Castletownbere: stone circle at Derreenataggart West (Cork)

*There are over two hundred stone circles in Ireland, of which almost half are to be found in Cork and Kerry. The circle at Derreenataggart West probably consisted of fifteen stones, nine of which are still standing. (not eight as Grose states in his text). The diameter of the circle is approximately 7.70 metres. Although it is known that stone circles belong to the Neolithic and early Bronze age, their function remains notoriously controversial. Much consideration has been given to their possible role in plotting the movement of the sun and the moon, so defining the seasons of the year, but, as one authority has pointed out, a complete circle is not needed for this. The architectural role of the stones, in defining and enclosing a specific space must surely be equally crucial. Like many of the early antiquarians, Grose believed they served as Druidic temples; modern scholarship still inclines to the view that they served a religious or ritualistic purpose of some sort. The painting shows the commanding position of the monument on a hillside above Castletownbere, with fine views across Bearhaven. The artist leaves us guessing what the man with the pick is threatening to do.*

# Druids Temple near Castle-town, Co:ʸ Cork.

About half a mile north west of Castletown, as you ascend the mountains, stands one of those circles of upright stones, commonly denominated Druidic Temples;[121] the circle at present consists of but eight standing stones, th'o it appears there were originally several more, as some loose stones lie scattered about near the area: the entrance was evidently on the east side, and the largest stone in the circle, is placed immediately opposite the west.

The interior diameter of the circle is 26 feet, and the ground appears raised towards the centre, but there is no vestige to be made out of there ever having been an upright pillar placed there.

The stones composing this temple are from six to eleven feet high, mostly of different breadth and thickness, all of them very ponderous, and unhewn blocks of brown mountain grit; nor on the closest inspection, can there be found on any of them the smallest indication of the Ogham character, so frequently to be found in the neighbouring Co:ʸ of Kerry on stones composing similar circles.

About one hundred yards south west, is the remains of another Druidic erection, which consisted of four large stones, but one of which is now standing; the largest of these is placed in the centre, and appears to have been raised much higher than the surrounding ones, th'o now fallen; this evidently had a connection with the larger circle, as an appendage to it, and used in like manner for the purposes of worship.

It were needless here to enter upon an investigation of the different opinions formed by antient and modern writers, respecting these circles, as a very learned disquisition is given to the reader by Doctor Ledwich in his introduction to the 1:ˢᵗ Vol:ᵐ of this work; and in his own Antiquities of Ireland.[122]

Contrary to the situation of other places of druidic worship in general, the eye is here permitted to wander abroad over pleasing objects, and is by no means confined to gloomy rocks or woods, for, from this eminence you command a view of the wide expanse of ocean, the western entrance into Bere-haven, with part of Bere Island, its Telegraph, and the Western redoubt, and th'o the modern erections here mentioned did not formerly grace the scene, yet it must have been at all times lively and interesting: these now form the background of the view here given.

Castletown is a small village situated on the shores of Bere-haven Bantry bay, and has in its neighbourhood many other curious specimens of Druidic antiquities.

D Grose

## 45. Bear Island: standing stone (Cork)

*The Greenane stone is located near the centre of Bear Island, with good views in each direction. Grose, impressed by its scale, took the trouble to measure it. He was also impressed by its shape, which he recorded with theatrical emphasis in his painting. Behind the stone in the middle distance lie the waters of Bearhaven and beyond is a rather volcanic-looking Hungry Hill. The purpose of standing stones continues to baffle modern archaeologists, much as it did the antiquarians around 1800. Few would subscribe to the eccentric opinions of Colonel Vallancey that they were designed for sun worship, but the possibility that they were intended as burial markers or boundary stones remains open. Indeed, a cist burial has been discovered close to a pillar stone at Furness (Kildare). The Irish word for a standing stone is gallán and the term 'Gowlawn stones' recorded by Grose is presumably some local corruption or misunderstanding of this.*

# Greenane Stone Bere Island Bantry Bay, Co:ʸ Cork.

Bere Island is of considerable size, and is placed in the mouth of Bantry Bay, six miles from the shores of Carbery on the south, and one from Ross Mac Owen on the North, forming the southern boundary of Berehaven, the best sheltered and most commodious harbour for Shipping on these shores, which are greatly indented and form innumerable nooks, and bays, from Cork harbour, to the mouth of the Shannon. The Island is nearly six Irish miles in length, and three in the widest part, is thickly inhabited, contains some very fine farms for the nature of the country, th'o of most rugged and unpromising appearance at a general view; during the war it was well fortified and held as a strong military station.[123]

The Greenane Stone derives its name from that division of the Island on which it stands, it is an upright unhewn rough pillar of eregular shape, eleven feet in height above the ground, but from its size and exposed situation, it must have had a considerable part of its length, sunk beneath the surface, to have enabled it to retain its upright position and to withstand the effects of time and storm, alth'o its thickness near the bace, is much worn away, and is now not more than half its original diameter. In the widest part it is now 3 feet 8 inches broad, and 1 foot 6 inches thick, formed of gray mountain stone, such as is commonly found on all parts of the Island.

It stands on an eminence between Ardagh hill and Ballinakilly both of which rise far above it, but so situated that the shade of neither of them can cover or osscure the stone, at any hour of the day, so that when the sun shines it has the whole of its rays, untill it descends behind the distant hills to the westward, its horizon in that direction. This circumstance and the name of the place and the neighbouring hill according to his translation of the Irish, seems greatly to favour Col:ˡ Vallanceys opinion that upright pillar stones were sometimes used in the worship of the Sun in pagan times. According to him Grain signifies the Sun and Graine a sacrifise, and the neighbouring hill (at whose foot it is) Ardagh the Hill of Fire, Ard being a hill, and Agh fire, so the Hill of fire, or of the fire;[124] and in aid of these the natives of the Island, translate the denomination of Greenane "the place of the Sun", or as they express themselves Tane Greanane; the Sun shines here.[125] They also tell you, that this stone, is exactly placed every way, in the centre of the Island, and on its being tried with an instrument by the writer of this article, it was found to be actually so stationed, within a few feet. To attain this exactness even with the trifling deviation mentioned, must have been attended with, and required infinite pains and trouble, as the Antient Inhabitants, or those who erected this stone, must have been in all human probability unacquainted with the use of Instruments fit for the purpose.

There is some reason to conclude from the nature of the ground round the pillar, that it was surrounded by a circle of other smaller ones, none of which are however now standing; it is a very conspicuous object on the Island being to be seen from the bay and haven, and from the peninsula, therefore commmanding a view of several druidic Altars and temples, several of which is to be found on it.

This stone is totally devoid of any Ogham inscription, this is rather singular as many of these kind of upright pillars which occur frequently in the neighbouring Co:ʸ of Kerry, have very deep inscriptions indented on their edges, very faithful views of these were taken by the late learned and engeneous M:ʳ Pelham, and have since been presented to the public in one of the numbers of the Collectenea de rebus Hibernicis. Authors vary greatly as to the use of these pillar Stones and for what purpose they were erected;[126] the Antient Irish set up pillars of Stone on many occasions, says the Author already quoted; some were inscribed with Ogham characters to mark the Cycles, others erected on the boundaries of districts, the common Irish call the upright pillars Gowlawn Stones; others say they were placed on the remains of illusterous [illustrious] men, after their bodies were burnt & collected in urns; but for a fuller account of these relics of antiquity I beg leave to refer my readers to Ledwichs introduction to the 1:ˢᵗ Vol:ᵐ.[127]

The view here given is taken from the South West, and presents in the back ground a distant view of Berehaven, Ross Mac Owen and Hungry Hill, with its "cloud cap't top".

D Grose

### 46. Bear Island: 'Druids' altar' at Ardaragh West 1 (Cork)

*The so-called Druids' altar near Rerrin village at the south-east corner of Bear Island is in fact a wedge tomb. With approximately four hundred recorded, this is the most widespread form of megalithic monument in Ireland. The name derives from the fact that the chamber is usually wedge-shaped in plan; it is normally wider and higher at the end where the entrance is placed. The gallery is constructed of orthostats or upright stones, supporting roofing slabs above. In some tombs, including that at Ardaragh West, the entrance 'portico' is separated from the main chamber by a 'septal' stone, a large upright completely blocking the way. The monument appears to have deteriorated considerably since Grose's time and it is not easy to equate his drawing with what is there today. His first plate shows the tomb from the south-east, looking inland towards one of the island's martello towers.*

# Druids Altar Bere Island in Bantry Bay, Co:<sup>y</sup> Cork.

It has been already noticed, that Bere Island abounds in Druidic remains, in fact a chain of them appears to run from east to west of its length, & from each of which may be seen, one or more of the rest.

The one now under consideration is the second in this line, from the east; it lies on the South shore of the Island, in what is call'd the peninsula, and is placed not far from the sea, but so situated, as not to command, a view of it from the spot;[128] the prospect however is by no means a confined one, particularly to the west, and in that direction rises the highest grounds in the Island.

From the upright Stones, and from the way the rest have fallen the figure plainly appears to have been originally, an oblong square Twenty four feet in length, and in breadth nine feet seven inches.

It lies nearly due east and west, the west end is roofed by a single stone, which measures in breadth Six feet and inclines in about an angle of 45 degrees; the height of the stones that form this roofed end is seven feet, five inches, and the width of the entrance, Two feet, three inches.

One stone forms the east side of the covered part, and is of great size and thickness, supporting entirely the weight of the large inclined roof.[129]

The remaining part of the oblong seems likewise to have been roofed, as appears from a flag of great size now nearly lying on the ground, measuring fifteen feet in length, and in breadth five feet four inches, which corresponds with the uprights on each side, th'o now fallen from their support;[130] under this is another flag of nearly the same dimentions which appears to have been the ground work or flooring of this very curious monument of antiquity. The whole is composed of rough unhewn gray mountain stone, of which there is a very fine quarry of loose flags at the foot of a neighbouring hill.

This and other similar remains proves beyond a doubt that this Island was inhabited from the very earliest periods of antiquity, and that those inhabitants were not few, is equally proved by the frequent occurrence of altars, upright stones and Circles, all equally antient, and for the purposes of religious worship, scattered over the face of it: but at the same time these prove the fact, a melancholy reflection arises therefrom, that in the present enlightened state of religion, when the knowledge of a Saviour has for so long a period banished the pagan rights of worship of Fire, Stones and Groves;

in such a tract of land, at the present day, but one place of Divine Worship should be found, and that one of the most wretched kind being no better than a thatched barn; on Bere Island there is but one Chapel of this description, and no Church.

The background of the 1:$^{st}$ plate presents the highest hills, or rather mountains in the Island, and in front, one of the Posts of defence, a Martello Tower and its advanced Battery;[131] the very distant hills are on the Island to the West.

(Plate 2:$^{d}$) Represents the North Asp:$^{t}$ of the Altar, and shows the flags that formed the flooring and roof now falling from its supports on each side.

## 47. Bear Island: 'Druids' altar' at Ardaragh West 2 (Cork)

*Grose's second painting of the wedge tomb illustrates the monument from the north-west, showing the entrance, described by Westropp in 1921 as 'a sort of portico of two stones leaning towards each other till they touch'. Wedge tombs are not easy monuments to describe, but in his text Grose makes a conscientious effort to place the salient details on record. Although the tomb at Ardaragh West has not been excavated, evidence from elsewhere reveals that most burials within them took place after cremation. A firm chronology is yet to be established, but details from one site suggest that such tombs were still in use as late as 1250-1000 B.C. The vigorous drawing of the stones, combined with the emphatic shadows, successfully conveys the powerful impact of this important megalith.*

## 48. Valencia Island: Cromwellian fort (Kerry)

*There are two Cromwellian forts on Valencia Island (which is in Kerry, not Cork), the more substantial being that at Fort Point. This is situated on a promontory at the north end of the island, about two miles from Knightstown, and it was built in 1651-2 to control the entrance to Valencia Harbour. On 7th December 1651 orders were given for a thousand veteran soldiers 'to land with all expedition at Valentia, that they may countenance the finishing of the fortifications, and be ready to fall upon the recovery of Dingle'. The walls follow a conventional star-shaped layout, though it is difficult to appreciate this from Grose's painting, with its low viewpoint. When he visited the island, the fort was in a state of semi-ruin, but it is clear from the text that some of the armoury was still in place. Grose also mentions the Napoleonic signal station at Bray Head, one of many that line the Atlantic coast of Ireland. In his painting of Fort Point, the artist has made a spirited attempt to show the waves, leaving the paper unpainted to indicate the surf. This 'negative' technique is combined with delicate washes of yellow, orange and green, which produce a warm glow on the buildings.*

# Fort in the Island of Valentia, Co:ʸ of Cork.

This Island is very little known from its very retired situation; it is however large and well cultivated, and contains a numerous population, and is the property of the Knight of Kerry; the revenue board have here a large establishment, for the accommodation of whom many good houses have been built which has greatly improved the Island.

It affords good harbour for Merchantman, and during the war had a Telegraph signal station,[132] erected on the highest ground, call'd Bray head — from this a very extensive view is commanded of a long stretch of coast to the right and left, with several Islands out at sea, the most conspicuous amongst which is the Skellough Rocks, famous for having on the largest, several antient religious erections.

Towards the mainland side, the prospect is most wild and rude, high mountains of uncouth outline, raising above each other, and bounding the view on all sides, but the sight of several roads intersecting these barren tracts in various directions, gives to the mind an idea of civilized intercourse, which greatly softens the rugged features of the scene, and takes much away from its dreary wildness.

This Island can boast of a Parish Church[133] near which is the ruins of an antient place of worship, with an extensive graveyard round it, and amongst several other decent memorials, is a stone over a gentleman who reached the very advanced age of 110; near this is a stone cross very rudely cut, and totally devoid of ornament.

Following the shores of the Island in this neighbourhood towards the eastward, on a rough point that runs into the sea, and forms one side of the Eastern entrance into the harbour, is to be seen the ruins of a Fort or Blockhouse, erected to defend the passage, and prevent the getting in of Shipping;[134] this point narrows the mouth to less than a quarter of a mile, and consequently must have effectually rendered the Fort efficient to the purposes, for which it was erected.

The Fort however is deficient in other most escential points, being entirely commanded by high ground, both on the main, and on the Island. It consisted of a Battery of Six Guns, the masonry remaining tolerably entire, together with two pieces of Iron Ordnance 24 pounders, one on the Battery, and the other amongst the rocks at its foot, below high water mark, where it was thrown some time back, through wantonness by the native inhabitants of the Island.

Within the Fort is a Barrack and Guard house, the walls of which with the Chimneys are still standing, these were calculated to hold as many men as was necessary to work the Guns and maintain the place; on the ground floor of the Guard house, is a dark dungeon, or black-hole. The Battery is strongly built, and the lime sement with which it was put together, has now become much harder than the stones it binds.

A short distance behind the Fort to the west, is a large square work with regular bastions at the angles, composed of earth, this incloses several ruins apparently of dwelling houses, the walls of which were semented together with mud; in this space is to be seen the remains of two ovens, one of them of considerable size; this seems to have been a fortified Camp, for a small force.

The approach to the Fort is very difficult, being a narrow neck of rough fragments of rocks, and the inhabitants say, in high winds it is covered by the sea, which makes a breach over it, and cuts it off. The name given to this building by the Islanders is Cromwells Fort, as having been erected and made use of by the Army of that Usurper; but it appears to be of a much more antient date, being very likely a Spanish station, as they had long the possession of the Coast on this side of the Kingdom.

It is however still probable that it was made use of by Cromwells army, who were certainly in this neighbourhood, and destroy'd the fine Castle of Ballycarbery not two miles off on the main; and that the fortified Camp above described was constructed by them, and occupied whilst they remained in this Island, as the ovens &c appear to be of a much later date than the Fort. Smith in his History of Cork is entirely silent in respect to this building.[135] Ware tells us the antient name of this Island was Dariry, and a modern writer says that Valentia derives its name from Spanish origin.[136]

D. Grose

## 49. Hungry Hill: stone circle (Cork)

*Antiquarian drawings play an important role in the study of Irish field monuments, hundreds of which have been sacrificed this century in the name of agricultural progress. The stone circle on the slopes of Hungry Hill is difficult to identify but it appears to be that at Curraduff, which was removed about 1970. According to local residents about five stones were standing at the time, the number shown in the watercolour. In his text Grose speaks of seven stones, with a further six lying nearby, making a total of thirteen altogether. This is about the average number found in the stone circles of Cork and Kerry, some of which have as few as five stones, others as many as nineteen. The artist was overwhelmed by the mountainous setting, claiming that 'no place could be better calculated for the theatre of mystic rights [sic] and magic incantations'. The overwrought depiction of the landscape suggests an enthusiasm for the 'Sublime'.*

# Druids Temple Hungry Hill Bantry Bay, Co:ʸ Cork.

If solemn scenery and seclusion from the haunts of men, could inspire with devotion the minds of the followers of the Druidic superstition, this place was well calculated to work up to phrensy the feelings of its votaries; here solitude reigned triumphant in all its horrors, and the surrounding objects could only inspire sensations of awe and gloom: indeed no place could be better calculated for the theatre of mystic rights and magic incantations, than this lone spot.

This Druidic Temple is situated at the South West foot of Hungry hill a lofty mountain 2160 feet perpendicular height above the level of the sea hanging immediately over Berehaven, in the midst of a valley intirely surrounded by lofty precipices except to the south, where they recede, yet even on that side the view is circumscribed and confined to the hollow. Hungry hill rises over it vast and terrific, presenting a collection of precipices and pinnacles formed by rocks of the most uncouth and fantastic shapes, piled on each other, wild beyond imagination.

This little valley being at present cultivated, affords some small relief to the eye, from those bleak and sterile mountains, that frown on every side, yet to add to the solemnity of the scene, and still more forcibly to impress the feelings, the ear is struck by the roarings of a mountain stream, that falls from the hill, rushing over precipices, and a succession of obstacles untill it joins the waters of the haven.

This Circle consists at present of seven stones inclining to the upright, with one in the interior of the sweep, now nearly covered with earth, but apparently of much greater magnitude than any of those that compose the circumference; six other stones are to be discovered that also formed part of the ring, th'o now overgrown with moss and weeds.[137]

The diameter of the circle is 26 feet, agreeing with the Temple beyond Castletown in this neighbourhood,[138] already given, the stones run from 4 to 6½ feet in height, and are of unwrought mountain grit.

The lands in this neighbourbood on the shores of Bere-haven are commonly denominated Ross mac Owen, accor[d]ing to Vallancy, Ross signifies a pleasant tract of country, Ware gives it as a verdant plane, or as some say a place where Heath or Broom grows, this last may be applicable, but the signification given of it by the inhabitants expresses a place abounding in grain;[139] nor is it improperly so named, for abundance of corn is grown in every little space amongst the rocks, that can afford soil for culture, and in many places the stones are cleared away, especially round the cabins and farm houses, which for such a wild country are commodious and comfortable.

The Temple stands something better than a mile from the shores of Berehaven.

## 50. Kilbeg Castle (Cork)

*The ruins of Kilbeg Castle were demolished in the early 1960s and no trace of the building survives in the open field that marks the site. It was evidently a fortified house of about 1600-40, with a massive chimney on the north side. The circular turrets or bartizans, corbelled out at two corners, are characteristic of the period, being especially common in the plantation castles of Ulster. A square tower, perhaps containing a staircase, can be seen to the right of the chimney. John Windele, the nineteenth-century antiquary, noted that the house was 40-50 feet in length and about 14-15 feet wide, so it was not a particularly large building. It stood within a square bawn and both Grose and Windele remarked on the deep ditches that surrounded it. In quoting a line from The Faerie Queene — 'the pleasant Bandon crowned with many a wood' — Grose must have been aware of the connection between Kilbeg and Edmund Spenser. The poet's daughter, Catherine, who died about 1635, married William Wiseman, who resided at Kilbeg Castle.*

# Kilbeg Castle, Co:ʸ Cork.

The Bandon River takes its rise in the Mountains of Carbery, it was antiently call'd Glasheen., and was stiled by the Poet Spencer ''The pleasant Bandon crowned with many a wood.''[140] Before it reaches the town of Bandon from whence it is now named, it flows through the beautiful park of Castle Barnard,[141] and between that place and the sea, its banks are adorned by several old Castles and fine seats surrounded with wood and well improved, together with the neat and romantically situated town of Innis Shannon, and well deserves the character given of it by the Poet.

On its nort[h] bank stands the subject now before us, about two miles below the town of Bandon, on elevated ground, commanding an extensive view over a well cultivated country up and down the river. It does not appear to have been a place of great strength, or military consequence, being rather a Castelated House than a Castle, it was however defended at two angles by small projecting turrets, that communicated with the enterior; it was also surrounded by a moderately broad ditch, intended as a dry one, but now partly filled with water. The building was formerly of much greater extent, and probably had defensible outworks, as may be conjectured from the old foundations now covered with earth and sod.[142]

As is invariably the case, this house is commanded by higher grounds a circumstance in the art of war, apparently quite neglected, by the builders of antient posts of defence.

We read of the lands of Kilbeg assigned by the 1:ˢᵗ Earl of Cork to his Son, the Lord Kinalmeaky, together with the town of Bandon-Bridge, and other manors.

D Grose.

## 51. Castle Conna (Cork)

*Castle Conna is situated on a rock overlooking the river Bride, five miles west of Tallow in County Cork (not Waterford as Grose thought). It is a well-preserved tower house of about 1500, more vertical in proportion than many buildings of this type. While it does not dominate the scene quite as emphatically as Grose suggests, it nevertheless forms a striking landmark in the area. The curiously-shaped fragment beside the tower appears to be a relic of the bawn. Castle Conna was an important Desmond stronghold and, as a Confederate fortress, was stormed in 1645 by the Earl of Castlehaven. Five years later it was bombarded by Cromwell. This is not one of Grose's more impressive paintings. The batter at the base of the tower is exaggerated and the windows bear little resemblance to their actual design. The perspective is abrupt, with the house at the right looking as if it has been squeezed into the picture as an afterthought. The fisherman, clad in a smart blue coat and wielding a handsome-sized rod, adds a welcome flourish to the work.*

# Castle Canna, Co:y Waterford.

The country in the midst of which this Castle is situated, is rich and highly cultivated, well wooded and watered, and affords many fine prospects; it stands on a rocky eminence over the small river Bride, that winds its serpentine course through this beautiful tract of land, and adds its tributary stream to the river Black-water.

It at present consists of one tall tower in good preservation the cliff on which it stands almost insulated by the river, a circumstance that must have added greatly to its defence; the building also appears to have been otherwise well fortified by strong surrounding walls, a fragment still remaining, together with the foundations which may be traced in several places.[143]

The river is here crossed by a neat bridge, from this the view given was taken, and near it is a small but well built Village, from w[h]ence the Castle derives its name, & through which the high road runs from Lismore to Cork.

D Grose.

## 52. Ballycarbery Castle 1 (Kerry)

*Because of its proximity to Valencia Harbour, Ballycarbery Castle was one of the major strongholds of the south-west. In 1597 Queen Elizabeth was advised to have great regard 'on whom she bestoweth the castle of Ballycarbrye and the haven of Bealynche (Valencia), which is a very large and fair haven, and in a remote place, dangerous to be in any man's hands that shall favor any common enemy'. Hitherto the castle had belonged to the MacCarthy Mór, the lords of southern Kerry, though for much of the time the building was occupied by the O Connells, who served as their constables. Some form of castle existed here in 1398, but the existing ruins appear to be a century or more later. The painting shows the castle from the west, with a creek in the foreground and the heights of Knocknadobar behind. The two-storey building beside the castle, which Grose thought served as 'offices', was in fact a relatively modern dwelling house of about 1700. It has now been demolished. The picture is impressively composed, the castle and mountains together making a powerful, if exaggerated, impact. In place of the usual well-dressed gentlemen, Grose has introduced a more humble figure carrying a creel. The clothes are nonetheless rather smart for a fishing expedition.*

# Ballycarberry Castle, Co:<sup>y</sup> Kerry.

That this pass into the enterior of the Co:<sup>y</sup> of Kerry, was considered of great consequence appears from the remains of this fine Castle which compleatly defended it, and must have been a strong barrier against the march of an invading army, before the use of cannon was known.[144] It crowns a gentle eminence, on a point of land nearly insulated by the Cahir river, and a mountain stream, up which the tide flows beyond the Castle.

The country behind it swells into high ground, which by degrees runs into lofty mountains that frown majestically on every side, except where they recede along the banks of the Cahir, and form the pass inland.

It was constructed with great strength, and every means of defence the nature of the fortification could afford, was not neglected. The principal part, or keep of the Castle, was an oblong square, with a projecting tower at the north angle, the whole surrounded by a strong Bawn or Court, the walls of which are pierced with loop holes for missive weapons, or musquetry, at regular distances, and is five feet thick. At the north west end of this bawn, appears the ruins of a long building never more than two stories high, without battlements, equally as old as the Castle, and communicating with the court by a small door, this probably formed offices.[145]

The upper stories of the keep were supported by a tier of remarkably strong arches which formed the ground apartments, one of these [in] the centre, was occupied by the grand entrance, which was on the north side, the gro[o]ves of the Portcullis communicating with the floor overhead, so that when the Port was let down, it must have descended with irresistable force.

The exterior walls of the north front remain pretty entire, but the south is entirely down, and the fragments lie scattered around in large masses, where they were thrown by the force of the Powder used in demolishing the building; which was accomplished by the Army of Oliver Cromwell: the fate of almost all the strong Castles in this Kingdom.

This Castle was probably one of M<sup>c</sup>Cartymores who was created Earl of Clan Care, and at the same time made Lord Baron of Valentia A:D 1565.

But before I take leave of this neighbourhood, I cannot forbear remarking a peculiar kind of Danish Fort, as they are commonly call'd, many of which are to be met with here in good preservation; they are built of loose stones without any kind of sement, but perfectly well laid, and with such regularity, as to show a smooth surface on the outside even to this day; which is the more worthy of notice, as the stones thus piled together are of a small size, and alth'o the batter is considerable, the close uniting of them causes so even a face, as to render the scaling of the wall unpracticable without a ladder. The one that came immediately under notice was upwards of 30 feet high at present, the diameter within the walls 32 paces, and the walls battering from a very considerable thickness to 21 feet at top, with a double banquet and parapet, capable of containing 50 men.[146] In the centre of the circle rose a small mound of stones covering what had been the entrance (but now blocked up with rubbish) into a subterranean gallery which apparently occupied the entire of the Fort.

This is one of the most perfect specimens of the Stone Lis or Fort to be met with perhaps in Ireland, many of them occur on these shores as well as on the Island of Valentia; here the observer can discover a line of them extending across the country, which must have been, when in good repair, a formidable line of defence, even with those missive weapons in use at that time.[147]

The workmanship of these Forts, are infinitely superior to any of those built of the same materials, to be found in the counties of Mayo & Galway and every way better calculated for defence.

Plate 2:[d] shows the South aspect of the Castle, on which side the Gunpowder acted with greatest force, large masses of masonry blown to a considerable distance, evinces the strength with which it was built, and the excellency of the sement used in those times.

The wild scenery around, imparts an air of grandure to these romantic ruins, and the idea of such a pile of building, in so solitary and remote a spot, with the total absence of any other erection that can form a comparison with it, adds much to its picturesque effect.

## 53. Ballycarbery Castle 2 (Kerry)

*It seems certain that Ballycarbery Castle was deliberately slighted by the Cromwellians, probably in 1651-2, when the entrance to Valencia Harbour was being fortified. The southern side of the building has collapsed, leaving the instructive cross-section that Grose has painted. The barrel vaults covering the ground floor are clearly visible, so too the narrow chambers in the turret to the right. Although Ballycarbery was one of the more ingeniously planned towers in the country, its remote situation means that it is not as well known as it deserves to be. More ivy has gathered on the walls and some chunks of fallen masonry have been removed; otherwise the ruins are little changed. Grose's description of the castle leads to a lengthy digression on the ancient stone forts of the west. He obviously paid a visit to Staigue Fort, less than twenty miles away, and it is odd that he did not include a picture of it in his book.*

D Grose.

## 54. Abbey Leix (Laois)

*It is surprising to find the great house at Abbey Leix, built around 1773-4 for Thomas Vesey, 1st Viscount de Vesci, included in a book on antiquities. Perhaps the hospitality was good, though it is more likely that Grose was attracted there by the name, for the house was built on the site of a Cistercian monastery, the history of which he would have known from Archdall's Monasticon Hibernicum (a picture of the house at Monasterevin, erected on the site of another Cistercian abbey, had been prepared by Daniel Grose for the second volume of the Antiquities). Nothing remains of the old monastery at Abbey Leix, apart from a fine tomb commemorating Malachy O'More, who died in 1502. Grose's picture is a pleasant though uninformative landscape, illustrating many of his favourite techniques. There are flashes of the tan colour in the foreground plants, and the waters of the Nore are painted with his characteristic stripes. The portrayal of the artist's companion shows the extent to which Grose struggled with figure drawing, once he abandoned a few stock poses. The accompanying text is largely taken up with praise for the de Vescis as improving landlords and contains a prescient warning about the peasantry's overdependence on the potato crop.*

# Abbey Liex, Queens Co:ʸ.

This noble domain and highly improved estate, is a striking example of what might be done in this country, if the noblemen, and great landholders would reside on their property, or by frequent visits make themselves acquainted with their tenantry, and by adequate encouragement render it worth their trouble to take care of the farms they occupy, to make improvements in agriculture, keep neat and comfortable dwellings, and to promote good conduct and cleanliness in their families. By finding something for these poor people to do in those times of idleness, so fatal to the peasantry of this country, a thousand unhappy effects would be prevented; the early attainment of their favorite food the Potatoe, renders them careless for the future, when once their crop is housed, and for the remainder of the year they continue idle, untill the season for again setting, this otherwise most desirable root, returns.[148] By the establishment of Manufactories on his estate the great proprietor would effectually remedy this evil, and every idle hand would get employment, and the head of a large family would find his riches in his children, even from an early period as children in such cases ever find ready employment.

On this estate Manufactories have been established, encouragement given to the Tenantry, neat farm houses in the English style, present themselves on every side, and improved agriculture cheers the face of the country. How praise worthy is such exertions! how much superior is lasting popularity gained from such a way of spending money, where it ought to be dispensed, far very far above the empty applause bestowed by strangers, on that magnificence and expensive pomp, displayed far from home, forgotten in a moment; the attainment of which, racks and leaves bare, the indigent cultivators of the soil, who have a right to look for some returns of fertilizing influence, from that stream drawn from their painful labours.

The domain of Abbey Liex is inriched by the fine river Nore, that flows through it, its banks crowned with noble woods, affording shade, shelter, and ornament; the antient Oak here spreads its ample arms across the stream, and the springing Trout feeds on the fly that drops from the leaves.

An Abbey was founded here to the honor of the Virgin Mary, A:D 1183, by Corcheger O'More, some say it was endowed much earlier. The founder filled this house with Cistertian monks, from the Abbey of Baltinglass, and was himself interred here.

The 7:ᵗʰ of May, A:D: 1421, a great slaughter was made near this Abbey by O'More amongst the retinue of the Earl of Ormond, then Lord Lieutenant; twenty-seven of the English were cut off, the chief of whom were Purcell and Grant; ten persons of superiour rank were made prisoners, and two hundred other men were saved by flying to this monastery. On the last day of February, 5:[th] Queen Elizabeth, this Abbey with some lands in this county, was granted to Tho:[s] Earl of Ormond, at the yearly rent of £6..16[s]:8[d] for thirty seven years, and afterwards at the rent of £10..5[s]. the lands belonging to this Abbey were then estimated at 820 acres.[149]

This truly noble family who now are the possessers of this beautiful Domain and residence, was created Viscount de Vescy of Abbey-Leix in the Queens Co:[y] 22:[d] of June 1776.[150] Not a vestage of this Abbey now remains,[151] in its place has risen an handsome modern house, which still retains the antient name. The River Nore was antiently call'd Eyrus.

D Grose

## 55. Cloghan Castle (Offaly)

*There are several places in Offaly with the name Cloghan (meaning stony place). The castle depicted by Grose lay in the village of Cloghan, on the road from Clara to Banagher. The ruins have long since been removed and few inhabitants of the village are aware that this was the site of one of the major fortresses of the Mac Coghlan family, the lords of Delvin. Recording the death of John Mac Coghlan in 1590, the Annals of the Four Masters report that 'there was not a man of his estate, of the race of Cormac Cas, whose mansions, castles and good dwelling houses were better arranged, or more comfortable than his'. Thirty years later the castle at Cloghan was described as the 'manner howse of Sir John Mac Coghlan'. A castle here was destroyed in 1548, so it is likely that the building depicted by Grose was its mid-sixteenth century successor. It appears to have had four storeys, with deep window embrasures on the upper level, furnished with aumbries or wall cupboards. The machicolis must have protected the principal entrance in the left wall. The roof is most unusual for a late-medieval tower house: there are no gables, and it looks as if it had a hipped roof, suggesting a seventeenth-century remodelling. Grose's text is not helpful at this point, being taken up with a digression on the Ulster plantations.*

# Cloghan Castle, Kings Co:ʸ.

Castelated houses were common in Ireland towards the middle of the reign of James 1:ˢᵗ and were first encouraged in the North by the orders of Conductors for the planting that Province, about the 7:ᵗʰ of that Monarch; when holders of 2000 acres of land were bound to erect a Castle on their lands, with a strong court or bawne about; and every possessor of a middle proportion i:e, 1500 acres, within the same time to build a stone or brick house with a strong Court or bawne about it: every possessor of the least proportion, that is 1000 acres, within the same time to make thereon, a strong court, or bawne at least.

Of the middle description was the Castle here given, it does not appear to have been of very great extent, th'o the walls display great strength & thickness;[152] of the bawne or court that surrounded it, there is now no remains, the stones as well as the fallen ruins of the Castle, having been cleared away, most probably for the purpose of erecting the neighbouring houses in the village, close to which it stands. The open space about it, is now occupied as a market place or Fair ground, and the more modern building adjoining the Castle appears to have been intended for a market house, but never finished, the building of which helped to dispose of the loose materials, belonging to the Castle.

History is silent in respect to this Castle, th'o in all probability it held out against, and suffered from Cromwells Army, as it evidently appears to have been demolished by gunpowder.

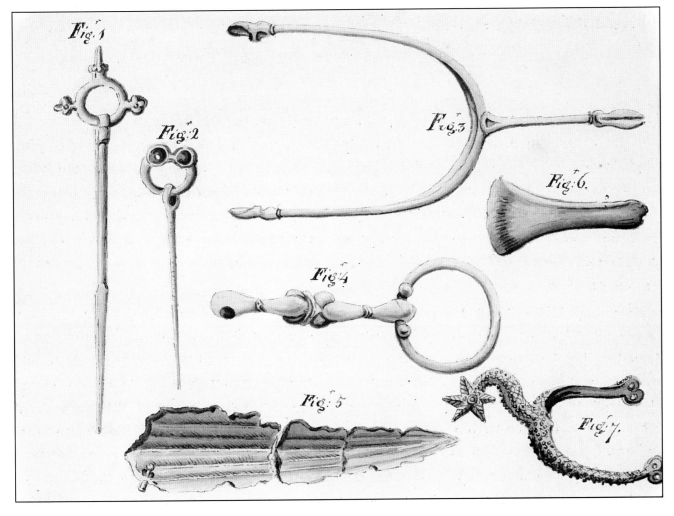

## 56. Miscellaneous Antiquities 1

*Daniel Grose obviously felt that a few drawings of ancient artefacts would enhance the antiquarian status of his book and broaden its appeal. In this illustration he includes a fairly heterogeneous collection of objects. At least three (and possibly all) of the pieces came from the private collection of William Bennison, who lived at Cairn House, three and a half miles south-east of Ballyconnell (Cavan). Daniel Grose was in the area in 1792, when he visited Drumlane, and this is probably when he saw the collection at Cairn. Figure 1 is a knobbed ring pin, probably of ninth-century date, about a dozen of which are known from Ireland. Figure 2 is a brooch pin and, as Grose explains, it was decorated with two settings for glass or amber studs. This is likely to belong to the eighth or ninth century. Figures 3 and 4 are drawings of Iron Age horse trappings and figure 5 is almost certainly the blade of a socketed bronze spearhead, associated with the later Bronze Age. Figure 6 is an early Bronze Age axehead and Figure 7 is an ornate rowel spur, probably of sixteenth- or seventeenth-century date. Several of these objects are now in the National Museum of Ireland and Grose's illustrations provide important clues about their provenance.*

# Miscellaneous Antiquities (Plate 1:<sup>st</sup>).

Fig:<sup>rs</sup> 1 and 2: antient Brooches or pins, used to adorn the hair of females or fasten the Fallen or Jacket worn by the Irish, these th'o in excellent preservation, must be of great antiquity, having been found in an earthen Coffin at Cairn the Seat of William Bennison Esq:<sup>r</sup> County of Cavan.[153]

These are not made of Gold, but of a composition so greatly resembling it, that on the first inspection, the observer would pronounce them of that precious metal; the heads are loose, and play in the shafts or pins, elegantly designed and well executed: Fig:<sup>r</sup> 2 was adorned with precious stones, as the empty sockets they were set in show, this is every way much smaller than the other, being but 4 Inches ⅛ long.

The longest, Fig:<sup>r</sup> 1, is 6½ Inches.

Fig:<sup>r</sup> 3: We have here a brass Headstall, used by the Irish Cavalry, it is very neatly executed, and well finished, in the long top or shaft, that rose over the horses head, is cut a deep groove, in which was placed an ornament, or plume of feathers, that play'd on a pivot, as the animal moved its head. At the lower extremities of the cheeks, are holes to receive the leather straps or thongs of the bridle, to which the bit and reins fixed, these holes are neatly concealed by projections, which adds much to the ornament of the work. From one extremity to the other it is 12 Inches long, and 6 ⅖ broad in the fork, at bottom.[154]

Fig:<sup>r</sup> 4: Is the brass Bit belonging to the head stall, it is of good workmanship well finished and close in the joints; the weight and size of this bears no proportion to the delicate formation of the other, or to the kind of horse (commonly call'd Hobbies) used by the Irish Cavalry, and must have been very heavy in the mouth of so small an animal. The jointed part of the Bit is 6 inches long and thick in proportion, and the ring to which the reins were affixed, is 3½ inches in diameter.[155]

In the time of Cambrensis the Irish had Bridles, but no Stirrups, Boots, or Spurs; when Stanehurst writ in 1584 they had no Stirrups, nor had Mac: Murrough in 1399 though a powerful Chief; as Spurs were not used untill Stirrups were invented, and it was late before the latter were known in this country, we are therefore enabled to detect the weakness of those antiquaries, who exhibit antique Spurs, as belonging to a very remote age:— so far Doctor Ledwich.[156] In 1499 a law was enacted by the parliament then assembled at Castle Dermot, against those, who, when they rode, used not Saddles. In 1596 the Irish Cavalry used the strong brass Bit. Stirrups were not brought into general use in Ireland till after the Reign of Queen Elizabeth A:D: 1601.

Fig:$^r$ 5: Is the head of a Javelin made of brass found in the same Coffin with the brooches, but in a much less perfect state of preservation; it was a very formidable weapon, and the wound inflicted by it must have been most dangerous, as it was highly raised in a ridge down the centre, and had two deep flutings on each side. What remains is 6 inches long, but it appears to have been longer, the socket is entirely gone and with it part of the blade. The most curious circumstance in this weapon, is a pin or rivit placed at the broadest end, running through the entire thickness, the most probable conjecture is, that to this rivit was fixed a swivel to which was fastened a cord or thong, held by the person who used the Javelin, this thong being rolled round the shaft gave to the weapon when darted a rotatory motion, and also served to return it to the hand when thrown at an object not far off.

This was in all probability one of those Javelins alluded to by D:$^r$ Ledwich in his introduction to Military Antiquities, with which as he says, the Irish Kerns was armed.[157]

Fig:$^r$ 6: Presents us with the brass head of an Hatchet certainly used as a military weapon: this head went through an eye in the shaft or handle, and might be used either to knock down or cut with; it was met with in digging for turf in a bog, these are frequently found, and are often fluted and ornamented with raised work.

Fig:$^r$ 7: Is a brass Spur of elegant workmanship, richly adorned, also found in a bog, from its shape it does not appear to be of very great antiquity; the rowel is of brass and much wrought.

# Miscellaneous Antiquities (Plate 2:<sup>d</sup>).

Fig:<sup>r</sup> 1: These very curious sculptures are to be seen at Holy-cross Co:<sup>y</sup> of Tipperary, they are executed in high relief, on a cornice on the outside of the west end of the principal chapel there; to conjecture what they allude to would be useless, they are evidently of Danish workmanship, and in high preservation;[158] the 1:<sup>st</sup> division represents the figure of the Wolf, so often to be found amongst their ornamental sculptures, and the favorite theme of Scaldic poetry;[159] he has a shaggy mane reaching to his shoulders, and is well designed, and proportioned. In the next is the branch of a tree seemingly the Laurel, finely executed, and in great preservation, the leaving sharp and prominent.

The 3:<sup>d</sup> and last division presents us with two Bulls, with their necks entwined in such a manner, that each Bull is looking towards his own tail, thus forming a knot. Runic knots were also a favorite ornament of those times, probably this was meant to represent one of these knots; the animals that compose it, are well proportioned and boldly executed.

Fig:<sup>r</sup> 2: Capitals of clustering pillars amongst the ruins of the Dominican Friary Youghal of elegant workmanship, and beautiful appearance, all highly raised, and Sharp.

Fig:<sup>r</sup> 3: Carved stone head in the yard of Kiltoghart Church Co:<sup>y</sup> Leitrim, no mention is made of any religious foundation being placed here, yet this and other similar relics prove, altho now only a parish Church, an antient erection adorned with sculpture did exist near this spot.

D:Grose

## 57. Miscellaneous Antiquities 2

*Despite Grose's claim for 'Danish workmanship', all three sculptures illustrated in this plate belong to the Gothic era. The frieze of animals comes from Holycross Abbey (Tipperary), where it is to be found on the exterior of the building, at the north-west angle of the north transept (about 1500). The 'shaggy mane' ought to have persuaded Grose that the first animal was a lion and his suggestion that the next pair are bulls implies a limited knowledge of animal husbandry. They are in fact unicorns, a medieval symbol of chastity. Grose even managed to draw their solitary horns, without recognising the identity of the animals. The drawing below illustrates foliate capitals of about 1300 from the Dominican friary at Youghal. The third piece of sculpture is a keystone of a window or door, embellished with the head of a bishop. This comes from the ruined church at Kiltoghert, a remote spot amidst the hills, two miles south-east of Leitrim. The stone is now incongruously cemented to a monument to Bishop Moran. It is a robust piece of fifteenth-century carving, somewhat distorted in Grose's painting. While the drawing of the mitre is quite accurate, the prelate's ears have been metamorphosed into locks of hair. Members of the Grose family were buried in Kiltoghert parish and it is just possible that this is where Daniel had his home.*

D Grose.

## 58. Strancally Castle (Waterford)

*Strancally Castle was situated in a spectacular position on a cliff above the river Blackwater, five and a half miles north of Youghal. The ruins of the massive tower seen in Grose's painting collapsed in the nineteenth century and what is left is almost inaccessible due to dense vegetation and the precipitous terrain. There are the remnants of at least two towers, one of them cut back into the side of the cliff. A more informative engraving of the castle was included in the second volume of the Antiquities. A lurid tale was told of this Desmond stronghold in the text of volume II, which describes a hole 'cut through the rock in the manner of a portcullis, down which he (the Earl of Desmond) cast the dead bodies...', evidently a rather melodramatic description of a latrine chute. In 1579 James FitzJohn, the last Geraldine owner of Strancally, joined the Desmond rebellion. The castle was soon captured by the Earl of Ormond, and James FitzJohn himself was executed in Cork two years later. In June 1645 the castle was besieged by the Earl of Castlehaven, surrendering within a few hours. It was evidently slighted by Cromwellian forces a few years later.*

# Strancally Castle, Co:ʸ Waterford.

An ample account has been already given of this fine river, yet too much cannot be said of those picturesque scenes it affords, which multiply as you proceed up the stream; amongst them, this now given is not one of the least pleasing, and if variety can charm, here contrasts the most striking present themselves; the rough and barren sides of a mountain of russet hue, the lively prospect of a well cultivated country yellow with grain; the antient Castle rising in proud preeminence looking defiance th'o in ruins, towards the peac[e]ful, snug and comfortable cottage, wood and water, these are all here to be met with. At present we can look upon these relics of former tyranny with tranquillity, and bless our happy constitution that circumscribes the power of the lord of the soil, within due bounds, and makes the Peer as accountable to the Law as the peasant.

Formerly this fortress could not be view'd with such feelings; the rebel Earl of Desmond here carried on the most cruel acts of oppression, to this place he carried the pray taken in his predatory expeditions; here he caused to be committed many a foul murder, still the theme of tradition. The view here given represents the north west aspect of the Castle, and shows that side least in ruins, as the gunpowder by which it was demolished seems to have acted entirely on the other side.[160]

In 1579 the Earl of Desmond carried off the effects of the Inhabitants of the town of Youghall which he had plundered, to this his Castle of Strancally, then possessed by the Spaniards; however in the same year the Earl of Ormond attacked the Castle, which the Spaniards upon his approach quitted, and fled over the Black-water, but he pursued them, and put many to the Sword.

The Castle of Strancally or Stronecally furnished by the lease 155 foot and 43 horse to the 1:ˢᵗ Earl of Cork — it being on the estate of Lord Dungarvan his eldest son.

The river Black water was antiently call'd Nem according to Ware and also Abanmor, that is the great water or river in the territory of Nandesi, or Desies, Ptolemy calls this River Daurona, and Necham, Aven-mor, of which he says —

> By Lismore town Avenmor river flows
> And at Ardmor into the Ocean goes —

It was sometimes also call'd Broad-water, and laterly Black Water.[161]

## 59. Rindown 3 (Roscommon)

*Daniel Grose's second view of the castle at Rindown shows the monument from the south-west, the way it is approached by visitors overland. The main gate, complete with portcullis slots, lies in the centre of the picture, with the ruins of the hall or keep towering behind. Most of the existing buildings appear to date from after 1272, when the castle was attacked and partly destroyed by Aedh O Conor, one of many attempts by the O Conor kings of Connacht to thwart the extension of royal power west of the Shannon. While this forceful painting, copied from a drawing by Lieutenant Grose, gives a good general impression of Rindown, the artist has given the entrance gate a pointed rather than a round arch. He has also exaggerated the height of the buildings and enhanced the vigour of the earthworks. Today, with the walls of the castle surrounded by dense thickets, the gate is no longer visible from this position.*

# Castle of Randown or S:$^t$ Johns, Co:$^y$ Roscommon.

The Monasticon Hibernicum tells us, there existed formerly a flourishing town at this place, and tradition corroborates this assertion, at present however not the smallest vestige of it remains. The situation must have been of consequence, when so large a Castle, and such extensive fortifications were thought necessary, and it is natural to suppose that so formidable a fortress, must always have had a numerous garrison, which would draw after them a resort of people, who were likely to settle in the neighbourhood, and by degrees accumulate into a considerable town. We read that this Castle was destroy'd by the Irish in 1272.[162] From the strength and magnitude of the Fortress many must have been the desperate struggles that took place here, evidences of which are still to be met with; digging near the Castle not long ago, a human skeleton was found, with the brass head of an Arrow sticking in the back part of the Scull, which without doubt had occasioned the death of the person there buried, who received that shaft, in some of the attacks made on the Castle.

The arms of the Antient Irish were in general made of Brass, their Javelin heads, axes and hatchets, were of the same metal, and numerous specimens have been dug up in bogs and other places; and drawings of some of these will be given in the course of this work.

The English monarchs endeavoured to encourage Archery in Ireland particularly Edward 4:$^{th}$ who ordered Bows to be provided by the Irish the length of the person who was to use them, together with shafts three quarters of the length of the Standard.[163]

The Irish used shortbows and arrows resembling those of Scotland. The view here given represents the S:W: Asp:$^{ct}$ and was drawn by Lieu:$^t$ Arthur Grose of the Royal Navy.

D Grose —

## 60. Kiltimon Castle (Wicklow)

*Daniel Grose was puzzled by the design of Kiltimon Castle and he was right to be suspicious. Although medieval in origin, it was rebuilt by Lord Rossmore in the eighteenth-century to serve as a folly on his estate. New battlements were added to the old walls, along with four turrets at the corners, and these together with the design of the doors and windows, underline the extent of the remodelling. Daniel was right in thinking Kiltimon was an ancient fortress, but in failing to note the amount of reconstruction, his limitations as an antiquary were sadly exposed. The castle is situated two and a half miles south of Newtown Mount Kennedy, beside the road leading into the glen of Dunran. The painting, with its combination of hills, woods and an 'ancient' ruin, is an exercise in romantic landscape rather than a serious antiquarian study.*

# Kiltimon Castle, Co:ʸ Wicklow.

The County of Wicklow is justly famed for its bold and picturesque scenery in which it abounds, in it nature has been prodigal of her most majestic beauties, groupes of lofty mountains, wooded glens, romantic waterfalls, and fine rivers, whose rocky banks are covered with thick woods; the Dargle ranks formost in the list, the Vale of Avoca has been the theme of the Bard,[164] and the many varieties of that charming stream, must ever be remembered with delight and pleasure: nor is the softer features of the cultivated landscape denied, the polishing hand of art has not been spared, and many fine seats, and improved domains adorns the face of the country.

The glen of Dunran is not one of its least striking features; the scenery it exhibits is bold and picturesque, its noble and worthy proprietor the late Lord Rossmore, with infinite taste laid hold of every local advantage it presented, to improve its appearance, beautiful drives are made through the hollow's and over the high grounds, and the judicious mingling of the different species of the Fir, and other forest trees, clothes the sides of the vallies with a variegated coat of green most gratifying to the eye.

A banqueting lodge, or Cottage has been built in a sheltered dell, its neat whitewashed walls forming a pleasing contrast to the green embowering shades that surround it.

Near the entrance of the Glen stands the "ivy-mantled tow'r", a drawing of which is here given; it was placed there as a guard to this pass, that formed one of the fastnesses of the country in which it so much abounds.[165] It consists of a large square insulated tower of considerable thickness defended at two angles by projecting turrets; these are not as usual constructed round, but are square, a circumstance that very seldom occurs:[166] some chimneys also remain, th'o the whole is greatly in ruins. Newtown Mount Kennedy the seat of Lord Rossmore is not far from this Glen, no pains has been spared to adorn this place, and they have not been thrown away, the gardens are uncommonly well laid out, and contain more glass than is often met with in this Kingdom.[167]

## 61. Sculptures at Glendalough (Wicklow)

*In 1779 William Burton Conyngham, employed two artists, Gabriel Beranger and Angelo Bigari, to make records of the seven churches of Glendalough. Henceforth this early monastic site became a favourite haunt of antiquarian artists. Copies of drawings began to circulate, which makes it difficult to know whether Daniel Grose drew these details for himself. The drawing at the top shows one of the now-lost imposts of the east window, for the subjects of which Grose provides a highly fictional explanation. Needless to say, it is unlikely the sculptures depicted a 'dog devouring a serpent' or St Kevin gathering a medicinal apple. The same carvings were drawn, marginally more accurately, by Beranger. The drawing to the right shows the chevron decoration of the east window, and the head at the bottom comes from a capital on the so-called Priests' House. All this work is Romanesque in style and belongs to the middle or later years of the twelfth century. Grose's confidence in the judgement of Ledwich, who assigned them all to the ninth century, was badly misplaced.*

# Sculptures at Glandelough or the Seven Churches, Co:<sup>y</sup> Wicklow.

A description has been already given of the Seven Churches, in the 2:<sup>d</sup> Vol:<sup>m</sup> of these Antiquities, it would therefore be superfluous, again to enter upon it, but the sculptures here given have not been touched upon, th'o others found there, have been ably handled by Doctor Ledwich in his introduction.

This sequestered glen is highly renouned in the annals of Irish Antiquity from the earliest ages, and bears rank as one of the most venerable remains the Island can produce.

Previous to the settling of the primitive christians in this neighbourhood, this Glen was supposed by the barbarous and heathenish natives to be peopled by evil spirits; and its lakes with monstrous and distroying serpents, who spread their devastations on every side: this was therefore singled out as a chosen spot, where the sanctity of the new religion might be placed in the most advantageous point of view. Saint Coemgene is the reputed founder of the Seven Churches, and the City, ruins of both [of] which may still be traced.[168] S:<sup>t</sup> Coemgene, Koemin, Caymin or Kevin, as related by Irish Antiquaries, was said to be descended from a noble family and born AD: 498, this saint received the Sacrement of baptism, from the hands of saint Cronan a priest, and at the age of seven years, he was placed under the care and tuition of Petrocus a briton who had passed many years in this kingdom, for the exersise of learning. Under this venerable man, our saint continued untill 510, when his parents Coinlogh and Coemhella, sent him to the cell of Dogain, Lochan, and Aeneas or Enna, three holy anchorites, with whom he studied a considerable time, previous to his embracing the monastic profession; after which he took on himself the Cowl, and retired to this wild Glen, where he wrote many learned works, particularly the life of S:<sup>t</sup> Patrick.

This saint is described as possessing such exquisite beauty of person that it was impossible for the softer sex, to behold him without experiencing the most violent love, and desire, in consequence he was so beset with their unhallowed flame, and importunities, that he fled society, and buried himself amidst these wilds.

Many curious miracles are told of this saint Kevin, the 1:<sup>st</sup> is drawn from an Icelandis M:S: and thus given us by D:<sup>r</sup> Ledwich.[169] There was says the M:S: in Ireland one, amongst the body of saints, named Koevinus a kind of hermit inhabiting the town of Glumelhagam (Glendalough) who when that happened, which we are about to relate, had in his house a young man, his relation greatly beloved by him. This young man being attacked by a decease [disease], which seemed mortal, at that time of the year, when deceases are most dangerous, namely in the month of March; and taking it into his head that an Apple would prove a remidy for his disorder, earnestly besought his relative Koevinus to give him one. At that time no apples were easily to be had, the trees having then began to put forth their leaves. But Koevinus grieving much at his relations sickness, and particularly at not being able to procure him the remedy required, he at length prostrated himself in prayer, and besought the Lord to grant him some relief for his kinsman.

After his prayer he went out of the house, and looking about him saw a large tree, a Salix or Willow, whose branches he examined, as if for the expected remidy, when he observed the tree to be full of Apples just ripe. Three of these he gathered and carried to the young man: when the youth had eaten part of these apples, he felt his disorder gradually abate, and was at length restored to his former health.

The tree seemed to rejoice in this gift of God, and bears every year a fruit like an apple, which from that time have been call'd S:$^t$ Koevins apples, and are carried over all Ireland, that those labouring under any decease [disease] may eat them; and it is notorious from various relations, that they are the most wholesome medicine against all disorders to which mankind are liable. And it must be observed, that it is not so much for the sweetness of their savour, as their efficacy in medicine for which they are esteemed, and as at first, for which they are sought.

Fig:$^r$ 1(x) Is a sculpture over the window of one of the Seven Churches, and contains an history of part of the life of S:$^t$ Kevin, and relates to the miraculous actions of that Saint. Here we see a Dog devouring a Serpent, this alludes to the destruction of those monstrous and terrible Serpents which inhabited the lakes & which were exterpated by Dogs as the legend says, employ'd by the saint, and endowed by him with supernatural powers;[170] on the opposite side is represented the Saint himself in the act of gathering the miraculous and medicinal apple, that so expeditiously performed the cure, on his young friend, as related at large in the Icelandic M:S:. The attitude and dress of the Saint is very remarkable, he wears an high pleated or radiated Cap on his head, round

(x) The Cathedral Window

his waist is hung a short garment resembling the Scottish Philibeg, and his legs are covered with something like buskins, the rest of his body appears naked: one hand is raised as expressive of wonder, whilst with the other he reaches towards the medicinal apple, several of which are seen on the tree close to him. This historical sculpture, at once convinces us, that these reputed actions of the Saint, were believed, and implicitly relied on as truth and were executed and placed here in order to hand down to posterity a lasting memorial of such wonderful events.

Many other miraculous legends are related of this Saint equally wonderful, which would far exceed our limits to recount.

Fig:[r] 2: Is part of the arch of the window alluded to in the description of Fig:[r] 1.

Fig:[r] 3: Is the Capital of a pillar found amongst the ruins.

Doctor Ledwich describes similar sculptures to these also found at Glandelough and gives them as work's of the 9:[th] Century, and there is no doubt his conjecture is founded on fact.[171]

Th'o rudely executed the sculptures are still sharp and prominent.

D Grose

## 62. Fenagh: the monastic church (Leitrim)

*Two ancient churches survive at Fenagh, one of which is the fifteenth-century building depicted in Daniel Grose's painting. The east window, constructed with four lancets and an oculus, is indeed a 'valuable specimen of gothic workmanship'. The tracery is recorded with unusual care, even the pointed trefoils within the circle being carefully defined. The decorative rings on the shafts, flanking the window, are placed below the half-way point, an anomaly exaggerated in the painting. Grose was much taken with the 'handsome monument' on the wall to the right, a pair of exceptionally fine eighteenth-century memorials. The central mullion of the window has been restored by the Office of Public Works and the great swathe of ivy removed. In one respect the painting is unusual in Daniel Grose's oeuvre, for the shadows, which he paints meticulously, are coming from the north. Either this is 'divine' light or the artist who made the original sketch (in this case Lieutenant Arthur Grose) was at Fenagh late on a summer's evening. Daniel himself visited Fenagh in the summer of 1792, when he prepared the general view of the two churches included in the second volume of the Antiquities (1795).*

# East Window of Fenagh Abbey, Co:<sup>y</sup> Leitrim.

It is the duty of the Antiquarian eagerly to snatch such valuable specimens of gothic workmanship from the grasp of oblivion, and by no means to pass by such very curious relic's of the taste of the artist of the ''olden times''.[172] Time has indeed been remarkably lenient towards it, and considering its great antiquity, it is now in wonderful good preservation. As nothing of its original design has been lost, at least of any consequence, its perfect state speaks for itself, and calls for no further description here. It is said, that this place in former ages could boast of a flourishing settlement in its neighbourhood, famous not only for its religious institutions, but for its College of divinity, to which resorted Students from every part of Ireland, as well as from every Kingdom in Europe: however at the present day, not a vestige of this large settlement remains.[173] On the right hand side of the window is the handsome monument of the Peytons and Reynolds families united, with an appropriate inscription.[174]

The country people in this neighbourhood show a well, about half a mile from the ruins, of which they relate the following wonderful tradition. The founder of this Abbey, (S:<sup>t</sup> Callin or Kilian) was one day walking with some of his holy brotherhood over this spot, and feeling himself fatigued and thirsty, he stooped down to pluck up a small tuft of rushes, in order with them to moisten his mouth, when wonderful to relate, a spring immediately burst up in the place, from whence he had pulled the rushes; at which the holy man quenched his drouth without further trouble.

To commemorate this miracle the saint immediately ordained that this holy well should become a station, and endowed it with many wonderful qualities, especially that of curing pains and aches, which it is supposed to retain to this day. A Patron or festival is held here annually in honor of the Saint, on S:<sup>t</sup> John the Baptists day,[175] stations, and penance is then performed, and vast numbers of people attend.

This view was taken by Lieu:<sup>t</sup> Grose of the Roy:<sup>l</sup> Navy.

## 63. Fenagh: portal dolmen at Fenagh Beg 1 (Leitrim)

*As well as studying the medieval buildings at Fenagh, Daniel Grose and his relative, Lieutenant Arthur Grose, made their way across the fields to the megalithic portal tomb at Fenagh Beg. Convinced that this was a Druidic altar, Daniel took a rather disdainful view of local beliefs to the contrary. The notion that dolmens were erected as temporary refuges by Diarmaid and Grainne in their flight from the enraged Fionn stems from one of the most popular episodes in Irish mythology. Fenagh Beg is in fact a portal tomb or portal dolmen, a type of monument of which over a hundred and sixty examples are recorded, predominantly in the north and north-west of the country. The burial chamber is often covered by a single capstone of enormous size, sloping down towards the rear, and this produces the sort of dramatic silhouette seen at Fenagh Beg. In preparing his finished painting, Daniel seems to have slightly misunderstood the sketches made at the site. Some of the stones have shifted position, as if one of the giants described in his text had returned to rearrange the monument. Nevertheless, it is quite accurate in general terms, though, as always, the artist has enhanced the drama of the scene.*

# Cromlech near Fenagh, Co:ʸ Leitrim.

As something of the wonderfull or romantic is always attached by the country people to such erections as these; the following story is related by them of this altar. A Giant once lived in these parts, who felt an illicit passion for another Giants wife his friend, and not being able to conquer its violence he at length found means to persuade the lady (who was named Grania, as he was Dermott) to elope with him from her husband: in their flight they were pursued by the injured party, and choosing the most unfrequented tracts in order to avoid ditection, they every night built one of these uncouth apartments to repose in. It still through the country bears the name of Leaba Dearmud is Graine(x) or Dermott and Granias bed.[176] A similar story is recounted of one of these erections near Castle Hyde in the County of Cork, calld Leaba Cally or the Hags-bed of which Smith in his History of Cork gives two good drawings.[177] This altar now consists of 6 upright unhewn stones, three of them supporting a huge flag, placed in an inclined plane[178] from which it derives its denomination, as Cromlech signifies literally a crooked stone, so call'd, not from any crookedness in its external superficies, but from the posture of inclination, generally given them in these altars. Crom-leagh also signifies an Altar stone, or the stone of bowing, or adoration,[179] as Crom in Irish, is to stoop; an author derives the word from the Hebrew Coerum-luach i.e. a devoted table or altar, but as in a former druidic subject I shall refer my reader for further information to D:ʳ Ledwichs introduction to the 1:ˢᵗ Vol:ᵐ.[180]

The tallest of these supporting pillars is 6½ feet, the rest of various heights and dementions, one large and very thick flag lies close to the rest, this was most probably also one of the uprights, and th'o but three of them at present sustain the inclined stone, it is likely it rested equally upon them all, and that the short ones have sunk or mouldered away from their original height.

It stands on elivated ground over a cliff or quarry, out of which in all probability the stones that compose this altar were taken; here the view is not confined, as is usually the Case, but has a wide range; near this place is a small lake, which is shown in the 1:ˢᵗ plate. There is another Cromlech of this description, but much more decay'd, on

(x) According to Vallencey Leaba is a flame or Altar, as Leaba-Diarmut, the Altar of Dermot — but Leaba is considered by the lower Irish as a Bed.

the lands of Letterfyan, in this County.[181]

The holy well alluded to in the foregoing article, is close to this place and the saint who ordered the spot to become consecrated, no doubt looked towards this heathen altar of worship, with an idea of its future sanctification, in so doing. This view was taken by Lieu:[t] Grose of the Roy:[l] Navy.

(Plate 2:[d]). This view represents the North Asp:[t] and displays the size and thickness of the inclined stone, which must be of great weight, and required infinite pains and trouble to place it in its present position.

The figure inclines to an oblong square, on the inside about 8 feet in length.[182] This view was drawn by Lieu:[t] Grose of the Roy:[l] Navy.

## 64. *Fenagh: portal tomb at Fenagh Beg 2 (Leitrim)*

*Grose's second painting of the portal tomb illustrates the monument from the more shaded, northern side. The piles of small stones shown on each side are probably field walls, but it is worth noting that the tomb was originally contained within an extensive cairn of loose stones. Whether or not this rose to the full height of the tomb, obscuring its stunning silhouette, is a matter of debate among archaeologists. Equally controversial is the date of such monuments, a problem which is unlikely to be resolved until more of them are excavated. Just beyond the tomb, as mentioned in the text, there is a steep cliff, where the ground drops abruptly into a marshy valley.*

### 65. *Aughry Castle 1 (Leitrim)*

*The last remnants of Aughry Castle were demolished some time ago, but its memory lives on as a reference point in the Shannon navigation charts. The castle was situated close to the shore of Lough Bofin, about half a mile west of the village of Dromod. Little is known about the design of the building, which Grose describes as a Scottish plantation castle, belonging to a family called Nesbitt. The date of 1640 accords well with the elaborate chimney and circular bartizan. It is not clear whether the buildings hidden in the trees to the right related to the seventeenth-century castle. The rock-strewn foreshore occupied by the fisherman has now been taken over as a marina for Shannon pleasure cruisers.*

# Aughry Castle, Co:ʸ Leitrim.

The noble river Shannon forms an extensive sheet of water call'd Lough Bofin as it flows past this Castelated house, which is situated on the banks of a small bay or inlet formed by a wooded point that extends itself some distance into the lake. The spot on which it stands is flat & low, very little raised above the level of the water, that inundates a considerable part of the neighbouring lands in the winter season, and even during summer; access to the Castle might be rendered difficult by a small stream, over which is a light bridge of one arch not far from the building; however to counter-balance these circumstances of defence, it is compleatly commanded from the S:E: by the hill of Drummod More, that extends along the river for some distance within half-Musquet shot.

But one side wall, & a small part of an angle of the main building, (in the centre of which is a lofty stack of Chimneys) at present remains; it was originally square, & as we are told perforated by a lofty Arch, which went through the thickness of the building into the Bawn or Court. It was defended at the angles by Matriculations [machicolations], and the remains of a round Tower stands near the West face a few yards from the Castle, this as also the large ruin is perforated with loop holes for musquetry, as well as embrazures for Cannon. This Castle was built by an ancestor of the Nesbett family who came into this country from Scotland, and obtained from the Government a grant of an extensive tract of land, as a reward for his Military services in this country A:D: 1640.

He held the rank of Field Officer & settled here with his wife & family; but rebellion left him not long in tranquility, it once again reared its head and this gallant & Loyal Officer joined the Army, & left the defence of his Castle & property to his wife and domestic's. This Lady was of a brave & lofty spirit & well did her actions bespeak her generous sentiments. Her courage was soon put to the proof, for her husband had not long been absent, when a general rising took place in the neighbourhood, and the Rebels (as is always the case) were joined by every loose disorderly person in the country. Thus collecting a formidable force, they laid seige to the Castle, which was gallantly defended by this truly noble Lady and her faithful people who for a length of time baffled every effort of the beseigers, but at last her store from within failing, & all supplies from without being cut off, she was obliged to surrender upon the most solemn promises of safe conduct to the Garrison of Cas:ˡᵉ Forbes about 8 miles off, at that time also bravely holding out, under the command of another Heroine, agains[t] the rebels. These promisses however solemnly given were falacious, for no sooner had they gained possession of the Castle, than they murdered the Ward, & set fire to it. The unfortunate M:rs Nesbitt was then large with child, her they goaded on with their Pikes, almost naked towards Cas:le Forbes, on the public road, but Providence in pity soon put an end to her miseries, and she expired from loss of blood and fatigue, before they had driven her half the distance. In the mean time the ruthless rabble spared nothing in the Castle, the robber here sought his prey & found his cupidity gratified. A Sheep steeler and his wife who lurked in the neighbouring fastnesses of the Country, were there amongst the rest; these people found the two infant sons of the family, bleeding and left for dead, whom they fortunately knew and finding compassion rise in their less flinty bosoms, bore them from the scene of Slaughter to their own obscure habitation, & saved their lives.

The unhappy Father on his return, after bravely executing his duty, found his Castle desolated, and as he thought the whole of his hopeful family murdered; he was accompanied by his Troop, with which he scowered the country round, and to his inexpressible happiness recouvered his lost Boys; their preservers having fled in panic from the souldiers.

It may naturally be supposed the generous Officer, on knowing the particulars, became anxious to reward the benefactors of his children; in vain every search was made, the man and his wife remained undiscovered: in the mean time prisoners were daily brought in, and many of them executed by Martial Law.

One day a large party came in, & the young heir from a curiosity natural to children went out to view them, and discovered his preserver, who was immediately liberated, placed in a place of safety, and a donation of 50£ yearly settled upon him, & his heirs for ever.

Thus was the heir of a truly Loyal and restectable [respectable] family preserved, and his descendants now possess the Eastate on which this Castle stands, and a very considerable tract of landed property besides, in this neighbourhood.

D Grose

## 66. Aughry Castle 2 (Leitrim)

*Grose's second view of Aughry is a well-constructed composition, with a twisted tree used to balance the boldly drawn ruins at the right. The strong shadows in the immediate foreground contrast with the great pool of sunshine on the grass in the middle of the picture. The view is more informative than the first painting. It shows that Aughry was a three-storey structure, in all probability having a rectangular plan, as Grose suggests. In neither painting does he illustrate the round tower mentioned in the text. This was presumably a turret surviving from the defences of the bawn. Grose gives the impression that the castle survived both the Great Rebellion of 1641 and the ensuing Confederate Wars, so it remains a matter of conjecture when this impressive fortified house fell into ruin.*

## 67. Grandison Castle 1 (Kilkenny)

*During the sixteenth-century Grandison (or Granny) castle was one of the principal seats of the Earls of Ormond, whose influence at the time extended over much of the south of Ireland. It consisted of a substantial five-storey tower, with an elevated hall projecting to the west. The tower has a beautifully constructed oriel window, visible on the right of Grose's painting, a window which offered spectacular views across the river Suir. Although the castle was founded in the thirteenth century, Bairbre Duggan has recently demonstrated that both the hall and tower were built by Piers Ruadh Butler, the 8th Earl of Ormond (1515-39), whose tomb is still to be seen in Kilkenny cathedral. The painting shows several interesting architectural features, including the upper doorways that led from the tower out to the parapets above the hall. The great cavity depicted in the wall of the tower, with an alarming crack above, was a portent of a collapse which occurred shortly after Grose had made his drawing.*

# Grandison Castle, Co:ʸ Kilkenny.

This large Castle th'o it does not appear to be older than the reign of James the 1:ˢᵗ its once vast strength, its battlements and towers, its enterior magnificence could not prevent its decay.[183]

> Vain transitory splendors! could not all
> Reprieve the tottering mansion from its fall?[184]

What can resist the devastating Iron hand of war, this noble fortress fell a victim, in its turn, to the Parliament forces, and shared the fate of so ma[n]y others in this kingdom. It stands in the neighbourhood of the town of Waterford, within view of the bridge; the river Suir washes the outworks of the Castle, above which for some distance the tide flows; it lies low, much commanded by the surrounding high grounds.[185]

The enterior of the Castle seems to have been fitted up with care, and ornamented with sculpture, particularly the windows of what may be judged to have been the apartment of state, or principal room of reception; the view here given displays this hall, and more of the chambers.[186]

The Keep of the Castle was an oblong square on one side of which is a turret of peculiar construction,[187] this being placed at one angle of the Bawne, formed one half of a face; the other angles were defended by round towers of great strength.

The antient name of the fine river Suir was Surius, and being joined by the Barrow, and the Nore, these united rivers, from thence derived the appellation of the three Sisters.

## 68. Grandison Castle 2 (Kilkenny)

*Two of these three sculptured panels, decorating the windows of the great hall at Grandison, are still in situ. Not for the first time, Grose's inadequacies as a draughtsman were badly exposed when he turned to sculpture, and, in giving the carvings a classical flavour, he conveys little impression of the original work. Although the artist failed to realise it, one of the panels depicts the archangel Michael holding the scales of judgement. Nor did the artist spot the Ormond coat of arms held by the neighbouring angel. The style and subjects of the carvings are closely related to early sixteenth-century tomb monuments, but it is surprising to find such religious subjects in the context of a fortified house.*

# Sculptures in Grandison Castle, Co:ʸ Kilkenny.

The windows already alluded to in the description of Grandison Castle, are lofty circular arches, adorned with light fluted columns much carved, that gives a great degree of richness to the work; within the arch is placed the sculptures here given. The first represents an Angel with wings expanded, and habited in long garments, personating Justice, with the Scales in one hand, and brandishing an enormous sword in the other; the balances are not however equal, in one of them is a something that makes that side preponderate; this figure is rather rudely cut and designed, th'o the carving still retains its sharpness.

The next displays an Angel very curiously habited with wings spread, this holds up, and points to a Shield, with an armorial bearing.

The third stone presents us with another angel, with wings spread, adorned with lozenge work on the pinions instead of feathers, this also holds in both hands a Shield, charged with some armorial bearings, and Characters I:N:R:I Jesus, Nasareni, Rex, Judeorum.[188]

## 69. Naas: parish church (Kildare)

*Despite Grose's impression that this painting illustrates the remains of the Augustinian priory, it in fact shows the parish church. The artist was, however, correct in observing that the building incorporated medieval ruins; his drawing clearly shows the blocked medieval arches. Dominating the church is the great west tower, financed by the Earl of Mayo, but left unfinished in 1781. An inscription inside records its construction with the words: RUINAM INVENI, PYRAMIDEM RELIQUI, MAYO MDCCLXXXI (I found a ruin, I left a pyramid, Mayo 1781). The tower is a rather brutal affair, blunt and short of detail. It is built of rubble masonry with ashlar dressings, a contrast which Grose as usual overemphasised. He also added an extra pair of windows to the stair turret at the left, but this lapse apart, the painting gives a good general impression of the formidably proportioned tower. It is disconcerting to discover that, only a few decades after construction ceased, Grose thought he was looking at an ancient work which had lost its upper storeys.*

# Priory of S:<sup>t</sup> John the Baptist Naas, Co:<sup>y</sup> Kildare.

That this was the most considerable monastic establishment in the town of Naas, we have every reason to conclude, and th'o the remains are not very extensive, yet what still exists, indicates its former respectability.

The stump of the Belfry or Steeple is a square of uncommon dimensions, and must have been proportionally high, and by this we may form a probable conjecture that when it was entire the rest of its parts corresponded and composed altogether a large building; the principal Chapel that joined this Belfry, has been converted into a place of Divine worship for the modern day, and is the only Protestant Church in the town: this is also of considerable size. The Yard is partly surrounded with buildings, some of which appear antient, and were probably once part of this Priory. In the 12[th] Century the Baron of Naas founded a Priory here, under the invocation of S:<sup>t</sup> John the Baptist, for Canons regular of the order of S:<sup>t</sup> Augustin.

1317 Thomas was Prior, to whom William de London made a considerable grant to this Priory.

1348 The Prior and Canons of this house did this year receive a Royal confirmation of their charters.

By an inquisition taken in the reign of Queen Elizabeth, it appeared, that five acres of land in Styvenstown in this county, and a mill in ruins, annual value 6:<sup>d</sup> parsel of the possessions of this hospital, were a long time concealed from the Queen by Edward Misset of Dowdingston.

By a patent dated October the 23:<sup>d</sup> in the year 1553, the possessions of this house, amounting to the yearly value of £35..18<sup>s</sup>..2<sup>d</sup> were granted to Richard Mannerying.[189]

Besides the Friary of the Mount already given, in the first part of the Antiquities, there was in the centre of the town of Naas a Dominican Friary, erected by the family of Eustace, under the invocation of S:<sup>t</sup> Eustachius; this has totally disappeared, and houses have been built on its site.

## 70. Elfeet Castle (Longford)

*Elfeet is a small fifteenth-century tower house on the eastern shore of Lough Ree. The tower was placed at the corner of a walled bawn, the outline of which is clearly shown in the painting. A road now passes through the middle of the bawn and considerable sections of the enclosing wall have been removed. The tower was evidently intact at the beginning of the nineteenth century, but half of it has now fallen, including the whole of the western side. It contained two superimposed barrel vaults, at basement and first floor level, and access to the upper storeys was by means of a straight, mural staircase. The sides of the tower measured approximately twenty feet, close to the minimum dimension prescribed in 1429 for the £10 castles of the Pale. The upper chambers at Elfeet commanded beautiful views across to Inchcleraun and the other wooded islands of Lough Ree. The tower on the horizon might have been suggested by the 'Clogás' on Inchcleraun. This picture, which is based on a drawing by the Reverend John Moore, is composed in a rather ambitious way, looking straight down a track towards the castle. As if aware of the problems with perspective, Daniel has introduced a horse into the scene, and to make things easier for himself it is shown from the side, being led across rather than down the road.*

# Elfeed Castle Loughree, County of Longford.

The beautiful banks of Loughree are adorned by many an antient Castle that still rears its threatning head th'o in ruins, over the flood that reflects back its shattered battlements, on its polished surface.

Elfeed is not more than a Pistol shot distant from its edge, and th'o not upon very elevated ground, is well seen from, and commands an extensive view of the lake. Far inland as this fresh water sea is, yet was it subject to the inroads of remote tribes, who visited its Islands and banks on predatory expeditions, inticed by the rich spoil the many Monasteries on them afforded, offering a ready and easy prey to their hands; fleets of Ostmen frequently penetrated to its furthest extremity, and the Munster Irish often came on the same errand. Under such circumstances it is no wonder we find Castle's multiplied on the banks of this Lake, some of them are at present nothing but a confused heap of rubbish already sunk into oblivion.[190]

The eye from the high ground above this Castle, commands a far extended view of the shores of the County of Roscommon whose undulating hills are covered with woods and rich in cultivation; the Islands scattered over the lake afford a pleasing variety, and imparts life to the scene, which is highly interesting, and gratifying to the lovers of the beauties of nature.

Ware and Cox are quite silent in respect of this Castle. The View here given was taken by the Rev:[d] John Moore.

D Grose

## 71. Carlow Castle

*This is an attractive townscape, with the castle filling the vista as we look down river. Daniel Grose never found it easy to effect a smooth transition from foreground to background and in parts of this picture the recession is fairly violent. Carlow Castle was erected in the thirteenth century to an interesting and unorthodox design, whereby the rectangular keep was reinforced by circular towers at the angles. Several Leinster castles follow this pattern. The introduction of the scheme has been associated with William Marshal, Earl of Leinster, who was active in Ireland between 1207 and 1213. There is, however, no documentary confirmation of this early date, and construction of the castle may have taken place considerably later. Having survived a Cromwellian onslaught in 1651, the keep remained intact until 1814, when it was partly demolished during the construction of a local lunatic asylum. The spire in the trees to the left belongs to the Gothic Revival church of St Mary's. Daniel Grose visited Carlow in 1792 and a drawing made on that occasion was included in the first volume of the Antiquities. The author explains that this second view 'was taken' in 1804, making it one of the few firmly dated drawings in the book.*

# Carlow Castle North Asp:<sup>t</sup>, County of Carlow.

This most beautiful river the Barrow abounds in many picturesque views and romantic situations, particularly as it speeds its course through the Counties of Carlow and Kilkenny, its banks are crowned with woods, several venerable Castles, handsome seats and ruined Abbeys; it takes its rise in the mountains call'd Sliv-Bloom and flowing in a fine stream, is joined by the rivers Nore, and Sure who also rise in the same neighbourhood, and when united were formerly denominated the Three Sisters; they fall into the sea near the Castle of Hook in the County of Wexford.

It was best known by the antients, under the name of Brigus or Birgus. This river reflected not on its surface a more venerable Castle than that of Carlow, or none more famed for the vicissitudes it underwent, some authors ascribe its origin to Isabel, the daughter of Earl Strongbow, and others to Lacy but be this as it may, an ample account is given of its antient history in the 1:<sup>st</sup> Vol:<sup>m</sup>.

The view here given is taken from the banks of the Barrow, and includes the Church, the Bridge, and great part of the town, with distant mountains rising in the back ground, forming altogether a most interesting prospect, presenting a great variety of pleasing objects.[191] This view was taken A:D: 1804 before the Castle fell.

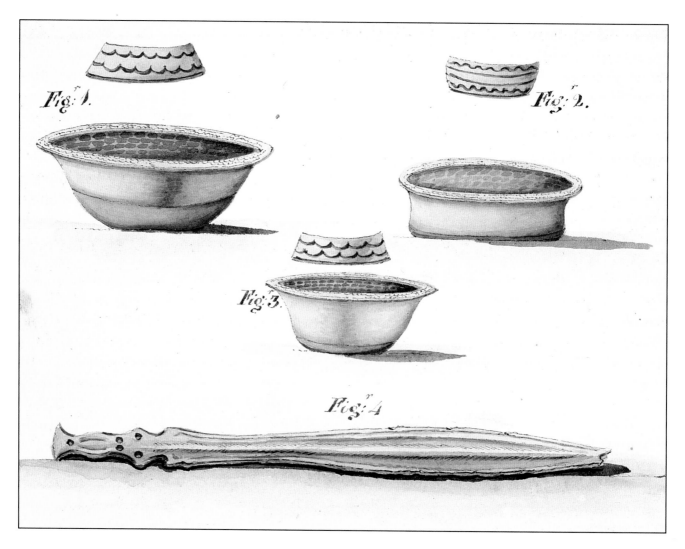

D Grose

## 72. Miscellaneous Antiquities 3

*The three brass bowls illustrated in this plate were found in a lake at Coolcholly, near Ballyshannon (Donegal) and they are now in the National Museum of Ireland. As Grose suspected, such basins are associated with distilling, often of an illegal nature, but his claim that they belonged to the Cistercians is far-fetched. It is likely they were manufactured in the sixteenth or seventeenth century. The fourth object, a bronze, leaf-shaped sword from County Kildare, belongs to the late Bronze Age. The gracefully drawn blade has a ridge running parallel to the edges and a clear ricasso or notch is depicted either side of the blade near the butt. The tang has a fish-tailed terminal and five unusually placed rivet holes. It has not been possible to identify the sword in public collections and it is a pity that Grose does not explain where he saw it. It is just conceivable that he owned this collection of objects himself.*

# Miscellaneous Antiquities (Plate 3:ᵈ).

In the course of summer 1802 in consequence of the great scarsety of fuel, some tenants of Tho:ˢ Dickson Esq:ʳ of Woodville near Ballyshannon Co:ʸ Donegall, for the purpose of getting some bog fir for fireing drained in some degree a small lake on the lands of Coolcally, near which is situated the Abbey of Asterroath,[192] not far from the town above mentioned. In this Lake were found the Pans of which drawings are given Fig:ʳˢ 1, 2, and 3; they are of three different sizes of a perfect circle, each smaller than the first, the largest being capable of containing the other two, one within the other. They are composed of the purest brass, apparently beatten out as the marks of the hammer are still to be seen on the interior surface which gives a degree of ornament to the work.

Fig:ʳ 1 is the largest being 2 feet 6½ Inches in Diameter and 11¼ Inches in height; the rim is ornamented with a double scallop, of which a Fragment is given over the pan— 1 Inch ⅝ broad.

Fig:ʳ 2 is the next in size & differs something in shape from the first is 2 foot 2-Inches in Diameter, 8⅜ Inches in height, rim 1⅞ Inches broad and differs from Fig:ʳ 1 in the ornament.

Fig:ʳ 3 is the smallest being 1 foot 9 Inches ⅓ in Diameter and 7⅛ Inches in height, the rim exhibits the same pattern as the first and is 1½ Inches in breadth. These pans being found so near the aforesaid Monastery, leaves us no room to doubt, that they belonged to, and were employ'd by the good Fathers who inhabited it, for the purposes of distilling Whiskey, a sufficient portion of which it is likely they thought absolutely necessary to their good living.

Fig:ʳ 4. This is a Brazen Sword, and was a Firbolgian instrument, from whence was taken the Irish Skene, as that word is evidently a contraction of the Saxon Segane, a short sword, the Irish Skene was sometimes a foot and an half long.[193]

The Sword measures 18¼ Inches in length, has flutings in the Centre highly raised, and swells considerably towards the point — it was found 13 or 14 feet deep in a bog in the Co:ʸ of Kildare.

D Grose

## 73. Cambo Castle (Roscommon)

*The exiguous ruins of Cambo castle, five miles south-west of Carrick-on-Shannon, belong to a small fortified house of seventeenth-century date. The most obvious clue to when it was built can be found in the pair of brick string courses, not visible in the painting. Only the east end of the house remains. The isolated stump of masonry to the left of the painting has disappeared and the top of the gable was pulled down quite recently by the local farmer. In the south wall is a doorway (shown blocked) and the square hole in the wall to the left is a drawbar slot. Failing to realise that this was the locking mechanism for the door, the artist has placed the slot too high. The horizontal 'V' shaped crack in the north wall marks the position of the first floor, but the massive vertical crack on the south wall seems to be a product of the artist's imagination, in this case Daniel Grose junior. Cambo lies in pleasant rolling countryside and, with the only means of access being a narrow lane, bordered by steep hedges, it still retains that 'sequestered situation' described by Grose in the text.*

# Cambo Castle, Co:ʸ Roscommon.

The sequestered situation of this Castle, amongst Bogs and Lakes, might we are led to imagine, have in some measure secured it against the devastations of war, but this appears not to have been the case, its defensible parts have all been destroyed and nothing but that portion of it used as a dwelling at present remains.

The moat by which it was surrounded still may be traced, and a small turret at one angle of the building, alone serves to denote it was once used for the purposes of war; it however shared in many of those vicissitudes so attendant on that dreadful scourge of mankind; and we read that an agreement was made with the Garrison of this Castle by the Lord Taaf, that upon an oath of fidelity, and to observe the Cessation, they should not be molested A:D: 1645. History is silent as to who were the original builders, or to what family it belonged, at the above mentioned period.

It lies low encompassed by lakes and bogs, and is rather difficult of access, yet an antient road may be discovered skirting the bog near which it stands; it is nearly half way between Elphin and Carrick on Shannon fully two miles from the main road. This view was taken by Dan:[1] Grose Jun.

## 74. Armagh Cathedral

*The Gothic cathedral of Armagh, founded in 1268, has been damaged on so many occasions that most of the medieval fabric has been obliterated. Daniel Grose's painting, based on a drawing by Benjamin Bradford, shows the cathedral before it was comprehensively remodelled during Cottingham's restoration (1834-40). The spire has now gone, so too the battlemented parapet above the nave. Gothic revival tracery fills the windows and ornate pinnacles bedeck the facades. The painting shows the building as it emerged from an earlier restoration begun by Archbishop Robinson in 1765-6. This primate was accused of removing the 'ancient and beautiful tracery windows' from the nave, which explains the plainness of the openings seen in Grose's painting. At this stage there was no clerestory, the roofs of the nave and aisles having been run together. The sculptured stone, discovered in 1805, is depicted on a pedestal to the left.*

# Cathedral Church Ardmagh, Co:<sup>y</sup> of Ardmagh Or Armagh.

This town has been famed in this Island from the earliest ages of Christianity for its monastic establishments, and the great Patron Saint of Ireland made this his principal seat, from whence he desseminated his holy Doctrines; and it in consequence acquired a proportional degree of celebrity. We are told it was this Saint that first built the city of Ardmagh, in the prosperity of which he took great interest, and to forward this he instituted Colleges, and after his time it became the principal seat of learning in this Kingdom, insomuch, that at one period according to Florence M<sup>c</sup>Carty the number of Students exceeded 7000. In consequence of this celebrity it was from the first the Archiepiscopal See of all Ireland,[194] but was not so established by a Bull from the Pope untill the year 1152 when he sent, in consequence of a dispute between it and the see of Dublin, John Paparo Presbyter Cardinal, entitled, Saint Laurentius a Damasco as Legate, who held a Synod, and delivered their Palls to the 4 Archbishops of Ardmagh, Dublin, Cashel, and Tuam, in the Abbey of Melefont, others say in that of Kells. The dispute above alluded to, originated from a Papal Bull granted to S:<sup>t</sup> Patricks Church Dublin, known by the name of Crede Mihe, about the year 1133. It is not to be wondered at, that this town and neighbourhood should abound in Monastic erections, accordingly we find mention made in history of several flourishing here; the Monasticon gives us as the principal one or Cathedral Church, the Priory of Regular Canons founded by S:<sup>t</sup> Patrick (who also founded several of the others) in the year 445 for regular Canons of the Order of S:<sup>t</sup> Augustine, dedicated to S:<sup>t</sup> Peter and S:<sup>t</sup> Paul, which continued for many ages, one of the most celebrated Ecclesiastical foundations in the world. The ground on which it was built being near the river Callen, abounded in Willows, that grew there, from whence it was called Druin Sailec, it was bestowed for this pious purpose on S:<sup>t</sup> Patrick by one Dair a man of great wealth and fame in this country; but from its elevated situation its name was changed to Ardmagh, that is the High field or Hill.

A:D:729 Flathbert son of Loingseach in the 7:<sup>th</sup> year of his reign abdicated the throne of Ireland, and became a Monk in this Abbey in which he died A:D:760. A:D: 1004 King Brien Borombhe with his Army remained a week in Ardmagh, and on his departure left a Collar of Gold weighing 20 Ounces as an Alms, on the great Altar of this Church. The same Monarch was entered in this Church together with his son Murchad, and the heads of Conaing his nephew and Mothlen prince of Desies who fell in the battle of Clontarf, they were brought here with great funeral pomp from the Monastery of Swords, the King was buried on the North side of the great Church in a large stone coffin by himself, and Murchad & the head of Conaing in another on the South.

A:D 1027, The Holy Staff of Jesus lodged in this Friary by S:$^t$ Patrick was broken. A:D. 1033 All the Inhabitants of Ardmagh were witnesses to a very great miracle namely blood was seen to run from the Shrines of S:$^t$ Peter & S:$^t$ Paul in this Church. This Cathedral together with the Town of Ardmagh was destroyd by fire nineteen times, and suffered from pillage no less than fifteen. This Friary was granted at the suppression of Monasteries A:D: 1612 to Sir Toby Caulfield Kn:$^t$ at the yearly rent of 5 Pounds Irish.

This Cathedral being in perfect repair at present, needs no farther description here.[195] The view here given was taken by Benj:$^{mn}$ Bradford Esq:$^r$.

D Grose

## 75. Armagh: Franciscan Friary 1

*Daniel Grose laboured under the false impression that the ruins depicted in this painting belonged to a nunnery founded by St Patrick in 457. In fact they are the remains of a Franciscan friary, founded on the edge of the city eight centuries later in 1263-4. Records of the friary's history are sparse, though it is known that in the fifteenth century one of the friars was killed in Cavan after being kicked by his horse. The community was suppressed at the Reformation, probably in the year 1542, and by 1551 the buildings had been turned into a barracks. The friary was burnt on at least two occasions later in the century. The 1601 map of Armagh shows it as a roofless ruin, and all that now remains are sections of the church. Grose's painting gives a relatively accurate impression of the west front, though the put-log holes, used for fixing the scaffolding, are not in the correct position and several have been omitted. Benjamin Bradford, who supplied the drawing, presumably had no idea what they were for.*

# Nunnery of S:ᵗ Lupita Ardmagh, Co:ʸ of Ardmagh.

It was noticed in the foregoing subject that S:ᵗ Patrick founded several Monastic establishments in and about Ardmagh; amongst which was the one presented, bearing [the] date AD 457. It was call'd Temple-na-Ferta, or the Church of the Miracles, and was given by the founder Saint, to his eldest Sister S:ᵗ Lupita, who presided over this Nunnery and was buried in it; the beginning of the last Century her body was found buried deeply amongst the rubbish of her antient seat in a standing position; two crosses were also descovered closely guarding the body before and behind. History is silent as to any thing further respecting this Nunnery,[196] which is rather surprising from its singular title, and the illusterous [illustrious] Saint who presided over it. The far advanced state of decay in which this remain appears bespeaks its very remote antiquity; it stands in the Primates Domain, almost shrouded in Ivy, and thickly surrounded by Trees and underwood, so much is it sunk into oblivion, that many of the residents in the town of Ardmagh could not point out the spot where these ruins are to be met with.[197]

The 2:ᵈ Plate represents an inside view, and displays the remains of several Arches but so entirely covered with Ivy, as totally to obscure their shape, and as the masses of ruin are so detached and broken, it would be impossible to form any conjecture as to its original general plan, however these arches appear to have formed the body of a large Church or Chapel. Both these views were taken by Benj:ᵐⁿ Bradford Esq:ʳ.

## 76. Armagh: Franciscan Friary 2

*The second view of the so-called nunnery shows the interior of the friary church, looking westwards down the nave. On the left, engulfed by vegetation, are two of the pointed arches that opened into the south aisle. With a length of 180 feet, Armagh was the longest friary church known in Ireland, but its proportions are inadequately reflected in the painting. Indeed the watercolour suggests a building of great width rather than one of great length. The abandoned friary served as a convenient quarry for local building, and very little dressed stonework survives amidst the rubble masonry. Photographs taken earlier this century, showing the walls almost totally obscured by ivy, bear out Grose's comment that the ruins were 'sunk in oblivion'. The vegetation has been removed by the Department of the Environment for Northern Ireland, who carried out an extensive programme of excavations in 1970.*

## 77. Lottery Castle (Westmeath)

*Lottery Castle lay on the south bank of the river Inny, not far from the point where it flows into Lough Ree. The ruins were demolished about thirty years ago during drainage operations on the river, carried out by the Office of Public Works. It is said to have been located near the 'Red Bridge', which probably marks the site of an ancient ford across the river. If it was not for Daniel Grose's reference to a vaulted basement, it would be hard to guess that this was a castle. It is difficult to make much of the architecture. The building was presumably a late-medieval tower house and it was set within a bawn and further defended by ditches. Although Grose may be correct in suggesting that this was an O'Farrell castle, it is equally possible that it was built by a local family like the Geoghans defending themselves against the O'Farrells. The painting is a valuable record of this obscure and already forgotton monument and the artist, seated in the foreground, deserves credit for making much of a not very promising site. By showing the castle from a low viewpoint, he has exploited the bizarre silhouette of the ruins and the precarious pinnacles of masonry.*

# Lottery Castle, Co:<sup>y</sup> Westmeath.

The river Inney flows into Loughree, and is a narrow but deep and rapid stream about 50 or 60 yards broad at its mouth, up which boats can pass; this very antient Castle stands on its right bank, on the Westmeath side, as it here seperates that County from Longford.[198] It is situated on an eminence immediately surrounded by extensive flats, overflowed in winter, which must have added greatly to its security and defended it against land attack. Whatever might have been its former strength and size, but little of it at present remains; none of the defensible parts of the building exist, and what is still standing appears to be part of the Keep, with two vaults underneath, both tumbled down in several places. The ditch however may be traced which entirely cut off the building from the main, and compleatly insulated it, there is also to be seen outside the moat, two detached works; the foundations of them still remain, these are surrounded by fosses nearly as deep as the ditch, these evidently appear as part of the defences. The Keep is so much in ruins, as to preclude any decision as to its original form; a large Elder Tree springs from the midst and seems to flourish as in scorn over this scene of desolation, and appears to glory in the contrast between its fresh and lively verdure, and the gray and mouldering ruins time has made; the rank nettle and broad leaved Dock lend their aid, and grow with wild luxuriance in and about the masses of masonry, a great portion of which they hide. History is silent in respect to the antient account of this Castle, which is but two frequently the case in this Kingdom which obliges the Antiquary who describes them, to have recourse to conjecture, Cox and Ware makes no mention of it, and tradition in this instance fails to afford any assistance. The O'Farrells were a powerful family in these parts and were probably the original propr[i]etors of this Castle, and we are led the more readily to form the conjecture, as this sept founded the Abbey of Shrule in this neighbourhood.[199] The Country on the opposite side of the water is rich and highly cultivated diversifed [diversified] with gentlemans seats and improvements.

The River Inney gives rise to a singular notion, that the fine stream into which it flows, did not formerly bear the name of the Shannon, till its union with the Inney, being before called only the Shann, and that from thence it incorporates with it a part of the name as well as its waters, and is call'd Shann-Inny or Shannen; thus some antient authors have it, but more modern writers entirely explode the idea.[200] This view was taken by Lieu:<sup>t</sup> Grose of the Roy:<sup>l</sup> Navy.

## 78. Athlone: north gate

*The first mention of the north gate at Athlone comes in 1578, when it was occupied as a residence by Robert Damport, provost-marshal of Connacht. It was constructed during the 1570s, a time when various schemes to improve the town's defences were under consideration. The design followed a standard form, with the square or rectangular tower set astride the town wall, a section of which is visible to the right. In Grose's time the wooden gates were still in position under the arch and the plaque containing the arms of Queen Elizabeth I can be seen above the entrance. Behind the buildings to the left is the tower of St Mary's church, the spire of which was removed about 1839. The small harbour in front of the gatehouse has been filled in, but the modern road still follows the curve of the old shoreline. With its incidental details — the boat, the wooden gates and the spectator gazing at the artist — this is one of the most rewarding pictures in Daniel Grose's book.*

# North Gate of Athlone, Co:<sup>y</sup> Westmeath.

This place has been the theatre of so many public occurrences of consequence that none who are in the slightest manner acquainted with the history of Ireland can be ignorant of those memorable events; it would therefore be a needless waste of time to enlarge upon them here, however it is necessary to give some description of the plate now before us, which represents the North Gate of Athlone. This outwork most probably bears date with the erection of the Castle (on which it was dependant)[201] and the other fortifications of the town, which underwent in the many agitations of this Country, the usual vicissitudes attendant on places of the kind. We read that the Castle of Athlone was built upon Abbey land under King John, who therefore granted in the year 1214 to the Monks the Tythe of the charges of the Castle to be paid to them out of the annual proceeds of the Ward.[202] We also find that Aug:<sup>st</sup> 30:<sup>th</sup> 1347 William FitzAndrew De Birmingham was made Constable of the Castle of Athlone, with all the lands, and tenements thereto belonging. This William Fitz Andrew de Birmingham, was the same who first built the Tower within the Castle of Dublin, which th'o afterwards rebuilt, still bears his name. One of the vicissitudes above alluded to, happened in 1572, when the Fortifications and Town of Athlone were burnt by the rebels headed by the O'Mores and O'Connors. This gate appears to have suffered much from Cannon shot, the holes of which show in many places, particularly in one large breach, where they seem to have taken great effect and notwithstanding the thickness of the wall, to have nearly penetrated through; these shot were probably received the 30:<sup>th</sup> of June 1691 when the fortifications of Athlone were battered by Gen:<sup>rl</sup> De Ginkle commanding the Royal Army. The Battlements that formerly defended the top of the Tower has disappeared, and it is internally as well as externally fast hastening to decay, the remains of a staircase however may still be seen; it was probably rebuilt or much repaired, during the Reign of Elizabeth, as her Arms and Initials are display'd on a square stone plate, over the Gateway, part of the town walls remain joining the Tower but equally in ruins. The Town of Athlone still retains its antient Character of a defensible place, modern fortifications having been erected, which together with its being so central in the Kingdom, constitutes it a post of considerable consequence. This view was taken by Lieu:<sup>t</sup> Grose of the Roy:<sup>l</sup> Navy.

## 79. Bethlem: house of Poor Clares (Westmeath)

*Daniel Grose was correct in thinking that the ruins at Bethlem were not 'of antient date'. The buildings here belonged to a community of Poor Clares, an austere, contemplative order, founded by St Francis and St Clare about 1212-14. During the religious revival of the early seventeenth century, a convent was established in Dublin, but the community was soon expelled from the city. The abbess, Cecily Dillon, brought her nuns to 'Bethlem', a remote spot on the shore of Lough Ree, where her father, Sir Theobald Dillon, had his estates. The surviving building appears to have served as living quarters, perhaps with a chapel on the attic floor above. Contrary to the opinion of Grose, there is no evidence that the nuns erected further stone buildings at the site. The nuns stayed at Bethlem for a mere eleven years, fleeing in 1642, when English regiments arrived at Athlone during the Confederate Wars. The community subsequently established itself at Galway, where the convent of Poor Clares retains a wooden statue of the Virgin and Child brought from Bethlem three hundred and fifty years ago.*

# Nunnery of Bethlem, Co:ʸ of Westmeath.

Here again occurs one of those instances of the defect of history so frequently to be met with in this kingdom, and which wraps up this and many other buildings, both monastic and military in obscurity and throws the Antiquary on tradition for necessary information. That it is the remains of a religious house, admits not of a doubt, but from the stile of architecture, and particularly the windows, it does not appear to be of a very antient date, however it is very probable the present building was erected from the ruins, and on the scite of a much more antient structure.[203] Tradition tells us this was a Nunnery, and that it consisted of three other buildings adjoining the large Chapel that remains, these a few years back were pulled down, in order to clear the land, and the rubbish removed, in doing which many old Coins and other curious Antiquities were found.

The country people say the Nuns sunk a large Pan of Gold, on a shoal that runs out from the land into Loughree in a direction towards Saints Island to which the Nunnery is directly opposite; this they pretend was a road that led to the Island, however there is not the smallest remains of it, nor was it possible that such a road could ever have existed, as All Saints is fully a mile from the shore, and there is three or four fathoms water in the passage, and no corresponding shoal from the Island.

The finding the antient Coins corroborates the conjecture formed as above and certainly proves a more remote antiquity, it very probably owes its foundation to the family of Dillon of Drumraney, who built the Priory of All Saints in King Johns time, with which they say it had communication, very likely the case, th'o not by means of the road.

The building stands low, about 150 yards from the Lake. This View was taken by Lieu:ᵗ Grose of the Roy:ˡ Navy.

D Grose

## 80. Rynn Castle (Leitrim)

*This small fifteenth-century tower house is situated within the Lough Rynn estate, two miles south of Mohill. The view was drawn by Daniel Grose junior, whose credentials as an antiquarian artist seem to have been limited. It is difficult to equate the drawing with what survives at Lough Rynn today. The castle is rectangular not triangular in plan and the exterior angles take an unusual rounded form. The entrance lay in the south wall, where there is a straight mural staircase leading to the upper floors. The ground storey was covered by a barrel vault, a section of which is shown in the painting. The viewpoint must be from the east, but on this side the wall of the castle survives to a height of about twenty-five feet, so such a view is impossible. Either Daniel adopted a highly imaginative approach or the castle has been reconstructed in this area. A window in the east wall has been rebuilt incorrectly and it is not impossible that the Earls of Leitrim tampered with the ruins during the nineteenth century, when it served as a convenient folly. The castle was probably built by the Mac Rannall family, who changed their name to Reynolds about 1580. Despite the inaccuracies of his son's drawing, Daniel Grose has used it to produce an attractive painting, with the steely-blue and grey-green washes evoking a hazy atmosphere on the lake.*

# Wryn or Rin Castle, Co:ʸ Leitrim.

It has been repeatedly remarked in the course of this work, that a short period of time will consign many of the antient fortresses of this kingdom to oblivion, and sweep away the small remains that now exist and "leave not a wreck behind". This is nearly the case with the Castle now before us which notwithstanding its advanced state of decay, appears once to have been a Military post of some importance, its foundations can still be traced with accuracy, and they present us with a triangular figure of some extent defended at the angles by square towers the quoins of which were rounded off, and the walls of considerable thickness.

It is situated on an irregular point of land, formed by several different lakes and secured by a moat, that cuts the peninsula in two, and into which the water still flows; access to the Castle was rendered still more difficult by three narrow Isthmuses which must be crossed before the moat could be approached, a circumstance of no small danger, as these narrows were compleatly under the guns of the Castle: it could only in one point be commanded by Artillery, and considering the nature of the surrounding country, intersected by Bogs and morasses, to make a road through which, capable of sustaining heavy Guns was, at the time this flourished, an almost Herculean labour; we may therefore safely pronounce this Castle to have been one of the best situated for defence, this province could produce.

Tradition tells us this fastness was erected by a Chief call'd Reynolds, and that it owes its destruction to Cromwells Army, who found means, notwithstanding every difficulty, to approach Cannon near enough to batter it to pieces. The fragment of the Tower that now remains, can admit of little description, it however displays the thickness of the walls, and shows the rounding of the angles, and even on this small portion, the effects of the Artillery still continue visible.[204]

The powerful Chief above alluded to, was ancestor to the family that now bears his name, of Letterfyan, and he not only held this strong-hold; but possessed a fastness of considerable respectability in, and on the banks of Loughscar,[205] in the neighbourhood of their present residence, the picturesque remains of which still exists and of which a plate is given in the first part of these antiquities.

Rin was probably one of those Castles, built by the Chiefs of this then wild country, for the purposes of securing their possessions from depredatory visitations, each chief of a name or sept, living in a state of continual warfare, with his neighbour.

If this was the case, this retired fastness was most undoubtedly well situated for security against surprise, and property once lodged here, could scarsely be removed if well defended. But Cromwell with indefatigable industry, found out and penetrated through every difficulty to these fortresses, which he naver spared, & there are but few Castles in this Kingdom that do not display, even in ruins, most evident marks of his destructive progress through it. Wryn or Rin signifies a point of land projecting into the water so, this is denominated Rin Castle, or the Castle on the Point; the principal Lake also derives its name from the Castle. A succession of Lakes communicating with each other, extend from this place and unite with the Camlin River in the County of Longford. This view was taken by Dan:[1] Grose Jun:[r].

## 81. Kilronan 'Abbey' (Roscommon)

The ruined church at Kilronan, six and a half miles north-west of Leitrim on the shore of Lough Meelagh, is best known as the burial place of Carolan, 'the last of the Irish bards'. This was an ancient parish church, not an abbey as Daniel Grose thought. Although the raking buttresses have been exaggerated, the painting gives a good general impression of the building, including details of the Romanesque doorway in the south wall. The curves of the fields and hills, together with the lively gait of the horse, lend a certain vigour to the composition and the handling of the cool blues and greys underlines the artist's skill at suggesting distance. The sprightly horse follows the path of the modern road from Leitrim to Sligo; the holy well of St Lasair, where lived a 'miraculous trout', is situated just to the left. Daniel Grose apparently knew Kilronan well and he was much impressed by the works of the local landlord, Thomas Tenison. Shortly after the view was painted, a splendid neo-Gothic mansion, Castle Tenison, was built beside the lake in the middle distance. This has been abandoned in recent years and is now lying derelict.

# Kilronan Abbey, Co:<sup>y</sup> of Roscommon.

After journeying through a dreary country for some miles, along a bleak road, across bogs and swamps, a view breaks in upon the weary traveller, for picturesque beauty and romantic scenery scarsely to be equaled in this or any Kingdom; heightened by the sudden contrast, and to a stranger, the more agreeable, being totally unexpected.

On ascending an eminence an extensive Lake presents itself immediately under the eye, spotted with planted islands, and surrounded by rising grounds, crowned with venerable woods, interspersed with sloping lawns improved by art, and tastefully laid out. On the right near the Lake, on the high road which winds itself gracefully through the valley is a small scattered Village, and a little further beyond, the remains of a venerable th'o not a very large Abbey,[206] immediately contrasted by a modern simple country Church with a comfortable Parsonage house both situated a few acres from the ruins.[207] Behind these still to the right, rise rude hills swelling by degrees into mountains with uneaven and indented sides, here and there inriched with groops of trees, and patches of underwood, the outline above waving and broken. In the centre of the Landscape on a fine sloping eminence over the Lake, in the midst of woods and lawns, rises with singular beauty the modern elegant Mansion of Tho:<sup>s</sup> Tennison Esq:<sup>r</sup> looking proudly superior over the surrounding country,[208] situated in a scene, and commanding a view difficult to equal.(x)

A little lower down the slope embosomed in groves stands this Gentlemans former residence, a pretty house built in the Castelated stile (a pleasing feature in the picture) with a farmyard, stabling &c, behind it.

The left hand shores of the Lake, are covered with noble woods, from amidst which peaps out another modern erection, belonging to the family already mentioned. The distance beyond these woods, the house and the Lake extends into a fine tract of Country, seen as through a vista, and bounded by lofty mountains rising in succession and vanishing into ether.

The Abbey principally consists of one large building or Chapel, with several smaller attached to it, the whole roofless, and in much decay; it is entered by a circular arch, ornamented with grotesque heads,[209] the east gable is much covered with Ivy, which

(x) This elegant Mansion was not built when this View was taken.

gives the building a venerable appearance.

In this Abbey was buried the famous Irish bard Carolan who so enlivened this country with his melodious strains, and his Scull was for some time preserved with great care, and viewed with equal interest, but of late it has disappeared, and report says it now adorns the Cabinet of Curiosities, belonging to a learned Gentleman in a neighbourhood County, many miles from this spot.[210] There was also, untill very lately, carefully preserved in this Abbey, the remains of a large Bell, formerly belonging to it calld Clough Ronan, or the Bell of Kilronan famous for its many miraculous virtues, and greatly reverenced through the surrounding country, and was most particularly famous for detecting falshood.[211] If this Bell was sworn by falsely, th'o broken and without a Clapper, it rung out, with so loud and dreadful a sound as to alarm the inhabitants round for a considerable distance, nor was this all, the parties so forswearing themselves, were sure either to die in the course of a year, or experience some other shocking punishment, that rendered them a striking example to posterity. Near the Abbey on the roadside, close to the Lake, under a beautiful Clump of antient trees, is a holy well calld Losser inclosed by a wall, and dedicated to the blessed Virgin, whose Patron or Festival is held here every 8:th of September the day of her Nativity.[212] In this well which is of the Clearest transparency the country people tell you, lives a blessed Trout, that has inhabited it since it first was made holy, and whatever devotee is so fortunate as to catch a view of this miraculous fish, is insured a happy reception amongst the good made perfect hereafter. Within a few Yards of the well is one of those antient arches called Tolmen, or the hole of Stone, this consists of two uprights supporting a heavy orbicular Stone that vibrates on the smallest touch, the whole about four feet high. These stones are held as sacred, and considered to possess a miraculous quality of curing disorders, especially pains in the back, and those who squeeze through the narrow aperture between the uprights, is sure of experiencing immediate relief; and many do resort to this spot to try the experiment. Authors can only guess at the use made of these passages by the Antients (M:r Borlace says) we have reason to think these were consecrated ritually, and considered as holy, and were supposed consequently to possess the most miraculous virtues: in fact that they were in all respects used as at the present day, for the same purposes, and believed to have the same blessed properties, as are still ascribed to them by the lower ranks of Irish, just as in the present instance. The Author of the Monasticon has omitted this Abbey in his list of Religious houses enumerated in this County, however in the addenda to that Work, we find mention made of a monastic establishment, denominated Kilronamna which he places in the adjoining Co:<sup>y</sup> of Leitrim, and as there is no remain so denominated in that County, we are led to imagine it must be this Kilronan;[213] it is there stiled an Hospital, Termon Irenagh, or Corbeship, endowed with Four quarters of land. Inquisition 27:<sup>th</sup> January 37:<sup>th</sup> Queen Elizabeth.

The mountains near Kilronan abound in rich Coalmines, which are at present worked and yield an excellent Coal for burning, in this neighbourhood are also the Arigna Iron works, these have been repeatedly set a going but have constantly failed, and are now unoccupied.

D Grose

## 82. *Molana Abbey (Waterford)*

*Given his taste for romantic settings, it is no surpise that the ruins at Molana made a big impact on Daniel Grose. The remains of the monastery, located on an island in the Blackwater, are now reached by a causeway, but the 'mouldering relics' are still covered by a canopy of trees, as they were when he visited the scene. During the twelfth century the ancient Irish monastery at Molana was changed into an Augustinian house, which survived until the Dissolutions of 1539-41. Some of the cloister buildings remain, as well as much of the church, the east wall of which leans out precariously towards the river. The best work is in the chancel, where there are a series of fine early Gothic windows. It is difficult to make much sense of the site from Grose's painting and he was clearly more impressed by the 'gloomy grandeur' of the place than its architectural merits. The gable on the right evidently represents the east wall of the church, but more buildings remain at the left than are shown in the painting. Wattle fishing weirs are still fixed in the river at this point and, in the two hundred years that have elapsed since Grose's visit, little has changed at this enchanting spot.*

# Abbey of S:ᵗ Molana, Co:ʸ Waterford.

This romantic ruin is situated on a small island in the Black water, not far from Temple Micheal, and about two miles and an half distant from the town of Youghall.[214] But little remains of this once magnificent Abbey, part of the walls of the nave and choir are however still standing, showing that the east window was lofty, and of considerable dimensions; by what remains we may judge of its former extent, and from its state of very great decay, of its remote antiquity.

It was built in the gothic stile of architecture, but the fragments of masonry are so covered with Ivy, and shrouded with trees and underwood, that its original figure is now totally lost.

This venerable remain strikes the eye of the observer with awe and reverence, the lofty trees that canopy its mouldering relic's, cast upon them a solemn shade imparting a gloomy grandeur to the scene, perhaps more impressive on the mind than was all its former monastic splendour. This was formerly called the island of Saint Molanfide, and also Darinis.

S:ᵗ Molanfide founded an Abbey here in the Sixth Century, for Canons Regular and was the first Abbot.

590 — S:ᵗ Fachnan, Mongach, or the hairy, being covered with hair at his birth, was abbot of this monastery.

S:ᵗ Gobhan was abbot of Darinis. The writer of the life of Saint Mocoemoge relates the following passage of the aboved mentioned S:ᵗ Fachnan, his Abbey and school. "Saint Fachnan lived in a monastery of his own foundation; there is a city grown up in which always continued a large seminary for scholars, which is call'd Ross Alithri." This saint is in an antient martyrology(x) calld Bishop and his festival is observed on the 16:ᵗʰ of August, on which day the espiscopal visitation is usually held.[215] He is still greatly revered by the papists, as the patron and tutelar saint of the diocess; they have a legendary tradition that he used to pray daily on the side of a hill, half a mile eastward of Ross, and that one day he left his Official or prayer book there, the night following happened to be very rainy, nevertheless the book was not wet for the angels (as the legend says) built a small chapel over it to preserve it. Raymond le Gross, who

(x) Martyr. of Cashell.

so highly contributed to the reduction of Ireland, is said to have been interred in this monastery.[216] Of the Monument of this Chief said to have been brought from S:ᵗ Molana, we have already made mention in our account of the North Abbey Youghall, but tradition is the only guide we have in appropriating that figure to his tomb.

History furnishes us with a long list of Abbots who successively governed this Monastery, with grants and various claims of lands &c — totally uninteresting.

On the suppression, Queen Elizabeth granted this Abbey and its possessions to Sir Walter Raleigh, who assigned to the Earl of Cork.

## 83. Annaduff (Leitrim)

*About a mile before Drumsna, the main road from Dublin to Sligo sweeps past the Protestant church at Annaduff, which Grose explained 'has been lately erected, but not yet finished'. As it was built with the aid of a loan from the Board of First Fruits in 1815, Grose was evidently writing his book some years after this. Members of the Grose family lived at Annaduff, for in 1817 the death was recorded of a Susanne Grose, aged 21, 'of Annaduff'. Just to the left of the Protestant church is what appears to be the old medieval parish church, evidently still roofed. Its east wall contains a remarkable fifteenth-century sculptured niche that Grose illustrates elsewhere in the book. There are no vestiges of the early Christian monastery recorded in the text. The drawing of Annaduff was prepared by Daniel Grose junior, who took plenty of liberties with the landscape. The river Shannon is too close to the church and the surrounding hills are not as undulating as the painting implies.*

# Annaduff or Annaghduff Abbey, Co:<sup>y</sup> Leitrim.

The Shannon is rich in picturesque prospects from this place, till it enters the Co:<sup>y</sup> of Longford, and the eye of the traveller as he journeys from Drumsna to Ruskey, a distance of Six miles, is regaled with a succession of beautiful views of that noble River, spreading into Lakes, whose shores are crowned with woods, diversified with cultivation, and broken by high grounds, swelling by degrees into mountains, as Slieuve Bawne is in view to the South, the greatest part of the way.

This subject, now a Parish Church, is situated close to the high road from Dublin, about a quarter of a mile from the pretty town of Drumsna, famous for its spaw [spa]. The old Church which was built on the scite, and out of the materials of the antient Abbey, is now in its turn gone to decay, and an handsome modern structure, has been lately erected, but not yet finished.[217]

Some of the antient ornaments have been preserved in the old Church, particularly the East Window, which is of a peculiar stile, very rarely to be met with, indicating its great antiquity; each corner of the building is also adorned with a grotesque head, so placed as to appear to support the roof.[218] We can learn nothing more of Annaduff than that an Abbey was erected here AD 766.[219]

However romantic Tradition is not idle here, the country people relate a legend that they firmly believe in, & no Blacksmith would be found hardy enough to live within half a mile of this Church. They say that the Saint who founded this Abbey, when he first came to the place, was denied a nights lodging by a Blacksmith who resided on the spot, this so displeased the holy man, that he immediately Prophecied that from that moment the sound of a Smiths hammer should not be heard for a year in continuance, near that Church. In consequence from that period, any Smith attempting to follow his trade within the proscribed distance, died within the year. This story of the Saint, savours more of the spirit of heathenish revenge in him, than Christian meekness and Charity. View taken by Dan:<sup>l</sup> Grose Jun:<sup>r</sup>.

## 84. Cloondara (Longford)

*Daniel Grose was enthusiastic about the construction of the Royal Canal, which reached Cloondara in 1817, a few years before he prepared his book. His view looks away from the canal, across the channel that drove the water wheel in the mill at the left. His main interest, however, lay in the ruined church, seen to the right of the picture, a simple rectangular building, probably of early thirteenth-century date. Built into its walls are an old millstone, along with a window head from an earlier church. 'The adjoining cell, which still retains its stone roof', is in fact a barrel-vaulted chamber inserted at a late date inside the west end. It probably supported a low tower. Just beyond the church, on the site now occupied by the large Catholic church of 1835, is a small building with its rafters exposed. The present layout of Cloondara is easily recognisable from the watercolour, though a line of trees now obstructs this particular view.*

# Abbey of Clone,— Cloono, or Cloonedra, Co:y Longford.

The good effects of intersecting this country by Canals is plainly discernable at this place, here the new line from Dublin forms a communication with the River Shannon,[220] and here we find a thriving little village, that bids fair soon to rise into a smart bustling town.

Within a few hundred yards of the Canal harbour one Lock opens the Shannon to Athlone, and Limerick, and the river Camlin that is navagable in the opposite direction, unites with that river by a cerpentine Course of about three miles, near the domain of Castle Forbes the Seat of the Earl of Granard, in a line towards Carrick, above which place the Shannon continues open for a few miles. We read of an Abbey of this name situated on the river Camlin, of which no authentic account can be found, except that it was founded AD 663.[221] As little can be said for it at the present day; its very great antiquity is very apparent and nothing remains but one large Chapel, and an adjoining cell, which still retains its stone roof, and near its mouth a flight of Stone steps, that led to apartments above. The building however appears to have been of much greater extent as here and there foundations may be traced; an enormous elder tree shadows great part of the ruins, & spreads its ample branches over many a rude grave, with which the inclosure round is much crouded.

The Camlin is here crossed by a good bridge of several arches, & about half a mile off the Shannon by Tarmon Bridge. The word Tarmon which frequently occurs, seems to have its origen from the God Terminus to whom the Heathens of old built Temples, as one who they believed, decided the differences of Countrymen in dividing of their lands; so that Termon was quasi Terminus as a boundary or possession limited, and distinct from the possessions of the Laity, from whence likewise it began to be called a Sanctuary.[222] Others think Termon denoted Terrum Monastrorum monks land. Thus far Ware. The parish of Tarmon or Termon Barry in which this bridge is, derives its name as above, i:e Saint Barrys district.

## 85. Kilbarry 1 (Roscommon)

*Daniel Grose was excited about Kilbarry, as he felt he had discovered an important monastery, unknown to Mervyn Archdall and other early scholars. Kilbarry was indeed the site of an early Christian monastery, said to have been founded by St Berach (anglicised by Grose to St Barry), who died in 615. Few reliable facts, however, are known about the history of the site and the notion that there were seven churches appears to be fanciful. The remnants of only two, or possibly three, churches can be identified amidst the modern graveyard that has enveloped the ruins. The buildings have deteriorated badly since the drawings were made. The first picture is a view from the north, showing in the centre of the picture the so-called 'Mad House', the building where the insane were brought in hope of a cure. An elderly inhabitant of Kilbarry today could recall only one person visiting the church in his lifetime to avail of the remedy, and that 'a very long time ago'. The building to the left was the largest church at Kilbarry, but most of it has now gone. If Daniel Grose junior, the author of the original sketches, can be trusted, it had a vertical moulding at the angle, suggesting a date around 1200. To enhance the ecclesiastical atmosphere of the scene, a ringed cross head has been placed in the foreground.*

# Seven Churches of Kilbarry, Co:ʸ Roscommon.

This remain is held in such veneration by the lower ranks of people, that its fame extends to a considerable distance round, and every one has some miraculous legend to relate of this holy place, each more wonderful than the first, a few of which will suffice with this description. Kilbarry signifies the burial place of S:ᵗ Barry, who it is said founded these Churches seven in number, and lies buried beneath the doorway of one of them, half in and half out of the building.[223] It is rather extraordinary that the Monasticon is totally silent respecting this religious establishment; Ware also in his Antiquities makes no mention of it, which is the more to be wondered at, considering its apparent extent and consequence. But its remote and secluded situation may in some measure account for the neglect, and it is hardly possible in a Kingdom like this, abounding with so many Monastic institutions, that some few amongst so great a number should have escaped these Authors notice. Under such circumstances we may be excused for being somewhat more copious in the description of a subject, as far as can be gathered never before meddled with, and for multiplying the drawings of a ruin exclusive of every other consideration, beautifully picturesque in itself. But to proceed. It is very apparent that Seven Churches did actually exist here, as the walls of four of them are still standing and the foundations, with fragments of the walls of the rest, can still be traced with the greatest ease.

These were most probably originally a station of the Culdees, who as it has been before remarked Selected the most retired and inaccessable situations for their abode. Kilbarry lies in the centre of a red Bog, that stretches along the river Shannon, and is nearly a mile from its banks, and the nearest road, in short, the bog compleatly insulates the spot of firm land on which the ruins, and the Village stands; and th'o modern civilization has at the present day, intersected every part of this country with roads, yet that was not the case at that very remote period, or even when the Monasticon was compiled.

This building or rather the Saint whose name it bears, also gave a denomination to the parish in which it stands; Tarmon Barry, which has been explained in the foregoing subject. Tradition tells us Saint Barry whose family name they say was Hanley, came to this spot in a most miraculous manner, sailing across the Shannon (widening into a lake of more than a mile broad at this place) on a large flag of Stone, which he stationed the brink to serve as a like conveyance to those religious people who had occasion to pass over, to and from Kilbarry. This wonderful stone continued to ply its friendly ferry for many years, till some unfortunate woman not paying due respect to its miraculous virtues, or being ignorant of them, ventured to bat linnen on it, a circumstance so derogatory to its dignity, that venting a dreadful cry, it sprung of itself into the Shannon, where it sunk in about three feet water, still to be seen deprived of its former buoyant quality. Saint Barry like his Comorban(x) Saint Kieran of Clonmacnoise, still retained after death an affection for the holy spot inhabited and beloved by him during his sojourn upon earth, and endowed it with many extraordinary privileges which continue even to this day. The Church or Chapel under which he is partly buried, is particularly favored by him. Any one having lost their senses by accident or otherwise, being put into this Church and sleeping in it for a few hours, comes out entirely restored, and of as perfect mind as any other; but on the contrary if any of the fair sex (to whom by the by S:t Barry appears to be no great friend) presumes even to enter it in her perfect senses, she immediately becomes mad, and never by any art can be recovered again. Many unfortunate wretches have actually been brought to this place to try the cure, and the neighbours insist upon it that the experiment has invariably been attended with success. A holy well is shown at this place, which was most particularly valued by the Saint, it was situated close to the Monasteries, and possessed many admirable or rather miraculous qualities, but again a female was guilty, and by some indecent insult towards this favorite spring, so provoked the guardian Saint, that at the instant he removed the well and a beautiful White thorn, that grew beside it, to the distance of several acres, where he has left it ever since undisturbed. But passing by many more Stories of like nature, all implicitly believed in, we shall relate a striking instance which may serve to show the great veneration any thing said to belong to this Saint, was and is still held in, by the lower orders of the people. There was preserved at this place till within a very short period a broken staff, and (as described) was most probably a pastoral staff or crook, belonging to Saint Barry, for his they say it was, and with it he exersised his Pastoral functions as a Bishop, for to that dignity tradition raises him.[224] This Staff or as it is call'd (y) The Garvally, th'o no longer kept at Kilbarry is still in being, preserving all its former virtues, and is stationed somewhere in the mountain of Sleuvebawn in this county. It is between four and five feet long, in thickness resembling a walking stick, bent at top like a Sheephook, and adorned with a human countenance. The fame of this Staff still echoes through the country round, like the bell of Kilronan, and the blessed Tree of All Saints, it can

(x) Comorban, Corba, Comorba (for it is variously read) signifies a Fellow Bishop — Wares Ant:qy.[225]
(y) This word is pronounced Garvally, Garvarry and some times Garbarry.

detect falshood and Perjury, and the wretch that is found wicked enough to swear falsely on the Garvally, is punished by having his face disfigured in a shocking manner, or in some other way that discovers his crime to all the world. The Garvally is still held in such high repute, that it is often sent for, from distant parts of the country, and never was known to fail, as the person to swear if guilty, flies, as none can be found bold enough to perjure themselves on Saint Barrys Staff.

These ruins cover a considerable space of ground, and is situated in the midst of a Village evidently built with the stones taken from the Churches, beautiful specimens of Sculpture frequently occurring in the walls of the cabins, the yard is surrounded by and thickly planted with trees, these prevent any distant view of the ruins, except within the yard, the Earl of Granard whose property it is, has caused these trees to be planted, which greatly adds to the picturesque beauty of the whole. The principal building is divided into two Chapels or Churches, the largest of them 33 by 11 feet, these th'o far gone in decay, still exhibit marks of former grandeur. The East window of the one above remarked, consisted of two Narrow lofty arches, the division considerably splayed on the inside; the whole ornamented within and without with rich carved work, which abounds throughout the ruins, many beautiful pieces of which, with the heads arms and shafts of Crosses lie scattered amidst the rubbish in every direction.

(Plate 1:[st]) Shows the North East Asp:[t] and is taken from near the West Gable of the double Church, and displays a general view of the ruins, as in it, part of all the other Churches may be seen. The yard and Churches were entirely surrounded by a wall part of which still remains: this view was taken by Dan:[l] Grose Jun:[r].

(Plate 2:[d]) Shows the North West Asp:[t] and brings in the principal building and the Mad House as it is termed, with its low doorway under which they say Saint Barry lies buried; the whole of this Church is overshadowed by large Elder trees, that grow within it, under the shelter of these at one end they have reared a small shed, roofed and thatched for the reception of Lunatics, who come for a cure; here a distant peep of the bog, with Lord Granards woods beyond, on the other side of the Shannon, may be had, between the Churches.

(Plate 3:[d]) Presents us with an inside view of the principal Church, showing through a breach in the wall part of the adjoining Chapel, and affords a beautiful glimps of the Shannon with the Mountain of Clanhugh rising in the distance.

The following dates are to be found on Tombstones in this Churchyard Viz:[t] 1508 and 1666.

## 86. Kilbarry 2 (Roscommon)

*In Grose's second view of Kilbarry, the main church can be seen at the left of the picture, with the artist in his blue jacket seated in line with the 'Mad House'. The latter had a lintelled doorway, but the dearth of architectural features makes it difficult to assess how old it was. This was where St Berach was reputed to be buried, his body lying 'half in and half out of the building'. The walls of this small oratory have now collapsed and the foundations are completely overgrown. It is now known locally as the 'Dark House'. Grose recounts that 'if any of the fair sex (to whom by the by St Barry appears to be no great friend) presumes even to enter it in her perfect senses, she immediately becomes mad and never by any art can be recovered again'. Grose provides a number of tales associated with Kilbarry, including one relating to the 'miraculous' crosier, which could 'detect falshood [sic] and Perjury'. This was the crosier of St Berach, purchased from its hereditary keeper by the Royal Irish Academy in 1863 and now preserved in the National Museum of Ireland.*

## 87. Kilbarry 3 (Roscommon)

*The presence of some Romanesque and Gothic carvings suggests that the architecture of Kilbarry was not as sparse and featureless as it initially appears. The principal church, now reduced to a couple of isolated walls, was lit by a pair of early Gothic lancets, shown in the third watercolour. The great crack at one side demonstrates that the ruins were in a precarious condition at the beginning of the nineteenth century, and almost everything shown in the picture has since collapsed. Kilbarry is thus a frustrating place for both the archaeologist and architectural historian. A considerable debt is owed to Daniel Grose for ensuring that the various churches, together with the local folklore, have not entirely vanished from the record.*

## 88. Miscellaneous Antiquities 4

*Two of the three carvings illustrated in this plate came from Kilbarry, but there is no sign of them there today. The stone decorated with interlaced animals and framed by lines of beading is a typical piece of Hiberno-Romanesque of about 1150-1200. Particularly distinctive are the figure of eight coils enveloping the two beasts, a motif which reflects the influence of Scandinavian 'Urnes' ornament. It is tantalising to learn that other stones, 'carved with equally strange devices' and commonly found during grave digging at Kilbarry, were tossed back into the ground. The drawing is sufficient to show that there was at least one church or cross at Kilbarry with high quality Romanesque carving. The second and much larger stone from the site, decorated with a standard late Gothic foliage pattern, can be assigned to about 1500. The third drawing, at the right, illustrates a remarkable late Gothic window or niche built into the east wall of the old church at Annaduff. The opening is now blocked by a mausoleum in the church behind. The original function of this arch, which is probably not in situ, is far from clear. The carved heads depict a king and queen and the gable is filled with Gothic foliage patterns. This fine piece of decorative carving is currently protected by a forest of nettles and brambles; close inspection cannot be undertaken without difficulty (and some pain).*

# Miscellaneous Antiquities (Plate 4:<sup>th</sup>).

(Fig:<sup>r</sup> 1) We have here a very curious Runic Knot found amongst the rubbish in the grave yard of Kilbarry, it is about 18 Inches square, but being partly buried in the ground, its thickness cannot be ascertained; it is hard to conjecture what it was, but from the small groove, in the upper corner, it appears to have composed part of some large piece of work, probably a copartment in the shaft of one of those crosses the heads of which lie scattered amongst these ruins; and we are told by the inhabitants of the surrounding Village, that in digging to make graves, many stones carved with equally strange devices are commonly found, these they pay no regard to, but throw them again into the earth.

It is well known that these Knots formed a favorite embelishment of the antients, a custom derived from the Danes, and there is scarsely a carved stone Cross, or other ornamental piece of Sculpture that is not adorned with one or more of these Runic Knots. The sculpture on this stone is highly raised and the design th'o so very complex may with little difficulty be made out, it represents two Sea Horses with their misshapen bodies strangely distorted and entwined together, and curiously interlaced with a knot of Ribbon which binds all their parts together.[226]

(Fig:<sup>r</sup> 2.) Represents a fragment of a Frize about three feet long, by one broad, found at the same place, the design is pretty and well executed, and is in high preservation.

(Fig:<sup>r</sup> 3) Is the very antient Window of Annaghduff Church, already alluded to in the description of that place, and appears to be part of the original building and of a stile rarely to be met with; the pillars that support the arch is upheld by two human heads wearing crowns, one that of a female, and the other a man with a beard. The rest of the ornaments are uncommonly well executed and alth'o not multiplied, has a grand effect, the whole is in tollerable good preservation. These 3 Figures were drawn from Sketches by Dan:<sup>l</sup> Grose Jun:<sup>r</sup>.

# Appendix:

Order of monuments as given in the original manuscript,
with original page numbers.

# Notes to the Text of Daniel Grose

The following notes are not intended to give complete bibliographical references to all the monuments mentioned by Daniel Grose. They are intended to alert the reader to the more blatant errors in the text and to provide some guide to the latest scholarly publications.

1. This comment appears to refer to Mourne (Cork), sometimes referred to as Mona, Gwynn and Hadcock (1970), 338.

2. It is difficult to know what Grose had in mind. The medieval cathedral at Elgin retains its two western towers in good vertical alignment. The crossing tower fell in 1711, long before Grose's time, Mackintosh and Richardson (1980), 43. When discussing Elgin, Francis Grose's *Antiquities of Scotland* (1789-91), II, 273-7, makes no reference to a leaning tower.

3. The Reverend Edward Ledwich, vicar of Aghaboe, who died in 1823. He was the author of the *Antiquities of Ireland* (Dublin, 1790) and wrote the text of Francis Grose's *Antiquities of Ireland* (London, 1791-5).

4. When Daniel Grose was a young man there was widespread interest in the voyages of Captain Cook, for which see Smith (1985).

5. The author is referring to William Wilberforce (1759-1833) and the abolition of slavery.

6. Grose is repeating one of the favourite antiquarian interpretations of dolmens, for a modern interpretation of which see Harbison (1988) and O'Kelly (1989).

7. The standing stone is at Broadleas (Kildare), *The Shell Guide*, 102. The paragraph has been taken from Edward Ledwich's 'Introduction to the Pagan Antiquities of Ireland' in Grose (1791-5), I, vi.

8. *Genesis*, XXXI, 46.

9. The Firbolgs or Fir Bholgs were one of the legendary peoples who invaded Ireland in prehistoric times; they are described in the pseudo-history known as *Leabhar Gabhala Eireann, The Book of The Conquest of Ireland* or the *Book of Invasions*, compiled in the twelfth century, MacCana (1983), 54-8. This passage is based on Ledwich (1790), 9-10, and Grose (1791-5), I, iv and II, iii.

10. Grose (1791-5), I, ix-x, xiii-xiv.

11. This paragraph is taken from Smith (1750), II, 403-4.

12. William Bennison evidently lived at Cairn House, a few miles south-east of Ballyconnell (Cavan). The Ordnance Survey notes for 1833 record a Mr John Bennison, High Constable of Cairn House (information from Mr Tom Barron of Virginia via Raghnall Ó Floinn).

13. The following section on sepulchres is from Ware (1764), II, 145-6.

14. Daniel's information about Samuel Hayes, who was M.P. for Wicklow and lived nearby at Avondale, comes from Ledwich's introduction to Grose (1791-5), II, vi.

15. The complex history of this sculpture, in particular the issue of whether the stone was intact or not in the eighteenth century, is discussed by Barrow (1972), 33-7 and McNab (1986), 354-5, 362. The stone was also illustrated in Ledwich (1790), plate II, p.39, where a different explanation of the iconography is provided: 'The one in the middle is a Bishop or Priest sitting in a chair, and holding a Penitential in his hand. On the right a Pilgrim leans on his staff, and on the left, a young man holds a purse of money to commute the penance'.

16. This is a reference to the 'Priests' House', Leask (Glendalough, n.d.), 18-20. The curious external arch at the east end of this building is clearly a late (eighteenth century?) concoction.

17. Such wooden effigies in fact date from the thirteenth and fourteenth centuries, A.C. Fryer (1924). Daniel is citing Grose (1773-6).

18. On several occasions Daniel mistook a lion for a dog. As a symbol of courage, the lion was normally found at the foot of knight effigies. For a modern discussion of medieval Irish tomb sculpture see Hunt (1974).

19. This slab is now at Ballymore Eustace (Kildare), Hunt (1974), I, 153. Daniel Grose described and illustrated the sculpture in *The Irish Penny Magazine*, I, no. 47 (Nov 23rd 1833), 373-4. There is also a sketch of the tomb by Daniel Grose, dated July 21st 1792, in the National Library of Ireland, Ms. 1976 TX, no.7.

20. Hunt (1974), I, 171-2.

21. Raymond le Gros died between 1189 and 1200 and both he and his wife bequeathed their bodies to the abbey of St Thomas, Dublin, Orpen (1911-20), II, 42. For Raymond's supposed connection with Molana see Gwynn and Hadcock (1970), 187. Daniel Grose's drawing was known to the Reverend Samuel Hayman, (1880), 342. Unfortunately Hayman does not tell us where he saw the drawing. He was incumbent of the parish of Douglas (Cork), which may be a clue.

22. The notion that crossed legs indicate a memorial to a crusader is a widespread, popular fiction, Tummers (1980), 117-126.

23. The tomb at Roscommon was described at greater length by Daniel Grose in the *Irish Penny Magazine*, II, no. 37 (Sep. 14th 1833), 293-4. For a modern account see Hunt, (1974), I, 216-7.

24. Hunt (1974), 130.

25. Daniel Grose has placed the introduction of brasses somewhat early. Brass was first used for inscriptions, and monumental brass images remained rare until the fourteenth century, P. Binski, 'Monumental Brasses' in Alexander and Binski (1987), 171-3.

26. There are four brasses of sixteenth-century date in St Patrick's Cathedral, Bernard (1903), 58-61.

27. The cadaver effigies in the churchyard of St Peter's Drogheda come from a tomb commemorating Sir Edmond Goldyng and his wife Elizabeth Flemyng, c.1500-25, Roe (1969), 15.

28. This passage refers to the late-Gothic sedilia at Holycross, which has an ornate canopy or (to use Grose's term) 'festoon', Stalley (1987), 200-2.

29. Grose appears to have had English canopied tombs of the seventeenth century in mind.

30. A watercolour of the upper section of the tomb at Newtown Trim, painted by Daniel Grose, is preserved in the National Library of Ireland, Ms. 1976 TX, no. 18. The design of the tomb is described by Jocelyn (1973), 153-66; see also Hunt (1974), I, 262 and Loeber (1981), 286, where the date 1586 is given for the tomb.

31. Grose is about a century too early in his date, see note 30.

32. *Anthologia Hibernica*, II (August 1793), 81-3. The Donadea tomb commemorates Sir Gerald Aylmer (d. 1634) and his wife Dame Julia Nugent (d. 1617), *The Shell Guide* (1967), 372; Loeber (1981), 275, suggests that it was from the same workshop as the O Conor tomb in Sligo. Grose has mistaken the date of Dame Julia's death with the date of the manufacture of the tomb.

33. Grose took the inscription from Smith (1750), I, 124, complete with errors. The correct reading is as follows: Here lieth anciently enterred the boddies of Richard Bennet and Ellis Barry, his wyfe, the first fovnders of this chapple, which being demolished in time of Rebellion, and their Tombe defaced, was reedified by Richard Lord Boyle, Barron of Yoghall who for reviving the memory of them, repaired their tombe, and had Tils Fi..........Rescve......in AN DNI 1619.. (the final part of the inscription is defaced). The tomb is attributed to Alexander Hills by Loeber (1981), 287.

34. The patronage of the Earl of Cork is discussed by Anne Crookshank (1971), 1288-90, from which the quotations in the caption are taken. The tomb is also discussed by Potterton (1975), 7, and Loeber (1981), 287.

35. Rather than a coronet, it is simply the Earl's hair swept back.

36. The inscriptions are gilded on black marble, not engraved on copper.

37. Grose has copied the inscriptions (incorrectly) from Smith (1750), I, 119-120. Smith also gives an extensive description, 121-3. The miniature figures have often been rearranged and specific identifications with members of the family are difficult to establish. The tomb was restored by the Duke of Devonshire in 1848, as indicated by an inscription on the outer southern edge of the monument.

38. It is in fact the medieval parish church.

39. The tomb is described at length in *Mainistir Shligigh, Sligo Abbey: Historical and Descriptive Notes on the Dominican Friary of Sligo* (Dublin, Stationary Office, n.d.).

40. The 'female figure' is identified as St Paul in the official guide, *Ibid*.

41. The discovery of the font and its removal to England is described by Rogers (1888), 129-131.

42. Grose's account of the history appears to be incorrect. He may be following Smith (1750), I, 250, who claims it was 'built by an Irish sept called O Shaghnassy'. For more modern accounts see Fuller (1907), 18 and Healy (1988), 290-2.

43. The friary may have been founded by a member of the Barry family, Gwynn and Hadcock (1970), 259-60.

44. Evidently a reference to the Irish word *cluaisíní*, meaning small shell fish, scallops, oysters etc.

45. The castle is described at some length in Healy (1988), 140-2. Kill-na-tworagh is presumably derived from *Cill na tourig*, i.e. church of the river Tourig.

46. Grose is taking his history from Archdall (1786), 81-2. For a recent historical summary see Gwynn and Hadcock (1970), 231.

47. Grose has confused the Franciscan friary with the medieval parish church of St Mary. Much of what Grose has to say about the church comes from Smith (1750), I, 118.

48. The Boyle monument was erected during the reign of James I in 1620.

49. There are 'atlas' figures on the exterior angle of the north transept.

50. The history and architecture of the church at Youghal are discussed in Leask (1955-60), II, 153-4 and III, 113; Gwynn and Hadcock (1970), 362. The chancel was re-roofed in the nineteenth century;

51. it was still open to the sky when seen by Lewis (1837), II, 729.

51. Grose took his information about the friary from Smith (1750), 117 and Archdall (1786), 81.

52. This is a popular local myth, without historical foundation.

53. *The Shell Guide* (1967), 462-3, gives the date of the clock tower as 1771. See also Craig (1982), 203.

54. The town walls are described by Buckley (1900), 156-61.

55. This is a reference to Tynte's Castle, Cockburn (n.d.), 20-1.

56. The next lines are taken from Smith (1750), I, 90-3.

57. For details of these buildings see Cockburn (n.d.) and Craig (1982), 203.

58. The castle at Two Mile Water, better known as Cornaveigh, is discussed by Healy (1988), 127. I am grateful to Tom and Mary Gibbons of Cornaveigh for helping me to locate the castle.

59. Wickerwork centering is explained by Leask (1964), 86-7.

60. Grose's etymology is suspect. Cornaveigh is likely to be derived from *Cor na bhFiach* (the ravens place), Healy (1988), 127.

61. The architecture of Mount Long is discussed at greater length by Craig (1982), 128. For the history of the house see Healy (1988), 278-9 and Fuller (1907), 16. The quotation given in the commentary comes from a letter of Tristram Whetcombe (1642) and is cited by Fuller (1907), 8.

62. This paragraph is taken verbatim from Smith (1750), I, 218.

63. The castle is discussed by Healy (1988), 269-70, who gives a different version of its history.

64. Grose has taken his information about a Carmelite friary from Smith (1750), I, 219. The friary was founded in 1314, long after the age of St Gobban, Gwynn and Hadcock (1970), 290.

65. *The Shell Guide* (1967), 343; Healy (1988), 286-7.

66. The next few lines are taken from Smith (1750), I, 241-2.

67. There are recent accounts of Charles Fort by Kerrigan (1977-9), 323-38 and Craig (1982), 161. There is also an excellent *Visitors' Guide* issued by the National Parks and Monuments Service of the Office of Public Works (1988).

68. The castle at Temple Michael is described in the Ordnance Survey Letters, Waterford, 156 (Royal Irish Academy). There are further details about its history in Redmond (1919), 94-7.

69. Grose appears to have misquoted Ware, who makes it clear that a cott was a boat 'formed out of an Oak, wrought hollow', Ware (1764), II, 180-1.

70. Gwynn and Hadcock (1970), 342, 327-8, give a brief historical outline of Rincrew and discuss the fate of the Templars in 1312 (not 1314).

71. Grose's account is dependent on Archdall (1786), 688, and Smith (1746), 88-9, where the account of the wooden centering is to be found. The friary is covered in Gwynn and Hadcock (1970), 46. The tower house is mentioned by Lewis (1837), I, 580.

72. Grose is here describing the 1780s block. For an account of Dromana see Bence-Jones (1978), 108-9.

73. After the death of George Mason Villiers in 1800, the Earl of Grandison did not reside permanently at Dromana until Henry Villiers-Stuart returned with his bride in 1826, as explained by de Breffny and ffolliott (1975), 190-1. This suggests that Grose made his visit between 1800 and 1826. I am grateful to Patrick Villiers-Stuart for advising me about the history of Dromana.

74. For a recent discussion of the sculpture at Tuam see Stalley (1981), 179-95.

75. Grose is evidently referring to Usher's Discourse of 1622, for a general account of which see *NHI*, III, 229, 567-8.

76. The account of St Jarlath is taken largely from Ware (1764), I, 602-3.

77. Grose is about 600 years too early in his dating, a point he might have realised if he had been able to read the inscriptions on the Tuam crosses, for which see Petrie (1850-3), 474.

78. The account of St Ciaran is taken from Archdall (1786), 380. For the history and associations of the various churches see Ryan, *Clonmacnois* (n.d.).

79. Archdall (1786), 379-92.

80. The next section is taken from Archdall (1786), 388.

81. This is from Archdall (1786), 386.

82. This church is now generally known as Temple Finghin. Grose's measurement of the round tower (seven feet) is correct, Barrow (1979), 177.

83. Grose is probably referring to the Norman castle beside the monastery, which was founded in 1216 by the justiciar John de Gray, bishop of Norwich.

84. An ancient name for Clonmacnoise was *Cluain Tiobraide* (meadow of the well). Grose is mistaken in thinking that *Cluain* signified a lurking place. *Cluain moccu Nóis* means literally 'meadow of the race of Nós', as Ware seemed to appreciate.

85. This house is described by Bence-Jones (1978), 86.

86. Grose was correct in thinking that this arch was the former chancel arch.

87. It is unclear what Grose is referring to here — possibly the remains of the Romanesque nave or the incomplete Gothic transepts. Some of the foundations of the latter were recently uncovered, Clyne (1987-8), 90-103. The Gothic choir of c.1312 is discussed by Leask (1955-60), II, 131-2.

88. The arches were the three former east windows of the Romanesque chancel, which are decorated with intricate sculpture. The whitewash no longer remains, confirming the suspicion that the sculptures were 'scraped' in 1861-3, Stalley (1981), 180-1.

89. The inscription was salvaged when the tower was being demolished and the Very Reverend James Grant informs me it is now in the Synod Hall.

90. The memorial tablet is not to the Dean of Tuam, Robert Echlin (1686-1721), but to his son John (1680-1763).

91. This gable is all that remains of 'Temple Jarlath', the remnants of a Premonstratensian house dedicated to the Holy Trinity, Gwynn and Hadcock (1970), 206.

92. Grose shows the arch blocked, apart from a small window. A lithograph in the National Library of Ireland (IR 7266 t 2) shows a doorway inserted under the arch, presumably a later alteration.

93. Not all the responds are circular in form.

94. Ledwich, 'An Introduction to Ancient Irish Architecture' in Grose, (1791-5), i-xiii.

95. The architecture of Manorhamilton is discussed by Craig (1982), 117, and Lewis (1837), II, 342. The quotation about the exploits and fate of Sir Frederick Hamilton is taken from the *Ordnance Survey Letters* (Royal Irish Academy), Cavan and Leitrim, 257, for which also see Borlase (1680), 88.

96. The castle at Rathcline has been inadequately published. The evidence for renovations in 1666-7 is given in Loeber (1981), 51, 77, 113.

97. The churches of Inchcleraun are described at length by Bigger (1900), 69-89.

98. For the life of St Diarmaid and the history of Inchcleraun, Grose relied on Archdall (1786), 440-1. For a more reliable modern survey see Gwynn and Hadcock (1970), 178.

99. This church is known as *Clogás an Oileáin*, for which see Bigger (1900), 81-3.

100. The quaker was a Mr Fairbrother, who presumably owned the island in the eighteenth century.

101. The history is taken from Archdall (1786), 441-2. For a modern account see Gwynn and Hadcock (1970), 193-4.

102. The importance of the architecture of this small house of Augustinian canons has tended to be overlooked and references in the literature are generally brief.

103. Two barrel-vaulted chambers, originally part of the west range, still survive.

104. Today there is no obvious trace of the stump of the stone cross or the remains of the 'porter's lodge'.

105. The churches on Inisbofin are described by Crawford (1917), 139-52.

106. Here Grose is referring to the Romanesque window, which is not shown in the paintings. The surrounding decoration was thinly incised and its appearance is not the result of excessive weathering.

107. There is no evidence to suggest there was a south transept as well as a north transept.

108. This paragraph on the history of Inisbofin is taken from Archdall (1786), 44. For a recent account see Gwynn and Hadcock (1970), 37, 199.

109. The identification of the ecclesiastical sites at Rindown is highly confused. According to Gwynn and Hadcock (1970), 215-6, a priory of St John the Baptist, belonging to the Knights Cruciferi, was situated about 200 yards north-west of the castle, but *The Shell Guide* (1967), 346, identifies this with the ruined church and graveyard at the north-west end of the peninsula, close to the farmhouse. Gwynn and Hadcock (1970), 207 also describe a Premonstratensian church of the Holy Trinity, the site of which remains unclear. Bradley (1985), 453, refers to a parish church of St Leonard. The remains to the south-west of the castle, illustrated by Grose, belong to a simple nave and chancel church, the standard form for a medieval parish church.

110. Archdall (1786), 617. The reference to Loughree is a mistake for Lough Key, Gwynn and Hadcock (1970), 205, 207.

111. Rindown Castle awaits a full survey and publication. There are brief discussions of the site in FitzPatrick (1935), 177-90, Claffey (1978), 11-14, Stalley (1978), 41-3, Barry (1987), 173-5.

112. Grose is here referring to the town wall which closes off the peninsula several hundred yards to the north-west of the castle.

113. The tower may have belonged to a windmill.

114. The section on the history of Rindown is taken from Archdall (1786), 617.

115. The siege of Clonmel is described in *NHI*, III, 347 and Borlase (1688), 230.

116. Grose was wrong in thinking a permanent Dominican friary existed at Clonmel, Gwynn and Hadcock (1970), 220, 232-3. Grose

confused the Franciscan friary with the parish church. His information about the friary came from Archdall (1786), 653. The ruins of the friary were incorporated into a complete rebuilding by W.G. Doolin, *The Shell Guide* (1967), 173.

117. It is no surprise that Grose could not find conventual buildings because he was looking at the parish church, not the Franciscan friary, as he thought. The history of the church is discussed at length in Burke (1907), 263-298.

118. The Roscrea cross is discussed by Henry (1970), 127-30, and McNab (1986), 430-5. The cross may be associated with Roscrea's claims for a bishopric in the twelfth century, Gwynn and Hadcock (1970), 95-6.

119. There is a brief comment about the Castle at Castletownbere in Lewis (1837) I, 307.

120. The account of the siege of Dunboy is taken almost word for word from Smith (1750), II, 86-90. There are a few mispellings and minor alterations.

121. The stone circle at Derreenataggart West is published by Ó Nualláin (1984), 20. For stone circles in general see Harbison (1988), 94-8.

122. Grose (1791-5), I, vi, and Ledwich (1790), 323-5.

123. During the Napoleonic Wars Bearhaven was an important anchorage for the British fleet.

124. The etymologies of Vallancey, here quoted by Grose, are suspect. Like several of the early antiquaries, Vallancey was excited by the notion of fire and sun worship. *'Ardagha'* in fact means 'high field'.

125. This appears to be an aural translation of *Taitníonn an ghrian ann* (the sun shines there); to non-Irish speakers *ghrian ann* would have sounded like *greanane* or *grianán* (the latter meaning a sunny spot, summer house or peak of a mountain).

126. The possible functions of standing stones are described by Harbison (1988), 96.

127. Ledwich in Grose (1791-5), I, vi.

128. The Druids' altar described by Grose is the wedge tomb at Ardaragh West, de Valera and Ó Nualláin, IV (1982), 36-7, Westropp (1921), 15-16. Wedge tombs are discussed in O'Kelly (1989), 115-22 and Harbison (1988), 100-2.

129. This is the so-called septal stone.

130. This is the original roof stone of the main chamber.

131. There are two martello towers on Bear Island, at Cloughalin and Ardigh, Enoch (n.d.).

132. During the Napoleonic era, signal stations were erected along the west coast, on the cliffs of Moher, Clare Island, Slieve League (Donegal) etc. The architecture of these square towers follows medieval traditions, even to the extent of their having bartizans.

133. The nineteenth-century Protestant parish church at Kilmore is now a ruin. It incorporated an older tower, Mitchell (1989), 91. According to Lewis (1837), II, 673, it was erected about 1815.

134. There is an aerial view of the fort in Mitchell (1989), 108; its design is discussed briefly by Kerrigan (1980-1), 135. For the reference to its construction in 1651 see S.M. (1914-16), 253 (Ballycarbery).

135. In discussing Valencia Island, which is in County Kerry, Grose appears to have confused Smith's volumes on Cork and Kerry. Mitchell (1989), 109, remarks that Smith does not appear to have visited Valencia Island.

136. According to *The Shell Guide* (1967), 452, the proper name of the island is *Oileán Dairbhre*. The name Valencia is an anglicisation of *Béal Inse*, the name of the adjoining sound.

137. I am grateful to the Cork Archaeological Survey and to Dr Ann Lynch for the suggestion that the stone circle described by Grose was that at Curraduff.

138. The reference is to the circle at Derreenataggart West.

139. Ware (1764), I, 583. *Ross* means wood, wooded headland, or headland.

140. Also quoted by Smith (1750), I, 219. The lines come from the fourth book of *The Faerie Queene*, canto XI, verse xliv, R. Heffner, ed., *The Faerie Queene* (Baltimore, 1935), 148. For the connection between the poet and Kilbeg see Henley (1928), 204.

141. Bence-Jones (1978), 62.

142. Healy (1988), 265 gives more details about Kilbeg.

143. There are brief accounts of Castle Conna, which is a National Monument, in Harbison (1970), 53 and *The Shell Guide* (1967), 434.

144. There is an extensive account of Ballycarbery Castle in S.M. (1914-16), 243-59. The quotation in the commentary about the strategic importance of the castle is cited on page 256.

145. S.M. (1914-16) mentions the 'ruins of a comparatively modern two-storeyed house' said to have been the residence of the Lauder family.

146. Grose may be thinking of Staigue Fort, seven miles south-west of Sneam.

147. There are three forts nearby at Leacanabuaile, Cloghanecarhan and Cahergall, Harbison (1970), 107.

148. A diet based predominantly on potatoes was uncommon in the eighteenth century, and, except for the very poor, it remained a subsidiary foodstuff. As the population grew in the early nineteenth century, dependence on the potato increased, especially among cottiers and those living in remote areas, Cullen (1968), 122-3.

149. Grose's information about the monastery is taken virtually word for word from Archdall (1786), 587.

150. Bence-Jones (1978), 1, gives a historical summary of the house.

151. This is not quite true, as there is the fine tomb of Malachy O'More, Hunt (1974), 198-9.

152. The castle at Cloghan lay in Castle Street, on the site of the old barracks, as indicated on the 6 inch Ordnance Survey Map. Brief references to the history of the castle will be found in Cooke (1875), 328-30, and Mac Cuarta (1987), 172, 176.

153. For William Bennison see note 12.

154. The dimensions and decoration of figure 3, a bronze Y-shaped pendant or leading piece, corresponds with a hitherto unprovenanced example in the National Museum of Ireland (Reg. no. W 157). It is illustrated in Raftery (1983), No. 158, fig. 57.

155. This is a link and one ring of a bronze snaffle bit of Iron Age type, its dimensions corresponding with an incomplete bit in the National Museum of Ireland (Reg. no. W 76), Raftery (1983), No. 37, fig. 16.

156. This paragraph is taken from Ledwich's introduction to Grose (1791-5), I, xxix.

157. Ledwich in Grose (1791-5), I, xxx.

158. The sculpture is on the west side of the north transept, Stalley (1987), 198.

159. Here Grose is quoting Ledwich in Grose (1791-5), II, vii.

160. Strancally Castle is discussed by Redmond (1919), 21-4, 91-4 and *The Shell Guide* (1967), 137. There is an engraving of the castle from the north in Grose (1791-5) II, 37. The watercolour from which it was taken is in Royal Irish Academy, 3C 29, no. 57. There is a different view in the National Library of Ireland, 1976 TX, no 133.

161. Ware (1764), II, 39. Contrary to Grose, O'Rahilly (1946), 4, identifies the Daurone (or Dabrona) with the river Lee rather than the Blackwater. *Aven-mór* (or *Abhann Mhór*, i.e. great river) is, however, likely to refer to the Blackwater.

162. *Annals of Loch Cé*, I, 471. For a bibliography on Rindown see note 111.

163. The preceding paragraph is taken from Ledwich's introduction to Grose (1791-5), I, xxxiv.

164. The reference is to the 'Meeting of the Waters' by Thomas Moore (1779-1852), *Irish Melodies, Thomas Moore* (London, 1834, 12th edition), 19.

165. *The Shell Guide* (1967), 395, dates the castle to c.1770. David Newman Johnson has pointed out that this is misleading, for as well as the archaeological evidence to the contrary, there is documentary evidence of a medieval castle here, belonging in the sixteenth century to a branch of the O'Byrnes. I am very grateful to David Newman Johnson for assisting me with the history of Kiltimon.

166. There appear to be remnants of four bartizans.

167. The history of Newtown Mount Kennedy is outlined by Bence-Jones (1978), 215. Lewis (1837), II, 441, explains how 'the late' General Cunningham, who was afterwards raised to the peerage as Baron Rossmore, expended upwards of £60,000 on plantations and improvements.

168. Coemgen is the old Irish version of Kevin. Grose has taken his information on St Kevin from Archdall (1786), 765. For a recent account of the early life of the saint see Barrow (1972).

169. The whole of the following account about the miracles of St Kevin is taken word for word from Ledwich (1790), 35-7.

170. This account of dogs and serpents is taken from Ledwich (1790), 38. *Philibeg* is another word for a kilt.

171. Ledwich in Grose (1791-5), II, viii and Ledwich (1790), 43-4. For a more recent account of the sculptures at Glendalough see Barrow (1972), 32-7 and Leask, Glendalough (n.d.), *passim*.

172. A more general view of Fenagh appeared in volume II of the *Antiquities*, Grose (1791-5), II, 62. The east window, the 'beautiful specimen of gothic workmanship', is dated by Leask (1955-60), II, 148-9, to the fourteenth century, though he admits it could be later. A date in the fifteenth century seems more likely.

173. The history of Fenagh is summarised in Gwynn and Hadcock (1970), 36.

174. The monument commemorates John Peyton (d. 1741) and his wife Jane Molloy (d. 1710) and Mrs Mary Taylor alias Reynolds (d.1731).

175. The birth of John the Baptist is celebrated on June 24th, his death on August 29th.

176. The story of Dairmaid and Grainne is told in Mac Cana (1983), 109-12.

177. The account of Labbacallee wedge tomb is taken from Smith (1750), I, 356 and II, 409-10. For more recent accounts see Leask and Price (1936), 77-101 and de Valera and Ó Nualláin (1982), 2-3.

178. The portal tomb at Fenagh Beg is described by de Valera and Ó Nualláin (1972), 73-4. For portal tombs in general see Harbison (1988), 52-6 and O'Kelly (1989), 92-7.

179. Cromlech was the old term for dolmen, a type of monument for which the terminology has been further refined, wedge tomb, portal tomb etc. *Crom* means crooked or bent and *leac* means flagstone. The notion that cromlech means the stone of bowing is a spurious etymology.

180. Grose (1791-5), I, vi-vii.

181. Letterfyan appears to be a reference to Letterfine, just over a mile west of Keshcarrigan on the road from Carrick-on-Shannon to Fenagh.

182. According to de Valera and Ó Nualláin (1972), 73-4, the chamber is 2.40 metres in length.

183. This comment, which is incorrect, is taken from the commentary in Grose (1791-5), II, 79, where Grandison is illustrated by an engraving showing the castle from the east.

184. The quotation is from Goldsmith's *Deserted Village*, lines 237-8, A. Friedman, ed., *Collected Works of Oliver Goldsmith*, IV (Oxford, 1966), 296. I am grateful to Professor John Scattergood for identifying it for me.

185. Grandison has been considered at length by Duggan (1991). For earlier accounts see Maher (1934), 50-1, Lanigan (1960), 29-31, *The Shell Guide* (1967), 457 and Harbison (1970), 131.

186. Duggan (1991) has argued that the hall was erected by Piers Ruadh Butler, the 8th Earl of Ormond (1515-1539).

187. Following the collapse of the keep or tower about 1823, it was restored at the expense of George Roche in 1827, as recorded on a plaque fixed to the west wall.

188. The sculptures can be compared with tomb carvings at Mothel (Waterford), Cashel (Tipperary) and Athboy (Meath), Hunt (1974), 233-4, 221-2 and 202-4.

189. Grose has taken his (irrelevant) information about the Augustinian priory from Archdall (1786), 335; for a recent summary of the house see Gwynn and Hadcock (1970), 189.

190. Grose's comments about Elfeet are anachronistic. The castle dates to the fifteenth century, at least four hundred years after the Vikings had ceased to be a threat.

191. A closer view of the castle was given in the first volume of the *Antiquities*, where there is also a brief account of the history of the castle, Grose (1791-5), I, 75-6. For further information see Lewis (1837), I, 261, Leask (1964), 37-9, Harbison (1970), 33, and Stalley (1971), 49.

192. The Cistercian monastery of Assaroe, Stalley (1987), 242.

193. This leaf-shaped sword can be identified as one of Eogan's class 4; a comparable arrangement of rivet holes can be seen on a sword in private posssession, Eogan (1965), No. 470, fig. 61.

194. Most of what follows is taken from Ware (1764), II, 58 and Archdall (1786), 14-30. For a modern summary of the history of Armagh see Gwynn and Hadcock (1970), 59-60.

195. The history of the fabric of the cathedral is discussed by Rogers (1888).

196. There is a brief history of the Franciscan friary (not nunnery) in Gwynn and Hadcock (1970), 242 and a more extensive account in Lynn (1975), 61-80.

197. The fact that Grose claims that many residents of Armagh did not know where the friary was situated suggests he visited Armagh in person and had to ask for directions.

198. For the identification of the site of Lottery castle and the information given in the accompanying commentary to the watercolour I am grateful to Mr Cecil English.

199. The Cistercian monastery of Abbeyshrule, Stalley (1987), 241.

200. As so often, Grose's etymologies seem far-fetched.

201. Grose was misled in his date for the north gate of Athlone, for which see Murtagh (1980), 92-3.

202. The monks of Athlone were given a tithe of the expenses of the castle in exchange for giving up land on which the castle was situated, *CDI*, I, 507, 508; see also Gwynn and Hadcock (1970), 110.

203. There is a brief account of Bethlem in *The Shell Guide* (1967), 78. See also Bagwell (1909), I, 323-6. An article on Bethlem by Liam Cox was published in *The Westmeath-Offaly Independent* for Friday 25th December 1981, p. 7. I am grateful to Mrs Jennifer Strevens for bringing this article to my notice and for helping me with other matters relating to Bethlem.

204. I am grateful to the staff of the Lough Rynn estate for furnishing me with information about the castle.

205. Letterfine House.

206. It appears to have been a parish church, not an abbey, Gwynn and Hadcock (1970), 366. Archdall (1786), 290-1, mistakenly assumes it was an abbey.

207. The Protestant parish church, which is still in good repair, was erected with the aid of a grant from the Board of First Fruits in 1788, Lewis (1837), II, 203.

208. Kilronan Castle or Castle Tenison, for which see Bence-Jones (1978), 176.

209. Grose is incorrect in thinking that the arch was decorated with heads. There is in fact a series of alternating cylindrical blocks.

210. *The Shell Guide* (1967), 95, reports that the skull of Carolan, who died in 1738, was displayed in a niche in the churchyard in the later eighteenth century.

211. This bell is not listed in the corpus of early Irish hand bells, Bourke (1980), 52-66. Dr Bourke informs me that he has not hitherto encountered references to this example.

212. The festival on 8th September at St Lasair's well was cancelled in the 1930s by the local parish priest, as it had become an occasion for too much drinking. It has recently been revived as a religious festival (information from Hugh Gibbons). The 'vibrating stone' or 'tolmen' is still regarded as a cure for back pains.

213. On this point Grose has been misled by Archdall (1786), 290-1. See note 206.

214. The ruins at Molana are described at length by Power (1932), 142-52. For a modern summary of its history see Gwynn and Hadcock (1970), 187.

215. The preceding historical section is taken from Ware (1764), I, 583.

216. Archdall (1786), 695.

217. The parish church was built with the aid of a loan of £1,600 in 1815, Lewis (1837), I, 28.

218. The reference to the grotesque heads at the angle of the roof appears to be a mistake. There are no such heads on the old church at Annaduff, but there are some at Fenagh, the building that Grose probably had in mind.

219. Gwynn and Hadcock (1970), 28, record the deaths of abbots of Annaduff in 767 and 792.

220. The Royal Canal reached Cloondara in 1817, Delany and Delany (1966), 86.

221. Archdall (1786), 438.

222. The account of the word 'Tarmon' is taken from Ware (1764), II, 233. In Irish the meaning of *termon* is, strictly speaking, a place of protection, equivalent to *terminus ad quem*, the boundary beyond which the law could not follow. In Roman religion the God 'Terminus' was associated with boundary marks.

223. St Barry is St Berach, the founder of the monastery, Gwynn and Hadcock (1970), 38. There is a discussion of the site in Barrow (1979), 179-80, where the evidence for the round tower, which fell in the 1770s, is given in detail.

224. The crosier of St Berach, known as *Gearr Beraich*, Crawford (1923), 171.

225. Here Grose misquotes Ware, who realised that *comarb* or *comharba* means successor to the founder, Ware (1764), II, 232.

226. The stone illustrated by Grose is of great interest since it is carved in the so-called Irish-Urnes style, for which see Stalley (1981), 184-8.

# Bibliography

ALEXANDER and BINSKI (1987): J.J.G. Alexander and P. Binski, eds., *Age of Chivalry* (London).

ARCHDALL (1786): M. Archdall, *Monasticon Hibernicum* (Dublin).

BAGWELL (1909-16): R. Bagwell, *Ireland under the Stuarts and during the interregnum* (London).

BARRELL (1980): J. Barrell, *The Dark Side of the Landscape* (Cambridge).

BARROW (1972): G.L. Barrow, *Glendalough and St Kevin* (Dundalk).

BARROW (1979): G.L. Barrow, *The Round Towers of Ireland* (Dublin).

BARRY (1987): T.B. Barry, *The Archaeology of Medieval Ireland* (London).

BENCE-JONES (1978): M. Bence-Jones, *Burke's Guide to Country Houses, I, Ireland* (London).

BERNARD (1903): J.H. Bernard, *The Cathedral Church of St Patrick* (London).

BIGGER (1900): F.J. Bigger, 'Inis Chlothrann (Inis Cleraun), Lough Ree: Its History and Antiquities', *Journal of the Royal Society of Antiquaries of Ireland*, XX, 69-90.

BORLASE (1680): J. Borlase, *The History of the Execrable Irish Rebellion* (London).

BOURKE (1980): C. Bourke, 'Early Irish Hand Bells', *Journal of the Royal Society of Antiquaries of Ireland*, CX, 52-66.

BRADLEY (1985): J. Bradley, 'Planned Ango-Norman Towns in Ireland', *The Comparative History of Urban Origins in Non-Roman Europe*, ed., H.B. Clarke and A. Simms (Oxford), 411-67.

BUCKLEY (1900): M.J.C. Buckley, 'The town wall of Youghal', *Journal of the Cork Historical and Archaeological Society*, VI, 156-61.

BURKE (1907): W.P. Burke, *History of Clonmel* (Waterford).

*CDI: Calendar Of Documents Relating to Ireland*, ed., H.S. Sweetman (London 1875-86).

CLAFFEY (1978): J.A. Claffey, 'Medieval Rindoon', *Journal of the Old Athlone Society*, II, no. 5, 11-14.

CLYNE (1987-8): M. Clyne, Excavations at St Mary's Cathedral, Tuam, Co. Galway', *Journal of the Galway Archaeological and Historical Society*, XLI, 90-103.

COCKBURN (n.d.): C. Cockburn, *Tourist Trail. A signposted Walking Tour of Youghal, Co. Cork* (Cork).

CONNER (1984): P. Conner, *Michael Angelo Rooker* (London).

COOKE (1875): T.L. Cooke, *The Early History of the Town of Birr* (Dublin).

CRAIG (1947): M. Craig, "Ken ye aught o' Captain Grose?", *Irish Book Lover*, XXX (Nov. 1947), 56-8.

CRAWFORD (1917): H.S. Crawford, 'The Churches and Monuments of Inis Bo Finne, County Westmeath', *Journal of the Royal Society of Antiquaries of Ireland*, XLVII, 139-52.

CRAWFORD (1923): H.S. Crawford, 'A Descriptive List of Irish Shrines and Reliquaries - II', *Journal of the Royal Society of Antiquaries of Ireland*, LIII, 151-76.

CROOKSHANK (1971): A.O. Crookshank, 'Lord Cork and his Monuments', *Country Life* (May 27th).

CROOKSHANK and GLIN (1978): A.O. Crookshank and the Knight of Glin, *The Painters of Ireland* (London).

CULLEN (1968): L.M. Cullen, *Life in Ireland* (London).

DE BREFFNY and FFOLLIOTT (1975): B. de Breffny and R. ffolliott, *The Houses of Ireland* (London).

DE VALERA and Ó NUALLÁIN (1972): R. de Valera and S. Ó Nualláin, *Survey of the Megalithic Tombs of Ireland*, III (Dublin).

DE VALERA and Ó NUALLÁIN (1982): R. de Valera and S. Ó Nualláin, *Survey of the Megalithic Tombs of Ireland*, IV (Dublin).

DELANY and DELANY (1966): V.T.H. Delany and D.R. Delany, *The Canals of the South of Ireland* (Newton Abbot).

DUGGAN (1991): B. Duggan, *The History and Architecture of Granagh Castle, Co. Kilkenny* (unpublished BA disertation, Trinity College, Dublin).

ENOCH (n.d.): V.J. Enoch, *The Martello Towers of Ireland* (Dublin).

EOGAN (1965): G. Eogan, *Catalogue of Irish Bronze Swords* (Dublin).

FITZPATRICK (1935): J.E. FitzPatrick, 'Rindown Castle, Co. Roscommon', *Journal of the Society of Antiquaries of Ireland*, LXV, 177-90.

FRYER (1924): A.C. Fryer, *Wooden Monumental Effigies in England and Wales* (London).

FULLER (1907): J.F. Fuller, 'Kinsale in 1641 and 1642', *Journal of the Cork Historical and Archaeological Society*, XIII, 1-18.

GROSE (1773-6): F. Grose, *The Antiquities of England and Wales* (London).

GROSE (1789-91): F. Grose, *The Antiquities of Scotland* (London and Perth).

GROSE (1791-5): F. Grose, *The Antiquities of Ireland* (London).

GWYNN and HADCOCK (1970): A. Gwynn and R.N. Hadcock, *Medieval Religious Houses, Ireland* (London).

HARBISON (1970): P. Harbison, *Guide to the National Monuments in the Republic of Ireland* (Dublin).

HARBISON (1988): P. Harbison, *Pre-Christian Ireland* (London).

HARBISON (1991): P. Harbison, ed., *Beranger's Views of Ireland* (Dublin).

HAYMAN (1880): S. Hayman, 'A drawing, by Grose, of a cross legged effigy, which was once at the Dominican Abbey, Youghal', *Journal of the Royal Historical and Archaeological Association of Ireland*, ser. 4, V, pt., 2, 342.

HEALY (1988): J.N. Healy, *The Castles of County Cork* (Cork).

HENLEY (1928): P. Henley, *Spenser in Ireland* (Cork).

HENRY (1970): F. Henry, *Irish Art in the Romanesque Period 1020-1170 AD* (London).

HERMANN (1986): L. Hermann, *Paul and Thomas Sandby* (London).

HUTCHINSON (1985): J. Hutchinson, *James Arthur O'Connor* (National Gallery of Ireland, Dublin).

HUNT (1974): J. Hunt, *Irish Medieval Figure Sculpture 1200-1600* (London and Dublin).

JOCELYN (1973): J. Jocelyn, 'The Renaissance Tombs at Lusk and Newtown Trim', *Journal of the Royal Society of Antiquaries of Ireland*, CIII, 153-66.

KERRIGAN (1977-9): P.M. Kerrigan, 'Charles Fort, Kinsale', *The Irish Sword*, XIII, 322-38.

KERRIGAN (1980-1): P.M. Kerrigan, 'Seventeenth Century Fortifications, Forts and Garrisons in Ireland: A Preliminary List (Part Two)', *The Irish Sword*, XIV, 135-56.

LANIGAN (1960): T.G. Lanigan, 'Granny Castle', *Old Kilkenny Review*, XII, 29-31.

LEASK and PRICE (1936): H.G. Leask and L. Price, 'The Labbacallee Megalith, Co. Cork', *Proceedings of the Royal Irish Academy*, XLIII, 77-101.

LEASK (1964): H.G. Leask, *Irish Castles and Castellated Houses* (Dundalk).

LEASK (1955-60): *Irish Churches and Monastic Buildings*, 3 vols., (Dundalk).

LEASK (Glendalough, n.d.): H.G. Leask, *Glendalough, Co. Wicklow, Official Historical and Descriptive Guide* (Dublin).

LEDWICH (1790): E. Ledwich, *Antiquities of Ireland* (Dublin).

LEWIS (1837): *A Topographical Dictionary of Ireland* (London).

LOEBER (1981); R. Loeber, 'Sculptured memorials to the Dead in Early Seventeenth-Century Ireland: A Survey from Monumenta Eblanae and Other Sources', *Proceedings of the Royal Irish Academy*, 81 C, 267-93.

LOVE (1962): W.D. Love, 'The Hibernian Antiquarian Society', *Studies*, LI (1962), 419-43.

LYNN (1975): C.J. Lynn, 'Excavation in the Franciscan Friary Church, Armagh', *Ulster Journal of Archaeology*, XXXVIII, 61-80.

MAC CANA (1983): Proinsias Mac Cana, *Celtic Mythology* (Feltham).

MAC CUARTA (1987): B. Mac Cuarta, 'Mathew de Renzy's letters on Irish Affairs 1613-20', *Analecta Hibernica*, no. 34, 109-82.

MACKINTOSH and RICHARDSON (1980): H.B. Mackintosh and J.S. Richardson, *Elgin Cathedral, The Cathedral Kirk of Moray* (Edinburgh, HMSO).

MCNAB (1986): S. McNab, *Irish Figure Sculpture in the twelfth century* (unpublished PhD dissertation, Trinity College, Dublin).

MCPARLAND (1985): E.J. McParland, *James Gandon, Vitruvius Hibernicus* (London).

MAHER (1934): J. Maher, 'Francis Place in Drogheda', *Journal of the Royal Society of Antiquaries of Ireland*, LXIV, 41-53.

MAXTED (1977): I. Maxted, *The London Book Trades 1775-1800* (Folkstone).

MITCHELL (1989): G.F. Mitchell, *Man and the Environment in Valencia Island* (Dublin).

MURTAGH (1980): H. Murtagh, 'The town wall fortifications of Athlone' in H. Murtagh, ed., *Irish Midland Studies; essays in commemoration of N.W. English* (Athlone), 89-106.

*NHI*, III: *A New History of Ireland, III, Early Modern Ireland*, ed. T.W. Moody, F.X. Martin and F.J. Byrne (Oxford).

O'KELLY (1989): M.J. O'Kelly, *Early Ireland: An Introduction to Irish Prehistory* (Cambridge).

Ó NUALLÁIN (1984): S. Ó Nualláin, 'A survey of stone circles in Cork and Kerry', *Proceedings of the Royal Irish Academy*, 84 C (1984), 1-78.

O'RAHILLY (1946): T.F. O'Rahilly, *Early Irish History and Mythology* (Dublin).

PETRIE (1850-3): G. Petrie, 'On two Irish inscriptions on the great stone cross of Tuam', *Proceedings of the Royal Irish Academy*, Ser. 1, V, 474.

POTTERTON (1975): H. Potterton, *Irish Church Monuments 1570-1880* (Ulster Architectural Heritage Society, Belfast).

POWER (1932): P. Power, 'The Abbey of Molana, Co. Waterford', *Journal of the Royal Society of Antiquaries of Ireland*, LXII, 142-52.

RAFTERY (1982): B. Raftery, *A Catalogue of Irish Iron Age Antiquities* (Marburg).

REDMOND (1919): G. O'Connell Redmond, 'The Castles in North-East Cork, and near its Borders', *Journal of the Cork Historical and Archaeological Society*, XXV, 21- 4, 91-7.

RICKMAN (1817): T. Rickman, *An attempt to discriminate the styles of English architecture from the Conquest to the Reformation* (London).

ROE (1969): H.M. Roe, 'Cadaver Effigial Monuments in Ireland', *Journal of the Royal Society of Antiquaries of Ireland*, XCIX (1969), 1-19.

ROGERS (1888): E. Rogers, *Memoir of Armagh Cathedral with an Account of the Ancient City* (Belfast).

RYAN, Clonmacnois (n.d.): J. Ryan, *Clonmacnois. A Historical Summary* (Dublin).

THE SHELL GUIDE (1967): Lord Killanin and M.V. Duignan, *The Shell Guide to Ireland* (London).

S.M. (1914-16): S.M., 'Ballycarbery Castle', *Kerry Archaeological Magazine*, III, 243-59.

SMITH (1985): B. Smith, *European Vision and the South Pacific* (New Haven and London).

SMITH (1746): C. Smith, *The Antient and Present State of the County and City of Waterford* (Dublin).

SMITH (1750): C. Smith, *The Antient and Present State of the County and City of Cork* (Dublin).

SMITH (1756): C. Smith, *The Antient and Present State of the County of Kerry* (Dublin).

STALLEY (1971): R. Stalley, *Architecture and Sculpture in Ireland 1150-1350* (Dublin).

STALLEY (1978): R. Stalley, 'William of Prene and the Royal Works in Ireland', *Journal of the British Archaeological Association*, CXXXI, 30-49.

STALLEY (1981): R. Stalley, 'The Romanesque Sculpture of Tuam' in A. Borg and A. Martindale, ed., *The Vanishing Past, Studies of Medieval Art, Liturgy and Metrology presented to Christopher Hohler* (Oxford), 179-95.

STALLEY (1987): R. Stalley, *The Cistercian Monasteries of Ireland* (London and New Haven).

STRICKLAND (1913): W.G. Strickland, *A Dictionary of Irish Artists* (Dublin and London).

TUMMERS (1980): H.A. Tummers, *Early Secular Effigies in England: The Thirteenth Century* (Leiden).

WARE (1764): W. Harris, ed., *The Whole Works of Sir James Ware*, 2 vols (Dublin).

WESTROPP (1921): T.J. Westropp, 'The promontory Forts of Beare and Bantry — II', *Journal of the Royal Society of Antiquaries of Ireland*, LI, 1-16.

WILDE (1870): W.R. Wilde, 'Memoir of Gabriel Beranger', *Journal of the Royal Historical and Archaeological Association of Ireland*, I, part 1, 4th Ser., 33-64.